Intermediate BIOLOGY

MULTIPLE CHOICE and MATCHING

Team Co-ordinator
James Torrance

Writing team
James Torrance
James Fullarton
Clare Marsh
James Simms
Caroline Stevenson

Diagrams by James Torrance

Hodder Gibson
A MEMBER OF THE HODDER HEADLINE GROUP

Orders: please contact Bookpoint Ltd, 130 Milton Park, Abingdon, Oxon OX14 4SB.
Telephone: (44) 01235 827720. Fax: (44) 01235 400454. Lines are open from 9.00 – 5.00,
Monday to Saturday, with a 24 hour message answering service. You can also order
through our website www.hoddereducation.co.uk.

British Library Cataloguing in Publication Data
A catalogue record for this title is available from the British Library

ISBN-13: 978-0-340-85060-2

Published by Hodder Gibson, 2a Christie Street, Paisley PA1 1NB.
Tel: 0141 848 1609; Fax: 0141 889 6315; email: hoddergibson@hodder.co.uk
First published 2003
Impression number   10 9 8 7 6 5 4
Year   2009 2008 2007

Copyright © 2000 James Torrance, James Fullerton, Clare Marsh, James Simms and
Caroline Stevenson

All rights reserved. No part of this publication may be reproduced or transmitted in any
form or by any means, electronic or mechanical, including photocopy, recording, or any
information storage and retrieval system, without permission in writing from the
publisher or under licence from the Copyright Licensing Agency Limited. Further details
of such licences (for reprographic reproduction) may be obtained from the Copyright
Licensing Agency Limited, of Saffron House, 6–10 Kirby Street, London EC1N 8TS.

Cover photo from Science Photo Library Ltd.

Typeset by Servis Filmsetting Ltd, Manchester.

Printed for Hodder Gibson, 2a Christie Street, Paisley, PA1 1NB, Scotland, UK, by
Martins The Printers, Berwick upon Tweed.

Contents

Preface ... iv

Unit 1 *Health and Technology*

1	What is Health and Technology?	2
2	Healthy Heart	17
3	Healthy Lungs	34
4	Healthy Body	53

Unit 2 *Biotechnological Industries*

5	Dairy Industries	74
6	Yeast-Based Industries	90
7	Detergent Industries	113
8	Pharmaceutical Industries	130

Unit 3 *Growing Plants*

9	Growing Plants from Seeds	152
10	Vegetative Propagation	171
11	Plant Production	192

| 12 | Specimen Exam Papers | 211 |

Preface

This book is intended to act as a valuable resource to students and teachers by providing a set of matching exercises and a comprehensive bank of multiple choice questions, the content of which adheres closely to the SQA Higher Still syllabus for Intermediate 1 Biology.

Each chapter corresponds to part of a syllabus sub-topic. The matching exercises enable students gradually to construct a glossary of terms essential to the course. The multiple choice tests contain various types of question. Some test knowledge and understanding, some test practical abilities and others test problem-solving skills thereby satisfying the requirements of Outcomes 1, 2 and 3 laid down in the syllabus' Statement of Standards.

The tests allow pupils to practise extensively in preparation for the examination. The book concludes with two 25-question specimen examinations in the style of the multiple choice section of the externally assessed examination paper.

Unit 1
Health and Technology

Unit 1 — What is Health and Technology?

Matching Test 1

Match the words in list X with their descriptions in list Y.

List X	List Y
1) blood pressure	a) diagram that represents the three essential aspects of good health
2) fat content	b) word used to describe the aspect of health that refers to parts of the body such as skin, teeth and heart
3) health triangle	c) word used to describe the aspect of health that refers to the state of mind and emotions
4) high tech apparatus	d) word used to describe the aspect of health that refers to the ability to form relationships with other people
5) mental	e) feature of the body that can be measured using a thermometer
6) physical	f) feature of the body that can be measured using pulsimeter
7) low tech apparatus	g) feature of the body that can be measured using a sphygmomanometer
8) pulse rate	h) feature of the body that can be measured using skinfold calipers
9) social	i) traditional equipment (e.g. thermometer) used to make a physiological measurement
10) temperature	j) advanced equipment (e.g. thermistor) used to make a physiological measurement

Chapter 1 What is Health and Technology?

Multiple Choice Test 1

Choose the ONE correct answer to each of the following questions.

1 Which of the following diagrams best represents the health triangle?

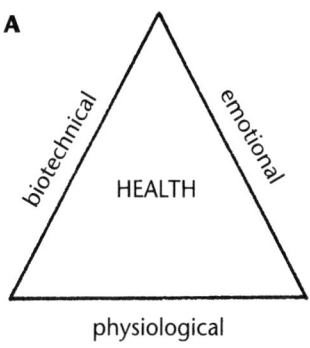 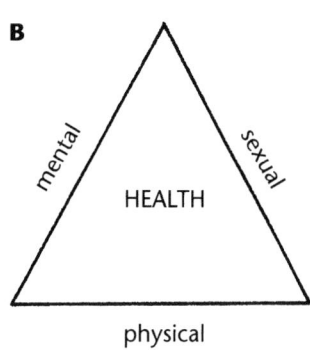

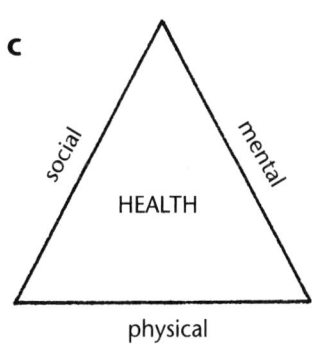 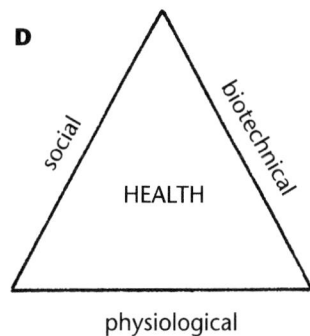

2 Which of the following contributes to **all three** aspects of good health?
   A taking a long hot bath before bed.
   B smoking a cigarette after lunch with friends.
   C drinking beer alone while listening to music.
   D going a cycle run with friends to a place of interest.

3 It is a sign of poor health to be
   A free from pain.
   B able to enjoy life.
   C free from disease.
   D tired all the time.

3

Unit 1 Health and Technology

Multiple Choice Test 1 continued

Questions 4, 5, 6 and 7 refer to the information in the following table only.

drug	medical use	psychological dependence after repeated use	physical dependence after repeated use
amphetamines	treatment of narcolepsy (tendency to fall asleep too easily)	* * *	*
barbiturates	treatment of insomnia (inability to get to sleep)	*	* * *
benzodiazepines (e.g. temazepan)	relief from anxiety	*	*
cannabis	possible treatment of multiple sclerosis in the future	* *	*
cocaine	local anaesthetic	* * *	
LSD	none	*	
opiates (e.g. morphine, heroin)	relief of pain	* * *	* * *

Key to dependence
  * = slight
 * * = moderate
* * * = severe

Chapter 1 What is Health and Technology?

Multiple Choice Test 1 *continued*

4 Which drug may be prescribed by doctors in the future for the relief of MS (multiple sclerosis)?

  A benzodiazepines.

  B cannabis.

  C cocaine.

  D LSD.

5 An 'upper' is a type of drug that stimulates a person and keeps him or her awake. Based only on the information in the table, which of the following could be described as an 'upper'?

  A amphetamines.

  B barbiturates.

  C benzodiazepines.

  D cocaine.

6 Which type of drug leads to both severe psychological and severe physical dependence after repeated use?

  A amphetamines.

  B barbiturates.

  C cocaine.

  D opiates.

7 Which drug leads to slight psychological but severe physical dependence after repeated use?

  A amphetamines.

  B barbiturates.

  C benzodiazepines.

  D cannabis.

Unit 1 Health and Technology

Multiple Choice Test 1 continued

Questions 8, 9, 10 and 11 refer to the following newspaper article.

People have been extracting a drug called salicylic acid from certain types of plant for hundreds of years. In 1763 it was obtained from the bark of the willow tree and records were kept of a trial that was done on 50 people. They were suffering a fever and salicylic acid brought relief to all of them.

By 1899 scientists had found ways of binding the chemical into pills. They named it **aspirin**. Aspirin was an instant success and remained the world's most popular painkiller until the 1950s. At that time 500 million tablets were being taken world-wide every year.

Then aspirin ran up against its first serious rival. This was paracetamol, a drug that was just as good at killing pain but, unlike aspirin, did not cause stomach bleeding in some of its users. Aspirin's sales dropped and continued to do so for years until further scientific discoveries about it were made. It was found that aspirin blocks the formation of a chemical needed to make blood clot. Clotting is important to seal bleeding wounds. However it is dangerous when it happens inside the body because the clot may stop blood flowing to a vital part of the body.

When a clot blocks the supply of blood to the wall of the heart, the heart muscle is starved of oxygen. This may cause a heart attack. Aspirin is found to

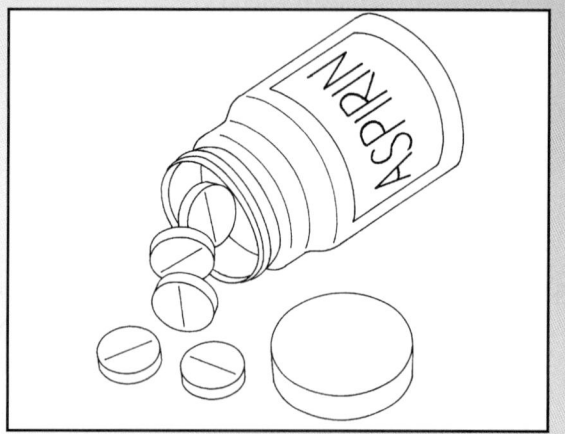

'thin' the blood making it take longer to clot. It therefore reduces the risk of heart attacks. Studies on a large number of high-risk patients have shown that regular doses of aspirin also reduce the risk of bowel cancer and strokes.

With such a wide variety of possible uses, aspirin seems little short of miraculous and today 100 billion tablets are consumed world-wide. However doctors warn healthy people *not* to take a pill a day. Only high-risk people should take it daily; low risk people would be taking medicine needlessly.

8 Which of the following would be the best title for this newspaper article?

    A Drugs extracted from plants.   C Aspirin the wonder drug.

    B The history of painkillers.   D A pill a day keeps the doctor away.

9 Aspirin is used to treat

    A pain.   B vomiting.   C stomach bleeding.   D bronchitis.

10 Aspirin is now being used to try to prevent all of the following **except**

    A blood clots.   B bowel cancer.   C heart attacks.   D athlete's foot.

11 By how many times has the world-wide use of aspirin increased from the 1950s to the present day? (Note: 1 billion = 1000 million)

    A 5.   B 20.   C 200.   D 500.

Chapter 1 What is Health and Technology?

Multiple Choice Test 1 continued

Questions 12, 13, 14, 15 and 16 refer to the following table which shows how a healthy lifestyle can help people to avoid certain serious illnesses. Each tick counts as a score of one positive point towards avoiding the illness.

serious illness	beneficial aspect of lifestyle					
	diet rich in fruit and vegetables	diet low in salt	diet low in fat	regular exercise daily	no smoking	little or no alcohol
heart attack	✔✔	✔	✔✔✔	✔✔✔	✔✔✔	
liver cancer	✔✔					✔✔✔
lung cancer	✔		✔		✔✔✔	
stroke	✔✔	✔✔✔		✔✔	✔	

Key to dependence
no ticks = zero reduction of risk of suffering illness
✔ = minor reduction of risk of suffering illness
✔✔ = medium reduction of risk of suffering illness
✔✔✔ = major reduction of risk of suffering illness

12 The risk of one of the serious illnesses is reduced by a major extent by consuming little or no alcohol. Which illness?
A heart attack.   B liver cancer.   C lung cancer.   D stroke.

13 The risk of one of the serious illnesses is reduced by a major extent by eating a diet low in salt. Which illness?
A heart attack.   B liver cancer.   C lung cancer.   D stroke.

14 The risk of two of the illnesses is reduced by a major extent by not smoking. Which two?
A   heart attack and lung cancer.   B   lung cancer and liver cancer.
C   liver cancer and stroke.   D   stroke and heart attack.

15 Which aspect of a healthy lifestyle makes a minor contribution to reducing the risk of a heart attack?
A   a diet rich in fruit.   B   a diet rich in vegetables.
C   a diet low in salt.   D   a diet low in fat.

Unit 1 Health and Technology

Multiple Choice Test 1 continued

16 Which aspect of a healthy lifestyle gives some protection against all four serious illnesses?
    A a diet rich in fruit and vegetables.   B a diet low in fat.
    C regular daily exercise.   D no tobacco smoked.

Questions 17, 18, 19, 20 and 21 refer to the diagram which represents a simplified version of a good night's sleep.

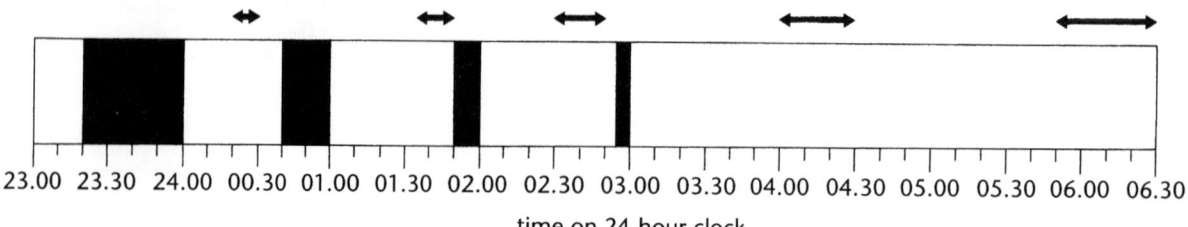

Key
☐ = period of 'light' (rapid eye movement) sleep
■ = period of 'deep' sleep
↔ = period of dreaming

17 The total number of minutes spent in deep sleep was
    A 75.   B 115.   C 375.   D 450.

18 The ratio of light sleep to deep sleep is
    A 5:1.   B 6:1.   C 8:1.   D 10:1.

19 What percentage of the time between midnight and 01.00 was spent in light sleep?
    A 20.   B 33.   C 40.   D 67.

20 It can be concluded that in this person, dreaming took place
    A during deep sleep only.
    B during light sleep only.
    C mostly during deep sleep.
    D equally during both light and deep sleep.

21 During which of the following times did the person do most dreaming?
    A 01.30–02.00.   B 02.30–03.00.
    C 04.00–04.30.   D 05.30–06.00.

Chapter 1 What is Health and Technology?

Multiple Choice Test 1 continued

Questions 22, 23 and 24 refer to the information in the following table.

physiological measurement	suitable equipment	
	low tech approach	high tech approach
blood pressure	mercury sphygmomanometer	digital blood pressure meter
body fat content	skinfold calipers	tracer analysis
body temperature	clinical thermometer	thermistor
pulse rate	stopwatch	pulsimeter

22 Which of the following should be chosen to measure pulse rate using low tech equipment?

   A thermistor.   B pulsimeter.   C stopwatch.   D digital blood pressure meter.

23 Which of the following should be chosen to measure body temperature using high tech equipment?

   A   thermistor.   B   pulsimeter.
   C   clinical thermometer.   D   digital blood pressure meter.

24 If you were carrying out tracer analysis, you would be taking a

   A   low tech approach to measuring blood pressure.

   B   high tech approach to measuring body fat content.

   C   low tech approach to measuring body temperature.

   D   high tech approach to measuring pulse rate.

25 Which of the following statements is true? Compared with high tech equipment, low tech equipment normally

   A   gives results faster and in more detail.

   B   is cheaper to assemble and run.

   C   is more complicated to set up and use.

   D   is more easily connected up to computers.

Unit 1 Health and Technology

Multiple Choice Test 2

Choose the ONE correct answer to each of the following questions.

1. Which of the following is a sign of good mental health?
   A positive attitude to life.
   B ability to get on well with people.
   C suitable weight for body height.
   D well exercised muscles.

2. Which of the following is a sign of good physical health?
   A feeling happy and contented.
   B having shiny, glossy hair.
   C feeling full after a big meal.
   D having an enthusiasm for life.

3. Which line in the following table gives three features that are important parts of a healthy lifestyle?

	drinking alcohol	taking time to relax	eating a balanced diet	smoking cigarettes	taking drugs	exercising regularly
A		✔		✔		✔
B	✔		✔		✔	
C		✔	✔			✔
D	✔			✔	✔	

Chapter 1 What is Health and Technology?

Multiple Choice Test 2 continued

Questions 4, 5, 6 and 7 refer to the information given in the following table only. It shows some of the possible effects of taking drugs during pregnancy.

drug	possible effect(s) of the drug on the unborn baby			
	physical abnormalities	reduced body weight	dependence on the drug	premature birth
alcohol	✔	✔		
amphetamines	✔	✔		
barbiturates	✔		✔	
cannabis				✔
heroin		✔	✔	
nicotine		✔		

4. If taken during pregnancy, which of the following drugs is most likely to cause physical abnormalities in the unborn baby?
   A barbiturates.   B cannabis.   C heroin.   D nicotine.

5. Which drugs could both cause the unborn baby's weight to be reduced?
   A alcohol and amphetamines.   B amphetamines and barbiturates.
   C barbiturates and heroin.   D heroin and cannabis.

6. The smoking of cannabis during pregnancy could lead to the baby
   A developing heart defects.
   B being lighter in weight than normal.
   C becoming dependent on the drug.
   D being born earlier than expected.

7. Which drugs could both lead to the baby suffering withdrawal symptoms at birth?
   A alcohol and amphetamines.
   B amphetamines and barbiturates.
   C barbiturates and heroin.
   D heroin and nicotine.

Unit 1 Health and Technology

Multiple Choice Test 2 continued

Questions 8, 9, 10, 11, 12 and 13 refer to the following newspaper article.

MDMA, the chemical in 'ecstasy' tablets which produces their effect, was first discovered in 1912. No use was found for it until the 1980s when marriage guidance counsellors discovered that it made their clients less hostile towards one another.

Although 'ecstasy' is now banned, it is still used illegally, especially among young dancers at night clubs. When people take 'ecstasy' they often find that their mouth goes dry, they feel slightly sick and their blood pressure goes up. Then a sense of calmness takes over, together with a strong feeling of friendliness towards everyone around. Much later that night or the next day, they often feel tired, sluggish and depressed. If they continue to take 'ecstasy' repeatedly over a long period, they are likely to suffer some or all of the following: anxiety, confusion, panic attacks and sleeplessness.

Because 'ecstasy' acts as a stimulant, the young people are able to dance for a long time in a hot disco without feeling exhausted. However they may become far too hot. Most of the 50 people who have died since 1988 after taking 'ecstasy' are thought to have died of heatstroke. Drinking water helps to prevent this by cooling down the body. However 'ecstasy' is thought to trigger release of a chemical that makes the kidneys hold back water. So in some cases, death may have been caused by excess body fluid making the brain swell up, crushing it against the inside of the skull. Call *that* ecstasy?

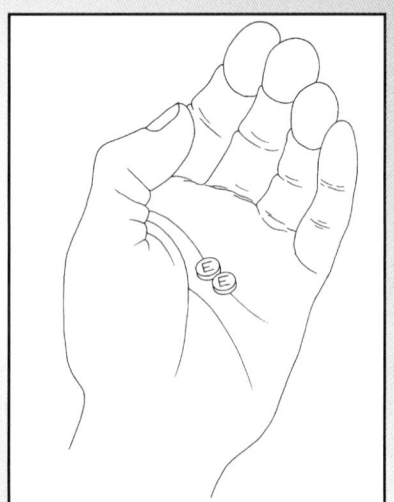

8 Which of the following is not experienced at first on taking 'ecstasy'?

A sickness.   B dry mouth.   C rise in blood pressure.   D drowsiness.

9 Which of the following words best describes the feeling experienced soon after taking 'ecstasy'?

A calm.   B anxious.   C confused.   D depressed.

10 Which of the following words best describes the feeling often experienced the day after taking 'ecstasy'?

A calm.   B relaxed.   C energetic.   D depressed.

11 Which of the following is often experienced by regular users of 'ecstasy'?

A anxiety.   B sleepiness.   C happiness.   D contentment.

12 Most of the 50 deaths resulting from the use of 'ecstasy' are thought to have been due to

A heatstroke.   B hypothermia.   C excessive sweating.   D muscular spasms.

Chapter 1 What is Health and Technology?

Multiple Choice Test 2 continued

13 A few people who drank excessive quantities of water after taking 'ecstasy' are thought to have died because

   A they were unable to sweat properly.

   B their bodies stopped producing urine.

   C excess body fluid damaged their brain.

   D excessive muscular activity led to a heart attack.

Questions 14, 15, 16, 17 and 18 refer to the accompanying diagram. It shows a risk chart for heart disease where each black dot counts as 1 point of risk factor. To work out a person's total score, you add together their score from each column.

14 A 41 year-old man who eats a diet containing much butter and fried food is 9 kg overweight. He also smokes 30 cigarettes every day. His total score in risk points is

   A 15.　B 16.　C 18.　D 19.

15 The risk of the same 41 year-old man (referred to in question 14) suffering heart disease is

   A average.　B moderate.　C high.　D very high.

16 A 16 year-old girl who does not smoke is 2 kg over her correct weight. She eats a diet low in fat and only has fried food very rarely. Her total score in risk points is

   A 0.　B 1.　C 2.　D 3.

17 The risk of this same 16 year-old girl (referred to in question 16) suffering heart disease is

   A very low.　B well below average.　C below average.　D average.

18 A man who smoked 35 cigarettes daily, ate a diet containing a small quantity of butter and fried food and was 5 kg overweight. He was found to have a total risk score of 15 points. His age (in years) must have been in the range

   A 21–30.　B 31–40.　C 41–50.　D 51–60.

Unit 1 **Health and Technology**

Multiple Choice Test 2 continued

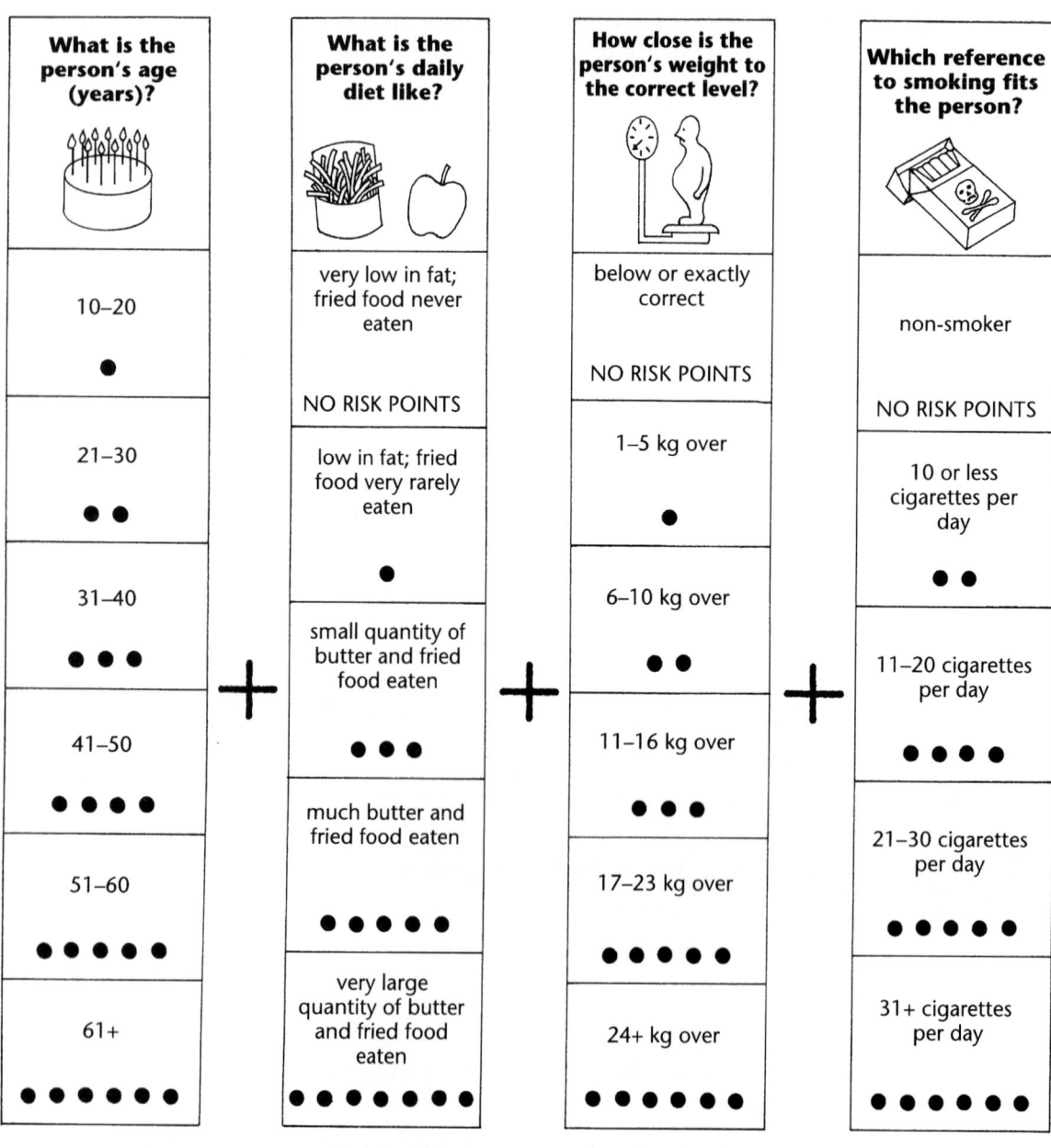

Key

total 0–1 risk points = very low risk of heart disease
2–4 risk points = well below average risk
5–7 risk points = below average risk
8–10 risk points = average risk
11–13 risk points = moderate risk
14–17 risk points = high risk
18+ risk points = very high risk

Chapter 1 What is Health and Technology?

Multiple Choice Test 2 continued

Questions 19, 20 and 21 refer to the following bar chart which shows how much sleep different age groups need for good health.

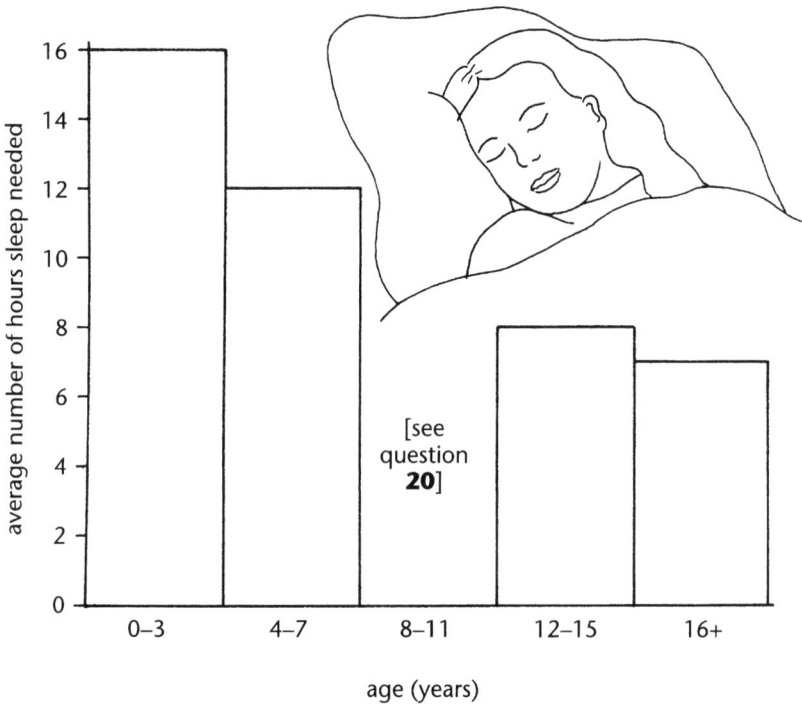

19 The average number of hours of sleep needed by a 5 year-old child is

A 7.   B 8.   C 12.   D 16.

20 The bar for age group 8–11 years has been missed out from the chart. It should have been

A 8 hours.   B 10 hours.   C 12 hours.   D 16 hours.

21 It can be concluded from this bar chart that as the young person's age increases, the average number of hours of sleep that they need

A increases.   B decreases.   C stays the same.   D varies from year to year.

15

Unit 1 Health and Technology

Multiple Choice Test 2 continued

Questions 22, 23 and 24 refer to the diagram of four pieces of equipment.

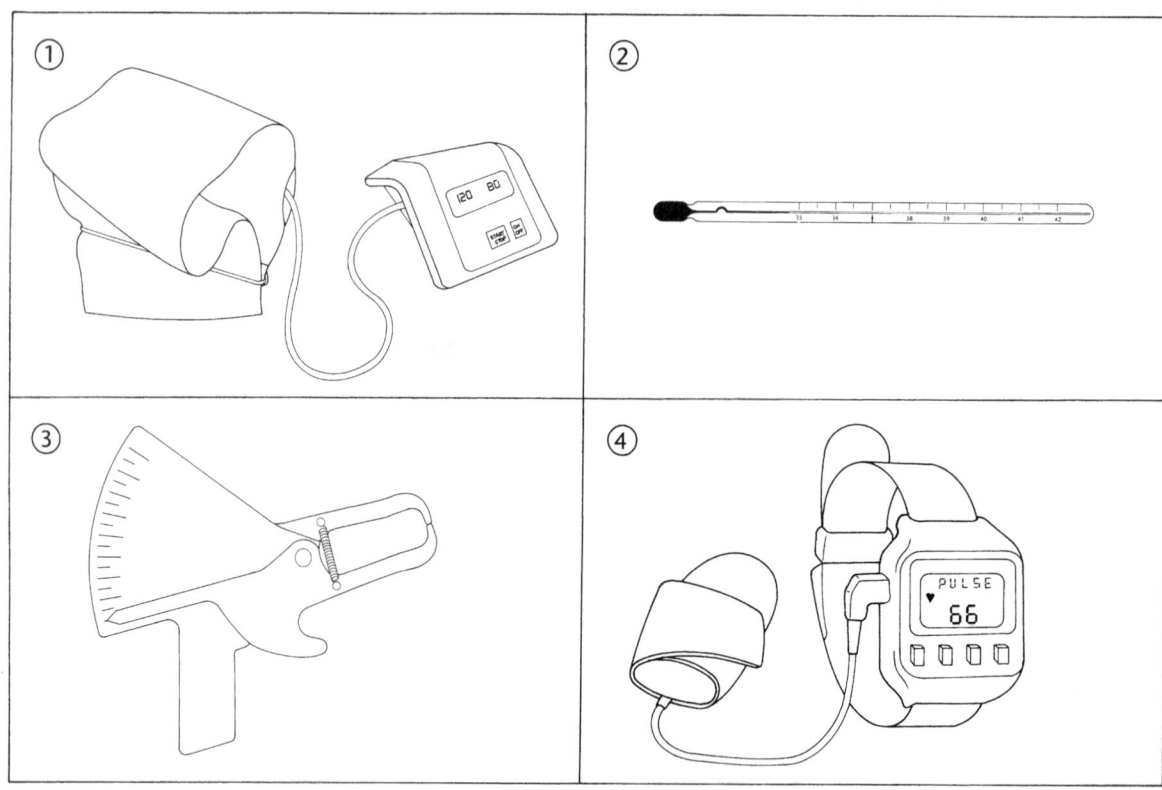

22 Which piece of equipment is used to measure body fat content?

   A 1.   B 2.   C 3.   D 4.

23 Which piece of equipment is used to measure heart rate?

   A 1.   B 2.   C 3.   D 4.

24 Which pieces of equipment both allow a high tech approach to making a physiological measurement?

   A 1 and 2.   B 1 and 4.   C 2 and 3.   D 3 and 4.

25 Which of the following statements is false? High tech and low tech equipment

   A both give valid measurements of the body's physiology.

   B are both reliable ways of obtaining accurate measurements.

   C differ in the cost of their production and operation.

   D are equally complicated to assemble and put into use.

Unit 1 2 Healthy Heart

Matching Test 1

Match the words in list X with their descriptions in list Y.

List X	List Y
1) artery	a) piece of high tech equipment used to measure pulse rate
2) capillary	b) structure made of two or more flaps that prevents backflow of blood
3) fitness	c) time taken for pulse rate to return to normal after a period of exercise
4) heart	d) blood vessel that carries blood towards the heart
5) pulse rate	e) physical condition of the body as indicated by the length of the recovery time
6) pulsimeter	f) muscular organ that pumps blood round the body
7) recovery time	g) tiny blood vessel that allows nutrients and oxygen to pass from blood to tissues
8) stethoscope	h) blood vessel that carries blood away from the heart
9) valve	i) measure of number of times that the heart beats per minute
10) vein	j) instrument used to listen to the heart beat

17

Unit 1 Health and Technology

Matching Test 2

Match the words in list X with their descriptions in list Y.

List X

1) anaemia
2) antibody
3) blood group
4) diabetes
5) heart attack
6) infection
7) iron
8) leukaemia
9) sphygmomanometer
10) stroke

List Y

a) instrument used to measure blood pressure
b) state resulting from invasion of body by disease-causing micro-organisms
c) chemical element essential for healthy red blood cells
d) blockage or bursting of a blood vessel in the brain that may cause brain damage
e) one of four types of blood represented by the letters A, B, AB and O
f) blood disorder where the number of red blood cells is lower than normal
g) protective molecules made by white blood cells to fight infection
h) blood disorder where the blood sugar level is much higher than normal
i) damage to heart muscle resulting from blockage of a blood vessel and lack of oxygen
j) blood disorder where the number of white blood cells is much higher than normal

Chapter 2 Healthy Heart

Multiple Choice Test 1

Choose the ONE correct answer to each of the following questions.

1. The heart is a muscular organ that
   A makes blood.
   B pumps blood.
   C filters blood.
   D stores blood.

Questions 2, 3, 4 and 5 refer to the diagram of the human heart.

2. Blood entering heart chamber 1 has a low concentration of oxygen. It has come from the
   A body tissues.
   B lung capillaries.
   C coronary arteries.
   D heart valves.

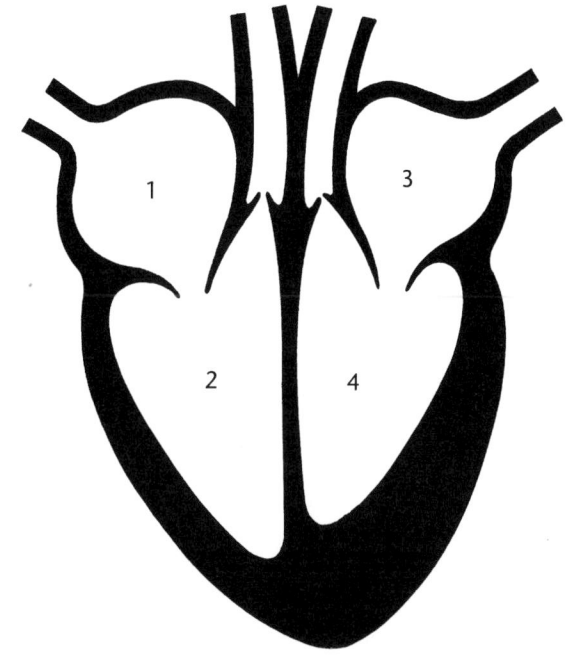

3. Blood ready to leave heart chamber 2 has a high concentration of CO_2 (carbon dioxide). It is about to be sent to the
   A head.   B arms.
   C kidneys. D lungs.

4. Blood entering heart chamber 3 has a high concentration of O_2 (oxygen). The last group of capillaries that it passed through were in the
   A head.   B arms.
   C kidneys. D lungs.

5. Blood ready to leave heart chamber 4 has a high concentration of O_2 (oxygen). It is about to be sent to the
   A body tissues.   B heart valves.
   C lung capillaries. D coronary veins.

19

Unit 1 Health and Technology

Multiple Choice Test 1 continued

6 The four pictures in the diagram represent part of a famous experiment carried out about four hundred years ago. It was done to show that blood in a vein always flows towards the heart and cannot flow backwards.

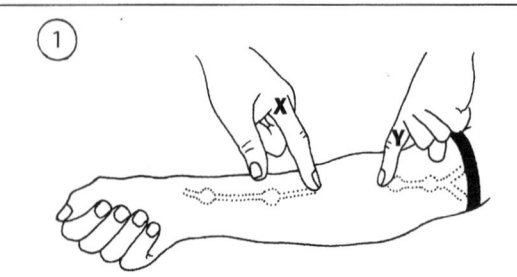

Finger **X** is kept in position while finger **Y** is used to push blood along the vein towards the heart.

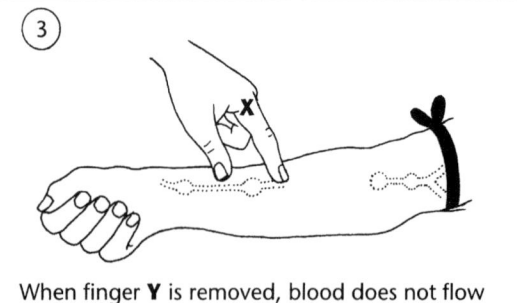

When finger **Y** is removed, blood does not flow back along the vein towards the hand.

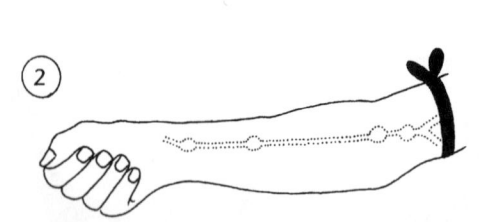

A scarf is tied tightly round the upper arm to show up a vein and its valves.

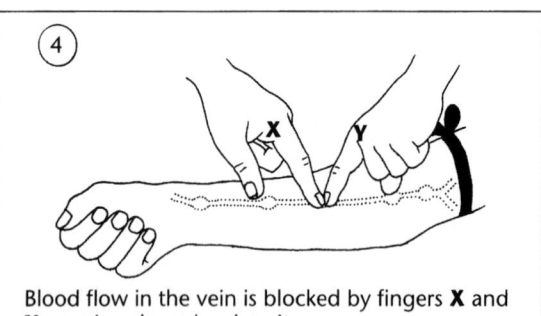

Blood flow in the vein is blocked by fingers **X** and **Y** pressing down hard on it.

The stages are shown in a mixed up order. The correct sequence is

A 2, 4, 3, 1.   **B** 2, 4, 1, 3.   **C** 4, 2, 1, 3.   **D** 4, 2, 3, 1.

Questions 7, 8 and 9 refer to the accompanying diagram. It shows a simplified version of the blood circulatory system.

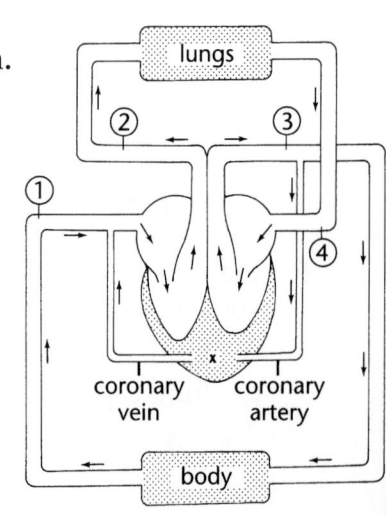

7 Veins are labelled

   A 1 and 2.   **B** 1 and 4.   **C** 2 and 3.   **D** 3 and 4.

8 Arteries are labelled

   A 1 and 2.   **B** 1 and 4.   **C** 2 and 3.   **D** 3 and 4.

9 Region X is made of

   A bone.   **B** tendon.   **C** muscle.   **D** cartilage.

Chapter 2 **Healthy Heart**

Multiple Choice Test 1 continued

10 Which of the following statements about capillaries is wrong?
   A   They link arteries with veins.
   B   They allow oxygen to pass from the blood to the tissues.
   C   They allow carbon dioxide to leave the tissues.
   D   They prevent waste materials passing from the tissues to the blood.

Questions 11 and 12 refer to the diagram of a stethoscope.

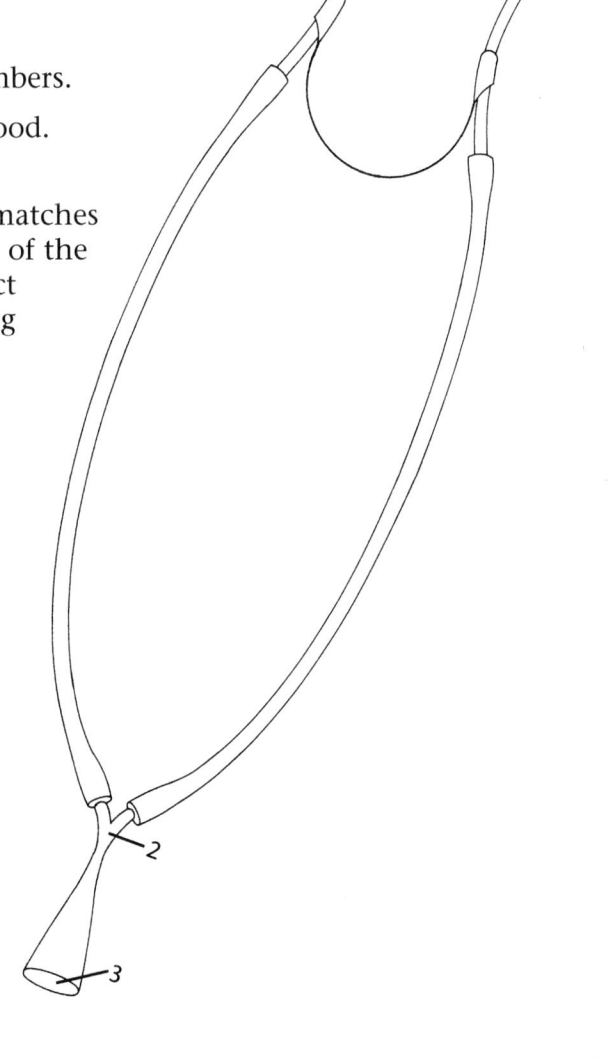

11 This instrument can be used to listen to a person's heart beating. It picks up the sound of
   A   heart valves closing.
   B   heart muscle contracting.
   C   echoes from empty heart chambers.
   D   heart chambers filling with blood.

12 Which line in the table correctly matches structures 1, 2 and 3 with the part of the body that they would be in contact with when the stethoscope is being used properly?

	chest	ears	fingers
A	3	1	2
B	2	1	3
C	3	2	1
D	1	3	2

21

Unit 1 Health and Technology

Multiple Choice Test 1 continued

Questions 13 and 14 refer to the following table which shows a girl's average pulse rate under different conditions.

13 What was the girl's pulse rate in beats per minute for standing?

   A 16.   B 32.   C 64.   D 80.

condition	average pulse rate (beats/15 s)
lying down	12
standing	16
walking	20
running	32

14 It can be concluded from the table that pulse rate decreases as the body becomes

   A faster moving.   B more tired.
   C more active.   D less active.

15 Pulse can be felt by pressing a finger tip against an artery near the surface of the body. At which place on the accompanying diagram would the girl be least likely to feel her pulse?

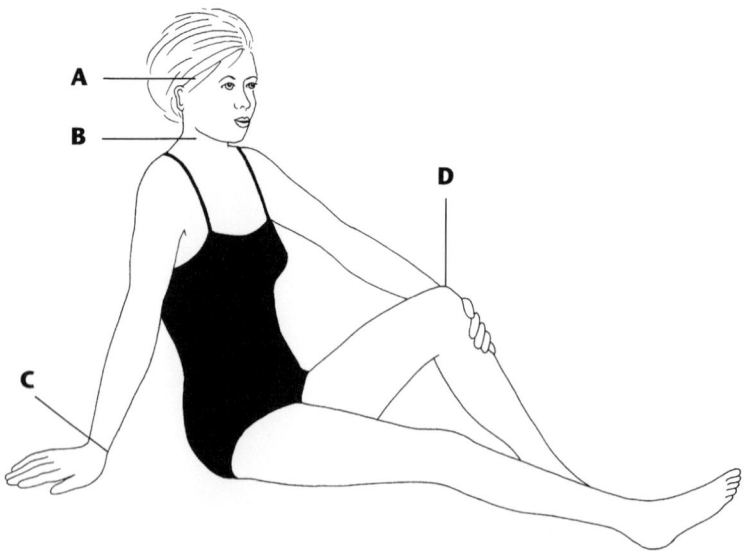

Chapter 2 **Healthy Heart**

Multiple Choice Test 1 continued

Questions 16, 17, 18 and 19 refer to the accompanying graph which charts the pulse rates of two boys over a period of time.

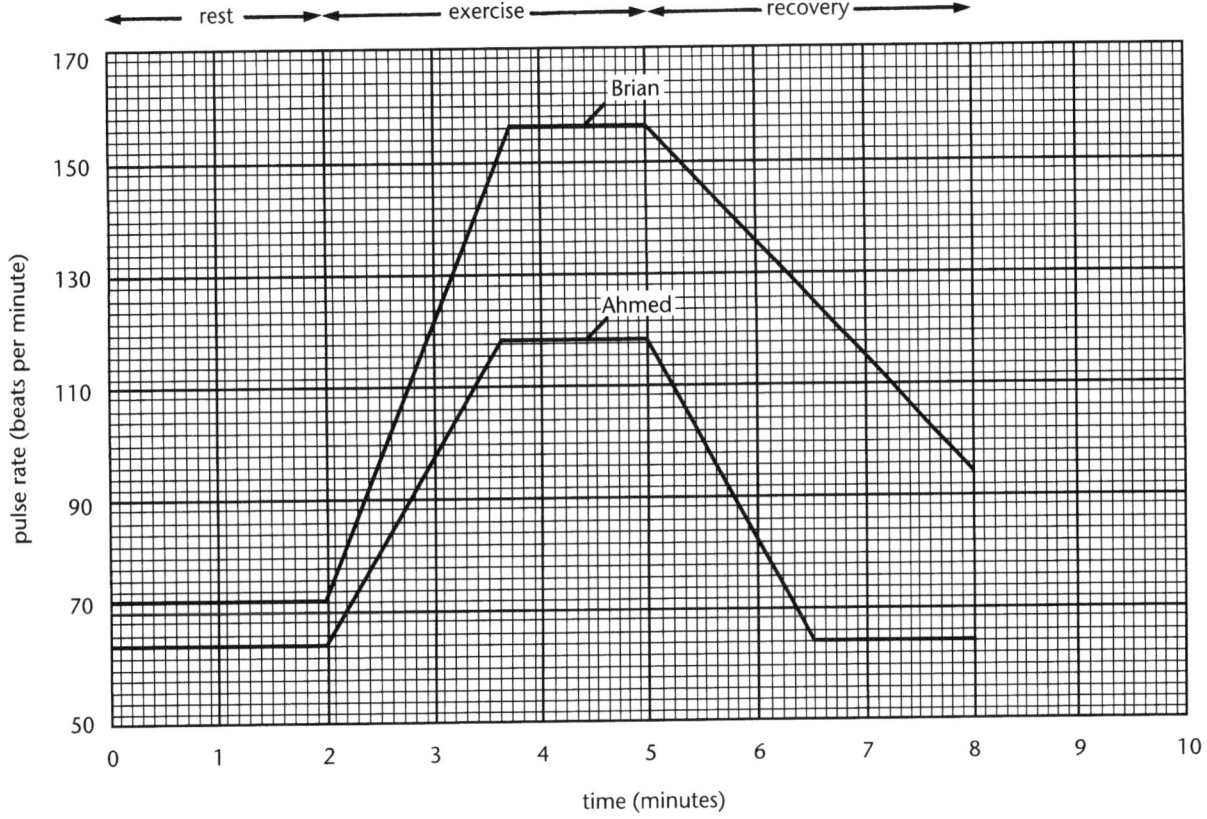

16 Which line in the first table gives the boys' resting pulse rates (in beats/min)?

17 How many minutes did it take for Ahmed's pulse to return to normal after exercise stopped?
A 1.5.   B 3.0.   C 5.0.   D 6.5.

	Ahmed	Brian
A	62	71
B	64	72
C	71	62
D	72	64

18 Which line in the second table gives the highest pulse rates (in beats/min) reached by the two boys?

19 If the trend continues, how much longer (in minutes) will it take for Brian's pulse to return to resting rate?
A 1.0.   B 1.5.   C 2.0.   D 3.0.

	Ahmed	Brian
A	156	118
B	158	119
C	118	156
D	119	158

Unit 1 Health and Technology

Multiple Choice Test 1 continued

20 Which line in the table opposite shows the results for exercising several times a week for two months?

	effect on resting pulse rate	effect on recovery time
A	↑	↑
B	↓	↑
C	↓	↓
D	↑	↓

Key
↑ = increase   ↓ = decrease

21 The bar chart opposite shows how blood pressure changes as blood flows round the body.

Which of the following conclusions cannot be drawn from this bar chart?

A Blood pressure is at its highest level as it leaves the heart.
B As blood moves from arteries to capillaries, the pressure drops.
C The pressure of blood in veins is lower than that in arteries.
D As blood moves from capillaries to veins, the pressure rises.

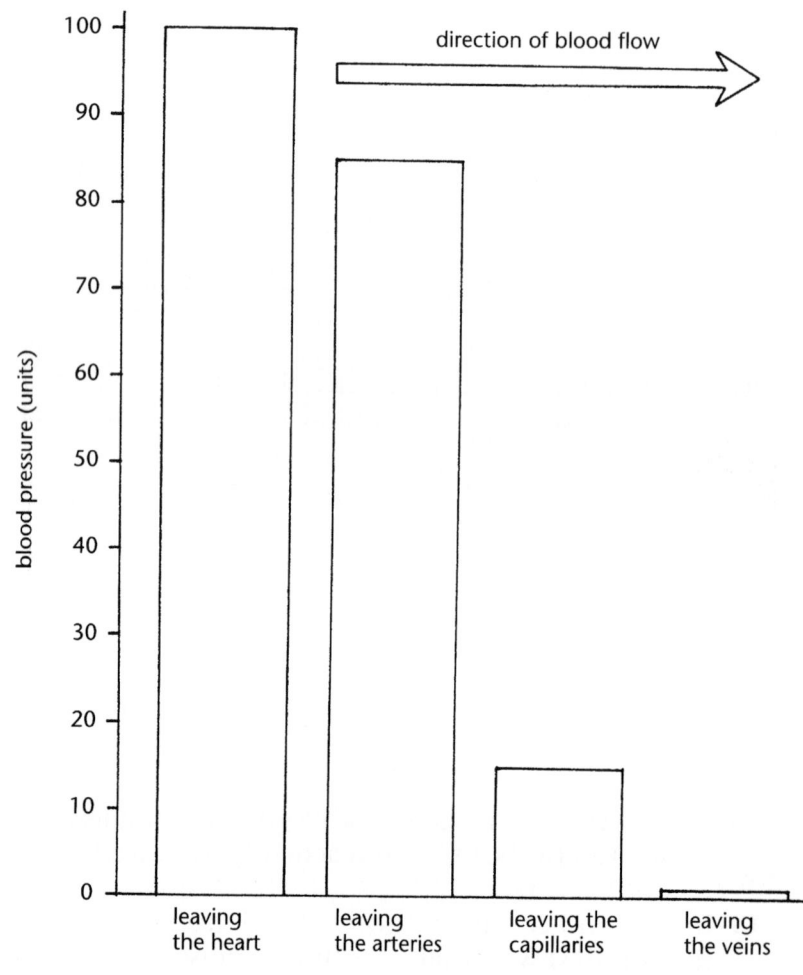

24

Chapter 2 Healthy Heart

Multiple Choice Test 1 continued

22 Which person in the following table is most likely to suffer high blood pressure?

person	overweight?	junk food eaten regularly?	regular exercise taken?	stress free lifestyle?
A	yes	yes	no	yes
B	no	no	yes	yes
C	yes	yes	no	no
D	no	yes	no	no

23 Which line in the following table is correct?

	condition	blood test
A	leukaemia	sugar content
B	HIV infection	presence of antibodies
C	diabetes	number of red blood cells
D	anaemia	number of white blood cells

Questions 24 and 25 refer to the following table.

nationality	blood group type (%)			
	A	B	AB	O
English	42	8	3	47
Welsh	38	10	3	49
Scottish	34	11	3	52
Irish	26	35	7	32

24 Most Scottish people are blood group

 A A.   B B.   C AB.   D O.

25 What is the nationality of the people whose percentage blood group types are represented by the bar chart?

 A English.   B Welsh.   C Scottish.   D Irish.

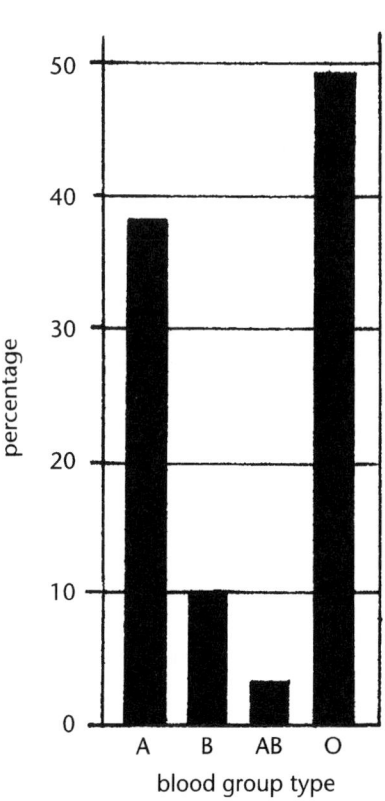

Unit 1 Health and Technology

Multiple Choice Test 2

Choose the ONE correct answer to each of the following questions.

1 The diagram shows the human heart.

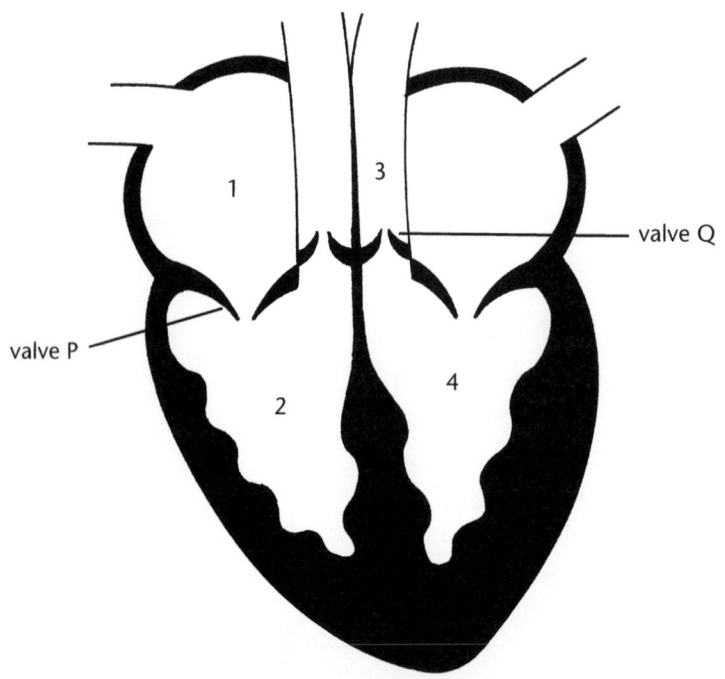

Which line in the following table is correct?

	valve P prevents blood flowing from	valve Q prevents blood flowing from
A	1 to 2	3 to 4
B	2 to 1	3 to 4
C	1 to 2	4 to 3
D	2 to 1	4 to 3

2 The function of the heart is to
  A pump blood round the body.
  B transport oxygen to the lungs.
  C send carbon dioxide to the body.
  D open and close valves in veins.

Chapter 2 **Healthy Heart**

Multiple Choice Test 2 continued

Questions 3 and 4 refer to the diagram of the blood circulation system in the human body.

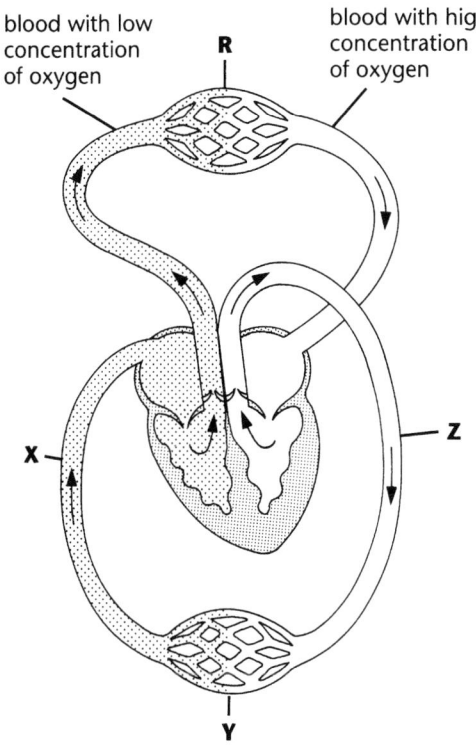

3 Which type of blood vessel would be found at positions X, Y and Z?

	X	Y	Z
A	artery	capillary	vein
B	capillary	vein	artery
C	vein	capillary	artery
D	vein	artery	capillary

4 Region R represents the position of the
   A lungs.   C intestine.
   B brain.   D coronary artery.

5 The table opposite gives four values of a boy's heart rate.

   His average heart rate (in beats/30 s) was
   A 33.   B 66.   C 72.   D 132.

trial	heart rate (beats/30 s)
1	36
2	30
3	32
4	34

Unit 1 Health and Technology

Multiple Choice Test 2 continued

Questions 6, 7 and 8 refer to the graph which shows the results of charting a boy's pulse rate before, during and after a period of exercise.

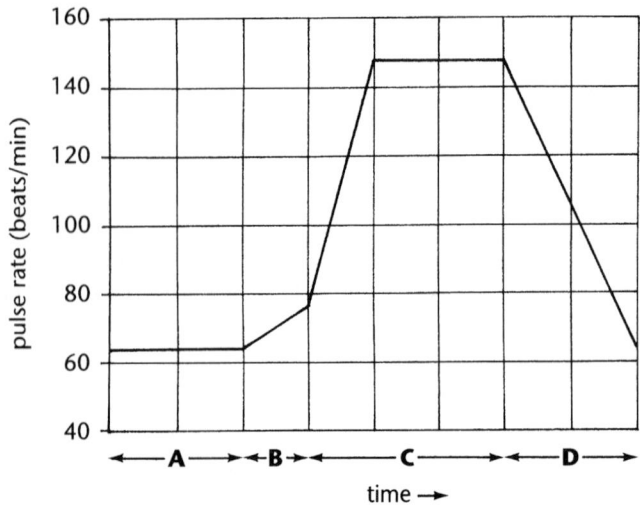

6 Which letter represents the warming up period?

7 Which letter represents the boy's resting pulse rate?

8 Which letter represents the period of recovery after exercise?

9 The diagrams show, in a mixed up order, the steps involved in setting up a type of pulse monitor.

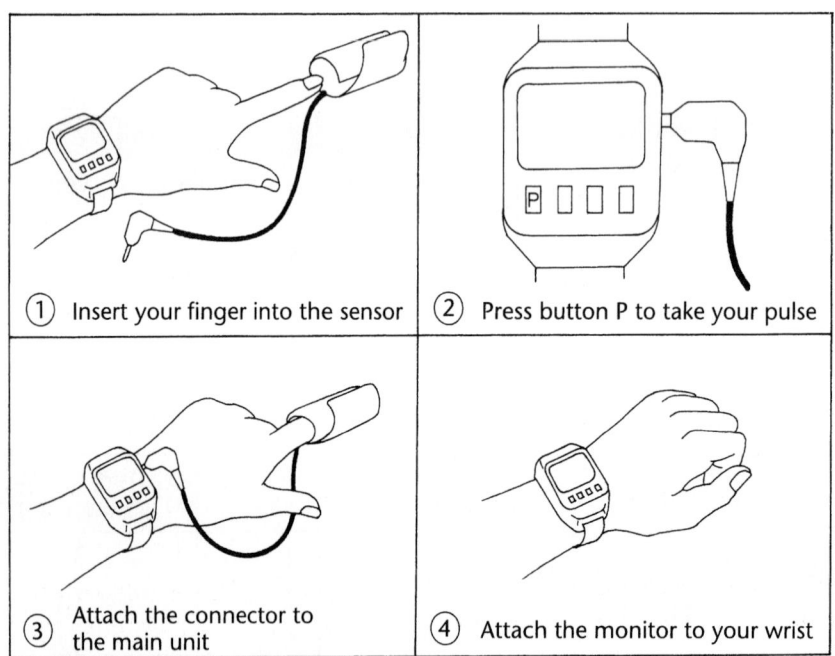

① Insert your finger into the sensor
② Press button P to take your pulse
③ Attach the connector to the main unit
④ Attach the monitor to your wrist

The correct order of the four steps is

A 1, 3, 2, 4.   B 1, 2, 3, 4.   C 4, 1, 3, 2.   D 4, 3, 1, 2.

Chapter 2 **Healthy Heart**

Multiple Choice Test 2 continued

Questions 10 and 11 refer to the data in the following table.

student	pulse rate (beats/min.)					
	before exercise	on stopping exercise	time after exercise(s)			
			30	60	90	120
Javaid	62	155	129	100	84	66
Stacy	66	146	134	112	89	68
Martin	70	148	126	108	85	72
Lesley	74	140	115	90	74	74

10 Which student is fittest according to this data?

　　A Javaid.　　B Stacy.　　C Martin.　　D Lesley.

11 Which of the following graphs correctly represents Stacy's pulse from the moment when she stopped exercising?

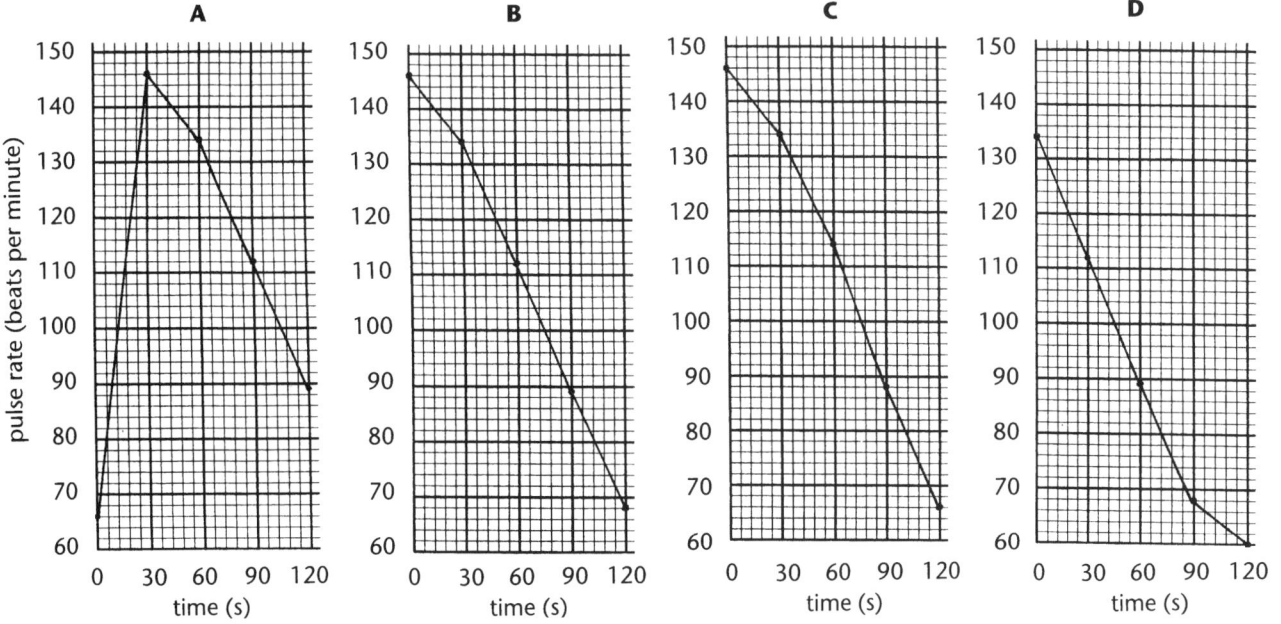

Unit 1 Health and Technology

Multiple Choice Test 2 continued

Questions 12, 13 and 14 refer to the chart below. It shows four levels of fitness targets and the rate at which the heart should be beating during exercise to reach these targets.

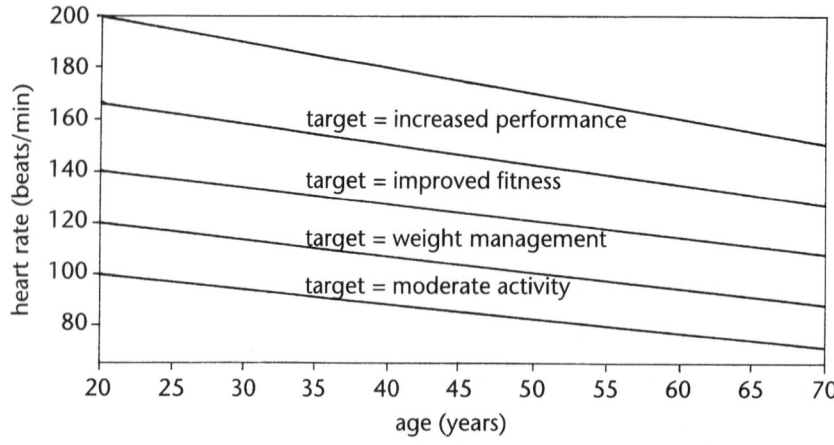

12 A 20 year-old woman wishes to increase her performance. Which range should her heart rate (in beats/min.) be in while she is exercising?

A 100–119.   B 120–139.   C 140–165.   D 166–200.

13 A 35 year-old woman exercised until her heart rate reached and stayed at around 120 beats/min. This was correct for the target that she had set herself. Identify the target.

A increased performance.   C weight management.
B improved fitness.   D moderate activity.

14 A man aged 50 wishes to improve his fitness. While he is exercising, his heart rate (in beats/min.) should be approximately

A 100.   B 120.   C 140.   D 160.

15 Which of the following pieces of equipment is used to measure blood pressure?

A heart rate monitor.   C pulsimeter.
B sphygmomanometer.   D stopwatch.

16 Blood pressure is normally at its lowest level when the person is

A walking slowly.   C sleeping soundly.
B driving quickly.   D exercising vigorously.

Chapter 2 **Healthy Heart**

Multiple Choice Test 2 continued

17 The diagram shows, in a simplified way, how the coronary artery supplies blood to the heart's muscular wall.

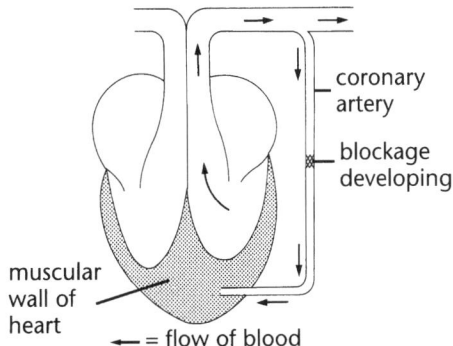

When a blockage develops in this artery, the person may be given a bypass to prevent a heart attack. Which of the following diagrams shows the result of an operation where the blockage in the coronary artery has been successfully bypassed?

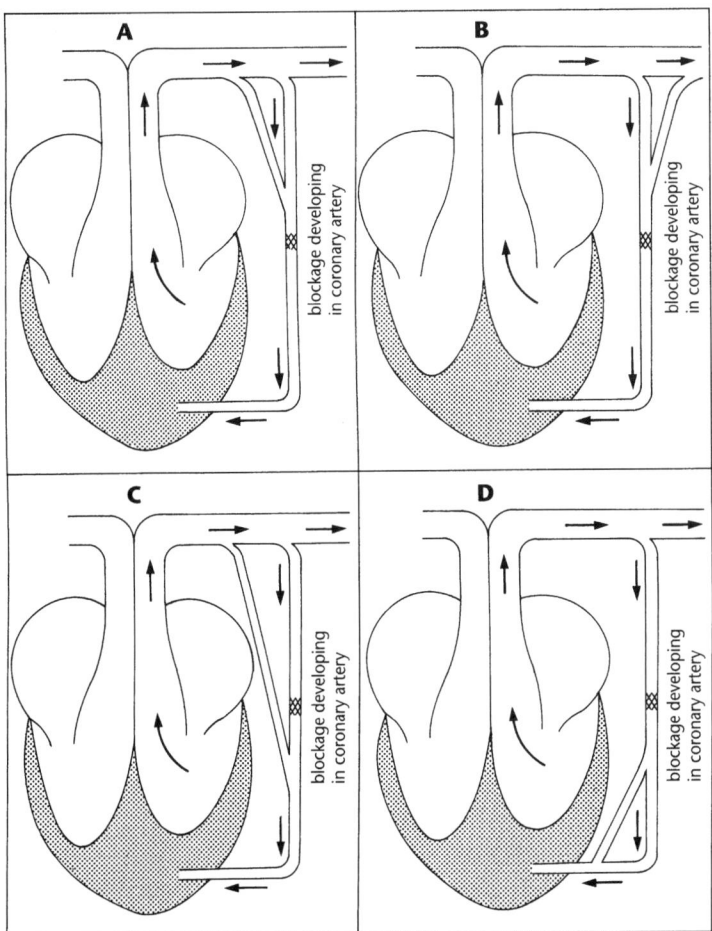

Unit 1 Health and Technology

Multiple Choice Test 2 continued

Questions 18 and 19 refer to the bar chart. It shows death rates from coronary heart disease in four different countries during the 1990s.

18 In which country did 210 women per 100 000 people die of coronary heart disease at this time?

A England.
B Finland.
C Scotland.
D USA.

19 In which country was the death rate for men more than three times that for women?

A England.
B Finland.
C Scotland.
D USA.

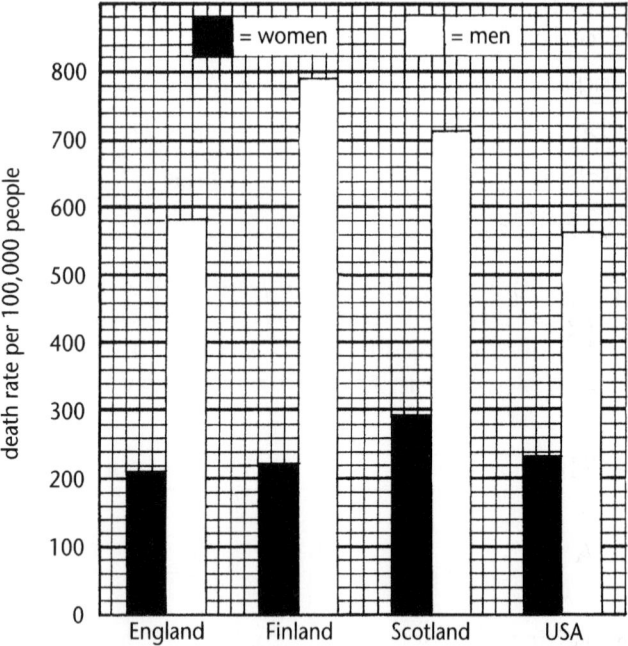

Questions 20, 21 and 22 refer to the following possible answers.

A anaemia.   B diabetes.   C measles.   D leukaemia.

20 Which of these conditions can be detected by testing the sugar content of the blood?

21 Which of these conditions can be detected by counting the number of white blood cells present in samples of blood?

22 Which of these conditions can be detected by measuring the iron content of the blood and counting the number of red blood cells?

Chapter 2 **Healthy Heart**

Multiple Choice Test 2 continued

Questions 23, 24 and 25 refer to the following table.

nationality	blood group type (%)			
	A	B	AB	O
Scottish	34	11	3	[X]
English	42	8	3	47
Irish	26	35	7	32
Welsh	38	10	3	49
UK average	35	[Y]	4	45

23 The percentage value that should have been entered in box [X] is

   A 16.   B 42.   C 48.   D 52.

24 The average value that should have been entered in box [Y] is

   A 16.   B 21.   C 64.   D 84.

25 Which of the following bar charts correctly represents the percentage blood group types of Irish people?

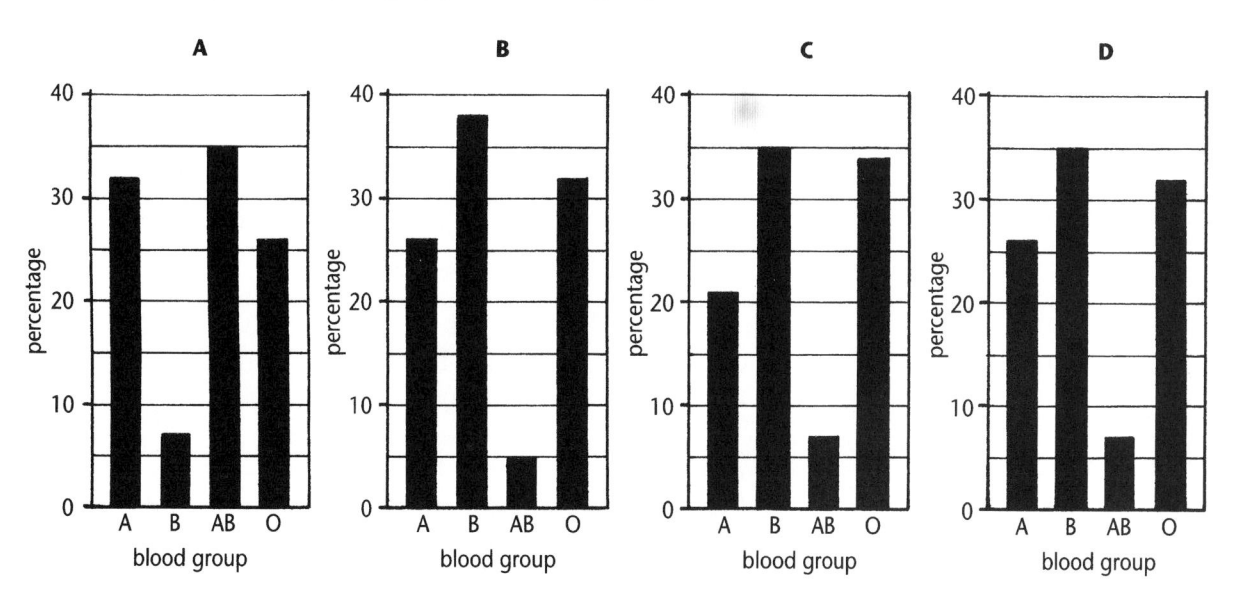

Unit 1 — 3 Healthy Lungs

Matching Test 1

Match the words in list X with their descriptions in list Y.

List X	List Y
1) air sac	a) tube connecting the back of the throat with the bronchi and allowing air to enter and leave the lungs
2) asthma	b) one of two branches of the windpipe that allows air to enter and leave a lung
3) bronchiole	c) one of two organs in the chest cavity needed for gas exchange
4) bronchus	d) respiratory condition involving wheezing and difficulty in breathing
5) gas exchange	e) abnormal growth (tumour) caused by uncontrolled cell division
6) lung	f) one of many small branches of a bronchus that ends in an air sac
7) lung cancer	g) one of many tiny bag-like structures in a lung needed for gas exchange
8) windpipe	h) movement of oxygen from an air sac into the blood and of CO_2 (carbon dioxide) from the blood into the air sac

Chapter 3 **Healthy Lungs**

Matching Test 2

Match the words in list X with their descriptions in list Y.

List X	List Y
1) breathing rate	a) poisonous gas present in cigarette smoke that combines with haemoglobin
2) carbon dioxide	b) apparatus used to measure vital capacity
3) carbon monoxide	c) measure of the maximum rate at which air can be forced out of the lungs
4) haemoglobin	d) volume of air that is breathed in and then out again during normal breathing
5) oxygen	e) maximum volume of air that can be breathed out after as deep a breath as possible has been taken in
6) peak flow	f) gas produced during respiration that leaves the body by being breathed out
7) spirometer	g) gas needed for respiration that enters the bloodstream from air sacs in the lungs
8) tidal volume	h) number of breaths taken per minute
9) vital capacity	i) chemical present in red blood cells that combines with oxygen

Unit 1 Health and Technology

Multiple Choice Test 1

Choose the ONE correct answer to each of the following questions.

Questions 1, 2 and 3 refer to the diagram of the human breathing system.

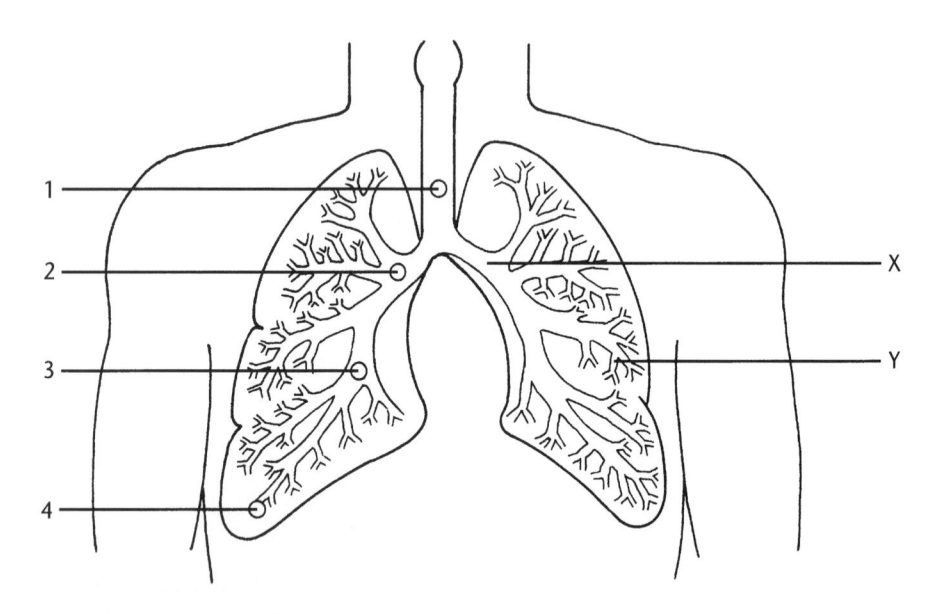

1 What is structure X called?
   A bronchiole.   B left bronchus.
   C right bronchus. D windpipe.

2 What is structure Y called?
   A bronchiole.   B left bronchus.
   C right bronchus. D windpipe.

3 An air sac would be found at position
   A 1.   B 2.   C 3.   D 4.

4 Which of the following correctly describes the form of gas exchange that takes place in a lung?
   A Oxygen and carbon dioxide enter the blood.
   B Oxygen and carbon dioxide leave the blood.
   C Oxygen leaves and carbon dioxide enters the blood.
   D Oxygen enters and carbon dioxide leaves the blood.

Chapter 3 **Healthy Lungs**

Multiple Choice Test 1 continued

5 During each period of 20 seconds, a boy was found to breathe in and out 5 times. This indicates that his breathing rate per minute was

A 4. B 5. C 15. D 100.

6 The first of the accompanying diagrams shows a set of apparatus that can be used to measure vital capacity. Which part of the second diagram shows the apparatus correctly set up and the person ready to breathe out?

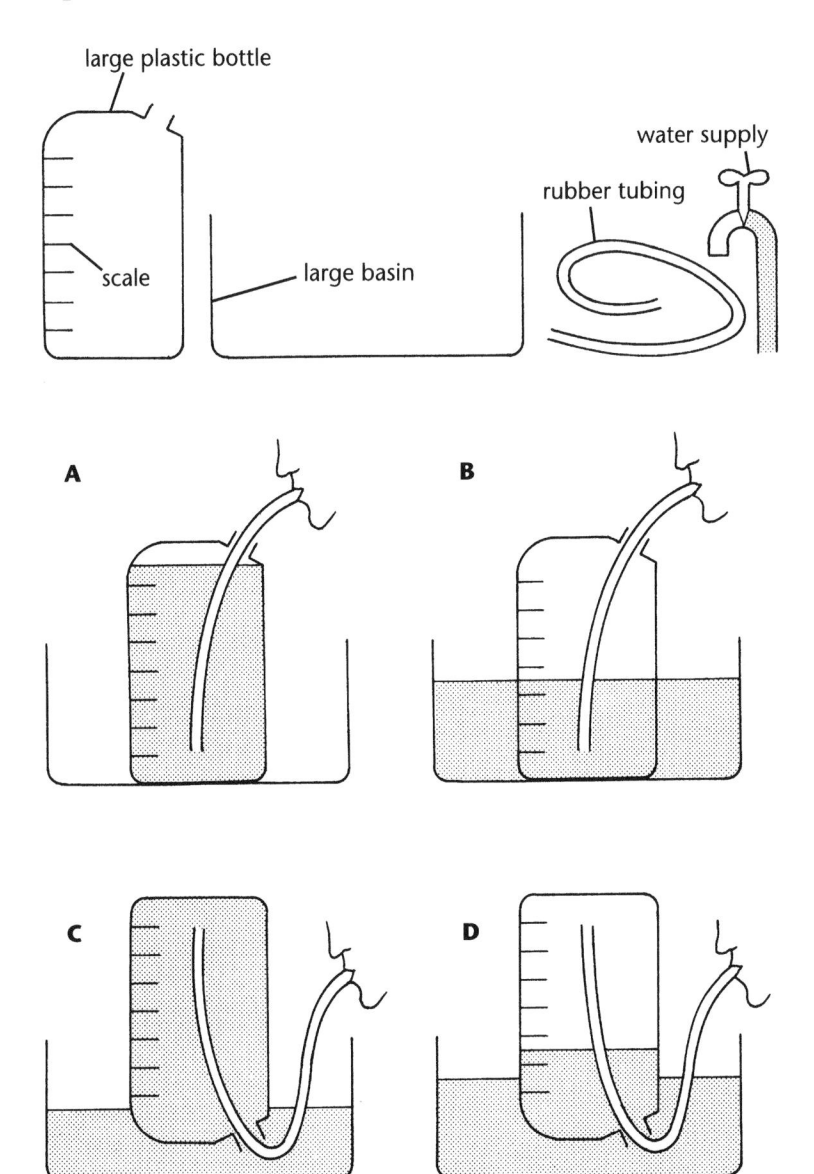

Unit 1 Health and Technology

Multiple Choice Test 1 continued

Questions 7, 8, 9 and 10 refer to the table opposite.

7 Between the ages of 4 and 14, vital capacity

  A increases in males and decreases in females.

  B decreases in males and increases in females.

  C decreases in males and females.

  D increases in males and females.

8 Between the ages of 36 and 60, vital capacity

  A decreases in males and females.

  B increases in males and females.

  C increases in males and decreases in females.

  D decreases in males and increases in females.

9 An average vital capacity of 4300 cm^3 would be typical of

  A an 18 year-old male.

  B a 19 year-old female.

  C a 19 year-old male.

  D a 20 year-old male.

10 The average woman aged between 51 and 55 would have a vital capacity equal to that of a girl aged

  A 11.   B 12.   C 13.   D 14.

age (years)	average vital capacity (cm^3) female	average vital capacity (cm^3) male
4	600	700
5	800	850
6	980	1070
7	1150	1300
8	1350	1500
9	1550	1700
10	1740	1950
11	1950	2200
12	2150	2540
13	2350	2900
14	2480	3250
15	2700	3600
16	2700	3900
17	2750	4100
18	2800	4200
19	2800	4300
20	2800	4320
21–25	2790	4270
26–30	2730	4150
31–35	2640	3990
36–40	2520	3800
41–45	2390	3800
46–50	2250	3410
51–55	2150	3240
56–60	2060	3100

Multiple Choice Test 1 continued

11 The apparatus shown in the diagram can be used to measure tidal volume of air breathed.

A boy breathed normally in and out of it six times. His exhaled air was collected in the plastic bag. The volume of air that he breathed out was 3.6 litres. This shows that his tidal volume (in litres) was

- A 0.6.
- B 3.6.
- C 6.0.
- D 21.6.

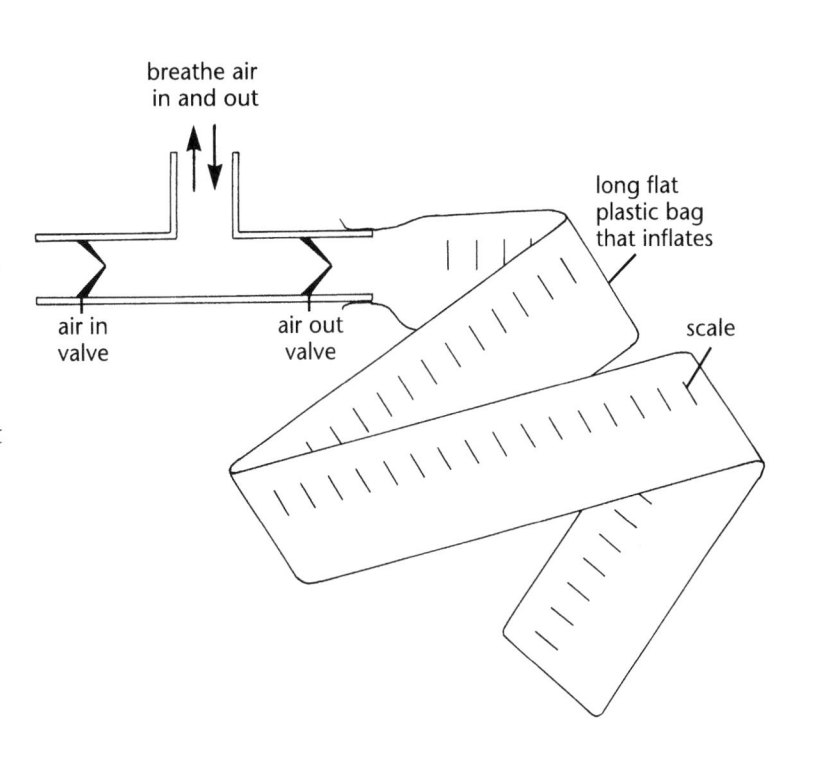

Questions 12 and 13 refer to the data in the following table.

student	tidal volume (cm^3)		
	trial 1	trial 2	trial 3
Sandra	500	460	600
Jack	580	490	480
Elaine	520	520	490
Michael	510	490	520

12 Which student had an average tidal volume of 520 cm^3?
- A Sandra.
- B Jack.
- C Elaine.
- D Michael.

13 It is important to repeat the experiment several times and calculate averages so that the results are
- A fair.
- B correct.
- C accurate.
- D reliable.

Unit 1 Health and Technology

Multiple Choice Test 1 continued

14 A girl sitting at rest was found to inhale, on average, 6400 cm^3 of air per minute. Four per cent of this air was absorbed into her blood as oxygen. What volume of oxygen (in cm^3) was entering her bloodstream per minute?

A 256.   B 1600.   C 25600.   D 160000.

15 The diagram shows five steps carried out during the use of a peak flow meter. They are in a mixed up order. The correct sequence is

A 2, 4, 1, 3, 5.   B 2, 4, 3, 1, 5.
C 4, 2, 1, 5, 3.   D 4, 2, 5, 3, 1.

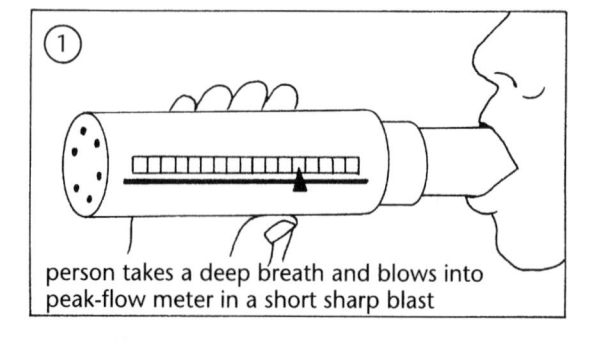

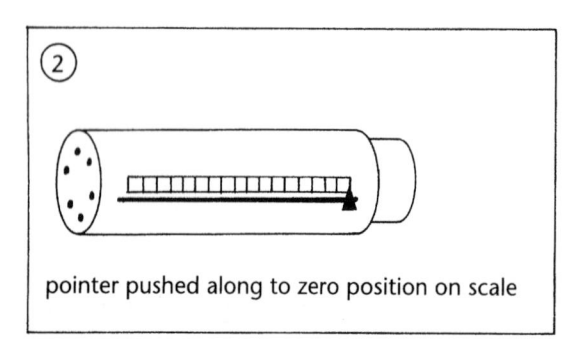

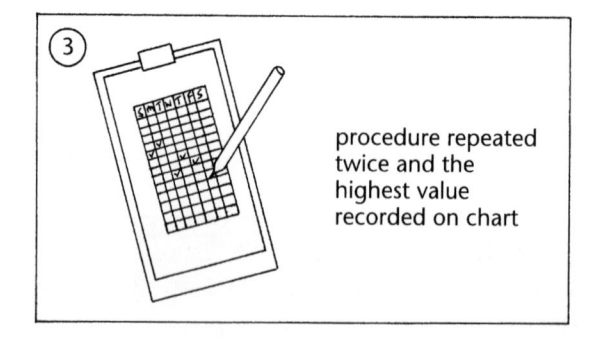

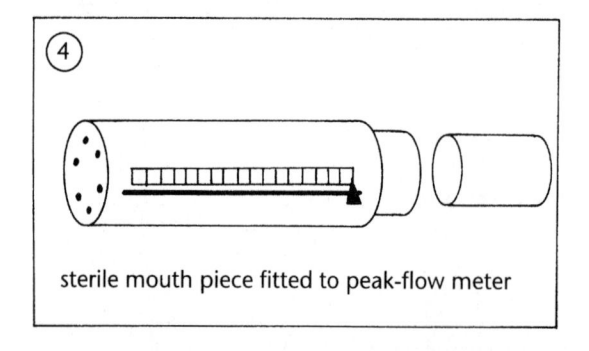

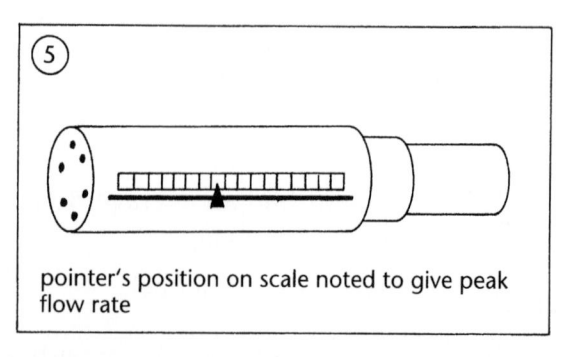

① person takes a deep breath and blows into peak-flow meter in a short sharp blast

② pointer pushed along to zero position on scale

③ procedure repeated twice and the highest value recorded on chart

④ sterile mouth piece fitted to peak-flow meter

⑤ pointer's position on scale noted to give peak flow rate

16 Which of the following conditions can be indicated by data obtained from the use of a peak flow meter?

A anaemia.   B diabetes.   C leukaemia.   D asthma.

Multiple Choice Test 1 continued

17 Which of the following is a gas that is present in cigarette smoke and reduces the oxygen-carrying capacity of blood?

   A tar.   B nicotine.   C carbon dioxide.   D carbon monoxide.

Questions 18 and 19 refer to the diagram of an experiment set up to collect tobacco tar by cooling cigarette smoke and making the tar condense.

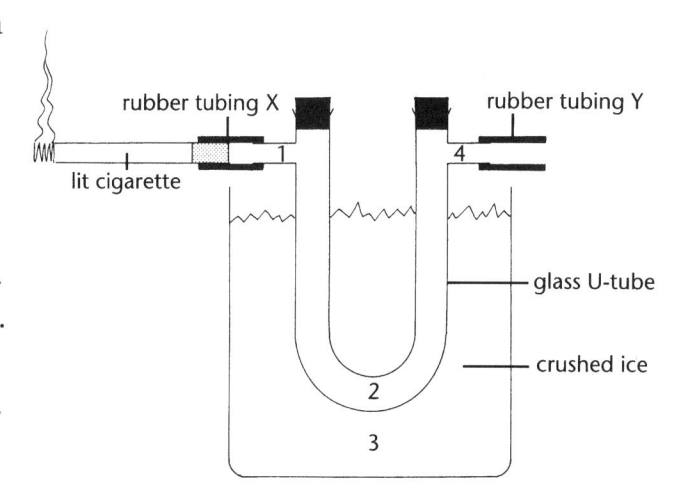

18 To make the experiment work, a pump must be fitted to

   A   rubber tubing X and air sucked out.
   B   rubber tubing X and air pumped in.
   C   rubber tubing Y and air sucked out.
   D   rubber tubing Y and air pumped in.

19 When the apparatus is correctly set up, most tobacco tar will gather at position

   A 1.   B 2.   C 3.   D 4.

Questions 20 and 21 refer to the bar chart which relates the average birth weight of babies to the smoking habits of their mothers.

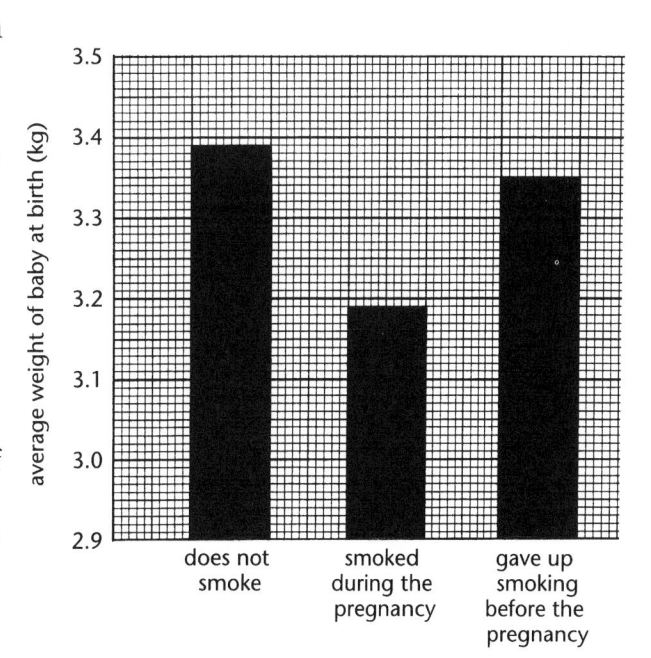

20 The average birth weight (in kg) of a baby born to a mother who has given up smoking before pregnancy was

   A   3.31.   B   3.35.
   C   3.50.   D   3.51.

21 On average, what is the difference (in kg) between the birth weight of a baby born to a mother who does not smoke and that of a baby born to a mother who smoked during the pregnancy?

   A   0.20.   B   0.22.
   C   1.20.   D   2.00.

Unit 1 Health and Technology

Multiple Choice Test 1 continued

Questions 22, 23, 24 and 25 refer to the data in the following table which shows the effect of cigarette smoking on the life expectancy of British men.

present age (years)	further years expected to live (life expectancy)			
	non-smoker	1–10 cigarettes daily	11–20 cigarettes daily	21+ cigarettes daily
25	49	44	43	42
35	39	35	34	33
45	30	26	25	24
55	21	18	17	16

22 The number of further years expected to be lived by men aged 55 who smoke 15 cigarettes a day is

   A 16.   B 17.   C 18.   D 25.

23 What is the present age (in years) of men who smoke 20 cigarettes daily and are expected to live another 34 years?

   A 25.   B 35.   C 45.   D 55.

24 On average, 25 year old men who smoke 1–10 cigarettes daily can expect to live to age

   A 44.   B 49.   C 69.   D 74.

25 Compared with non-smokers, the number of years by which 45 year old men who smoke 21+ cigarettes per day reduce their life expectancy is

   A 5.   B 6.   C 21.   D 24.

Multiple Choice Test 2

Choose the ONE correct answer to each of the following questions.

1. Air entering the lungs passes through the following structures in the order
   A windpipe ⟶ bronchus ⟶ bronchiole ⟶ air sac.
   B bronchus ⟶ windpipe ⟶ air sac ⟶ bronchiole.
   C air sac ⟶ bronchiole ⟶ bronchus ⟶ windpipe.
   D windpipe ⟶ bronchiole ⟶ bronchus ⟶ air sac.

Questions 2 and 3 refer to the diagram of the results from an experiment where a student's normal breathing rate at rest was recorded for 40 seconds.

2. The student's rate of breathing (in breaths per minute) was
   A 8.   B 12.   C 16.   D 24.

3. The volume of air (in cm^3) breathed in during one breath was
   A 600.
   B 700.
   C 3600.
   D 3700.

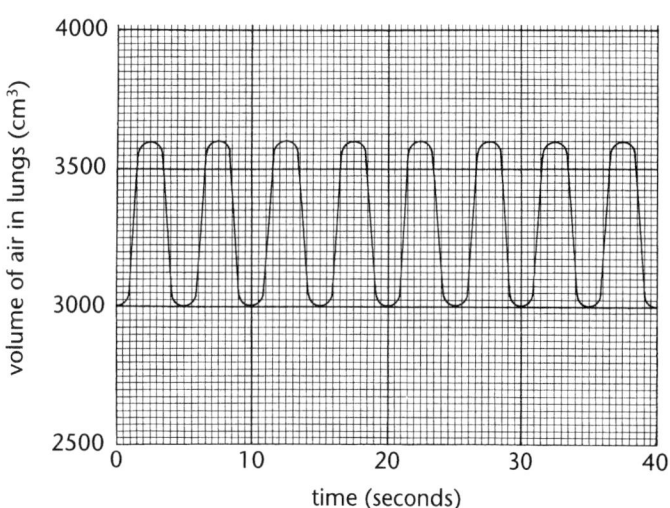

4. The efficiency of gas exchange in the lungs is improved by
   A eating.
   B resting.
   C smoking.
   D exercising.

Unit 1 Health and Technology

Multiple Choice Test 2 continued

5 The diagram shows an instrument called a spirometer. It is used to measure vital capacity.

The following steps give the procedure for using the spirometer but in a mixed up order.
1) Hold nose and breathe out fully through the mouthpiece.
2) Move outer ring (X) until pointer is at zero on the scale.
3) Read measurement of vital capacity on scale.
4) Fix sterile mouthpiece on to spirometer at position Y.
5) Take a deep breath.

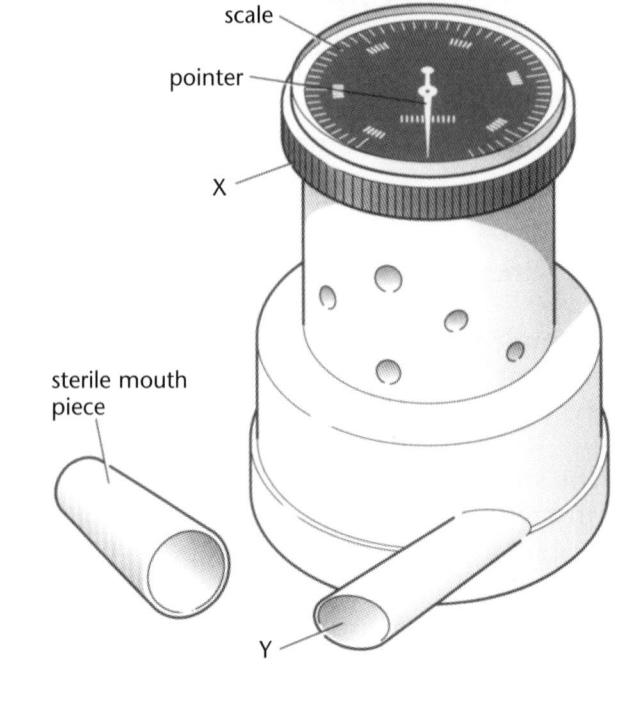

The correct order of these steps is
A 2, 4, 5, 3, 1.   B 3, 2, 4, 5, 1.   C 4, 2, 5, 1, 3.   D 5, 2, 4, 3, 1.

Questions 6 and 7 refer to the following table which gives data about the vital capacity of four students of similar age and build.

student	vital capacity (l)			
	trial 1	trial 2	trial 3	average
Frank	3.8	3.5	3.8	3.7
Imran	4.2	4.3	4.1	[X]
Harry	5.5	5.4	5.6	5.5
Nita	3.8	[Y]	4.2	4.0

6 The reading that should have been inserted in box [X] is
   A 4.1.   B 4.2.   C 4.3.   D 4.4.

7 The reading that should have been inserted in box [Y] is
   A 4.0.   B 4.4.   C 12.0.   D 13.2.

Chapter 3 **Healthy Lungs**

Multiple Choice Test 2 continued

Questions 8 and 9 refer to the following information. The volume of air entering and leaving the lungs can be measured using a piece of apparatus in which a pen moves up and down on a revolving drum. It draws a line graph as the person breathes in and out. An example is shown in the accompanying diagram where the person was at rest during period X. She took in the deepest breath that she could and then exhaled it during period Y.

8   Which lettered arrow in the diagram represents **vital capacity**?

9   Which lettered arrow represents **tidal volume**?

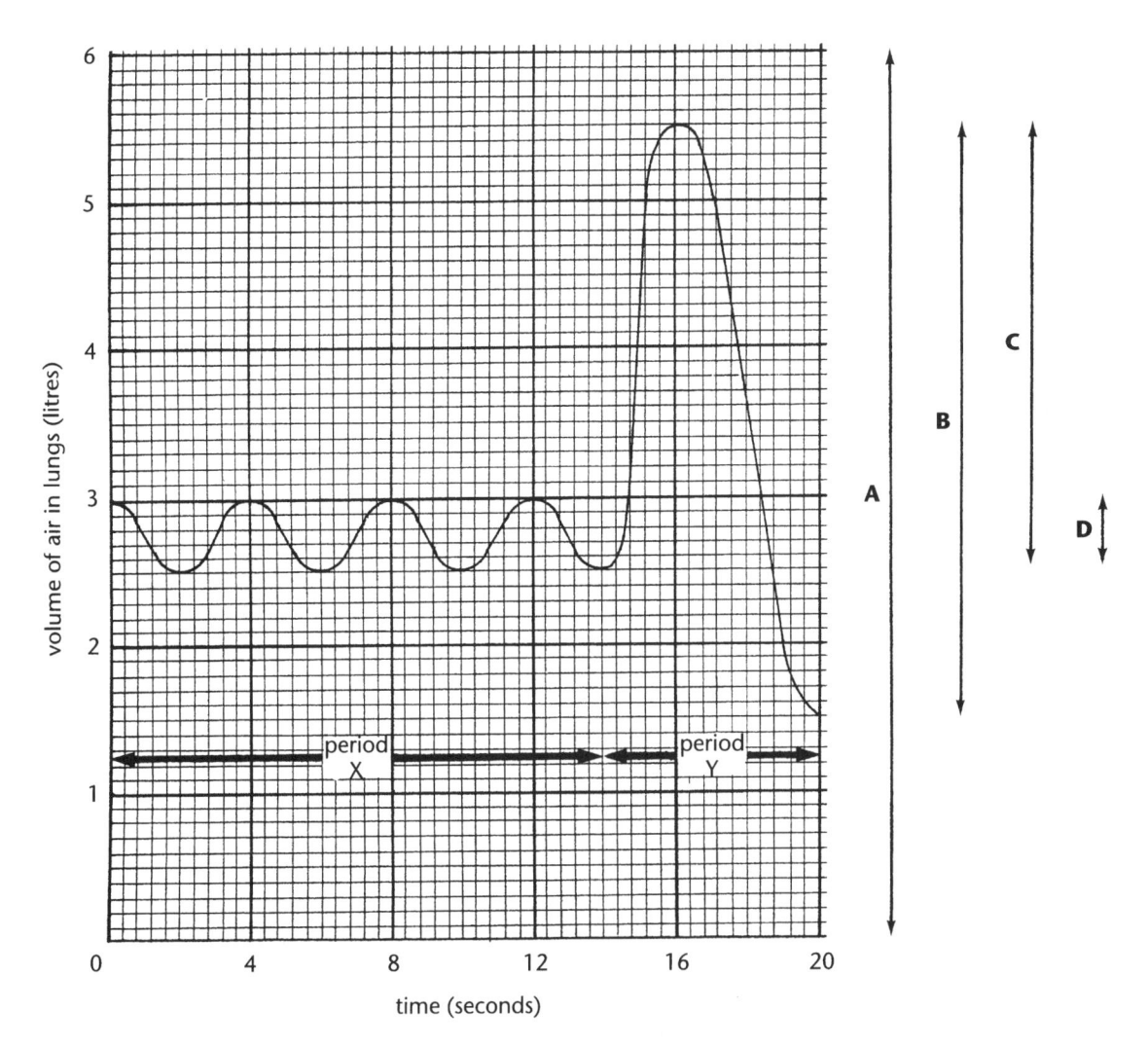

Unit 1 **Health and Technology**

Multiple Choice Test 2 continued

10 The pieces of apparatus shown in the first of the diagrams below, when fitted together, can be used to measure the tidal volume of a person's lungs.

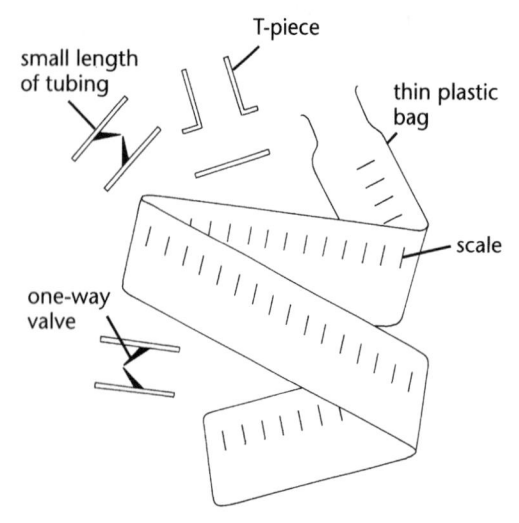

Which part of the second diagram shows the equipment correctly set up?

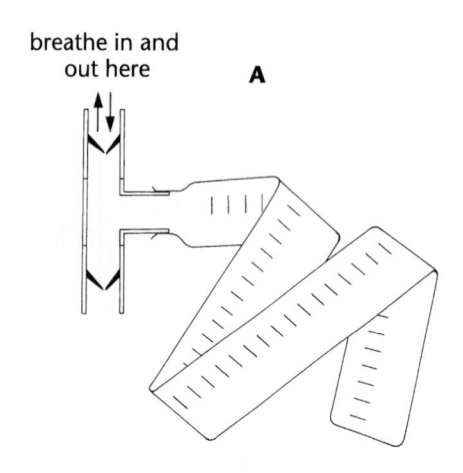

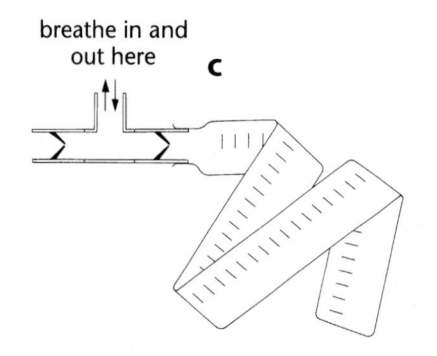

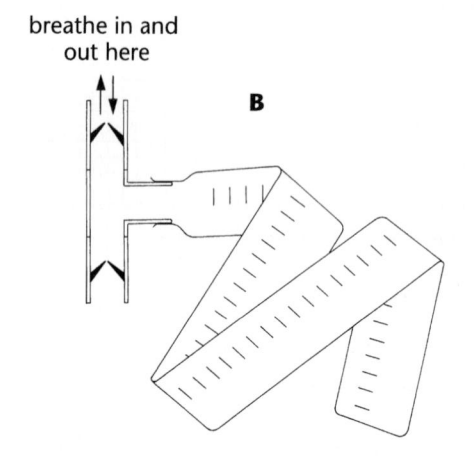

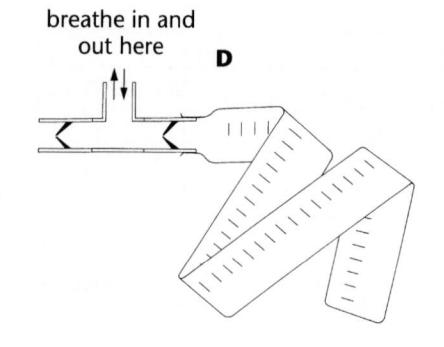

Chapter 3 Healthy Lungs

Multiple Choice Test 2 continued

Questions 11, 12 and 13 refer to the data in the table obtained from an athlete during training.

activity	average volume of each breath (l)	rate of breathing (breaths per min.)	volume of air breathed per minute (l)
resting	0.5	12	6.0
jogging	1.5	24	[see question 11]
running a race	2.5	36	90.0

11 The volume of air (in litres) breathed per minute during jogging would be

   A 16.0.   B 25.5.   C 36.0.   D 48.0.

12 The percentage increase in rate of breathing from jogging to running a race is

   A 33.   B 50.   C 67.   D 200.

13 The ratio of volume of air (in litres) breathed per minute by the athlete running a race to that breathed per minute at rest was

   A 3:1.   B 5:1.   C 15:1.   D 84:1.

14 The girl in the diagram has taken in a deep breath and is about to blow into the flow meter in one short sharp blast.

What is the error in her procedure?

   A She should have set the pointer at the zero mark on the scale.

   B She should have taken a normal breath not a deep one.

   C She should be holding the peak flow meter with her hand over the end.

   D She should have gently breathed in and out of the peak flow meter several times.

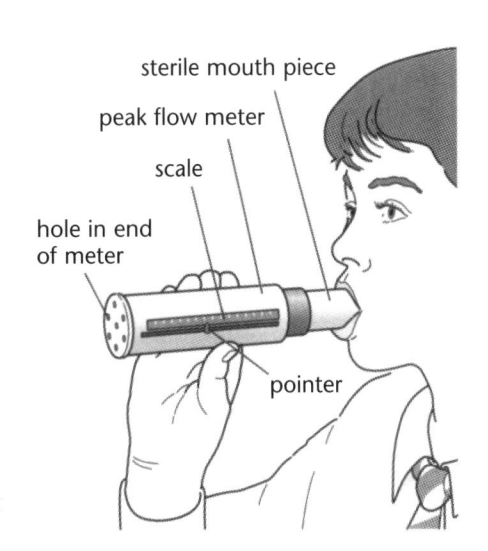

Unit 1 Health and Technology

Multiple Choice Test 2 continued

Questions 15 and 16 refer to the chart which shows the peak flow readings recorded by a sufferer of asthma over one week.

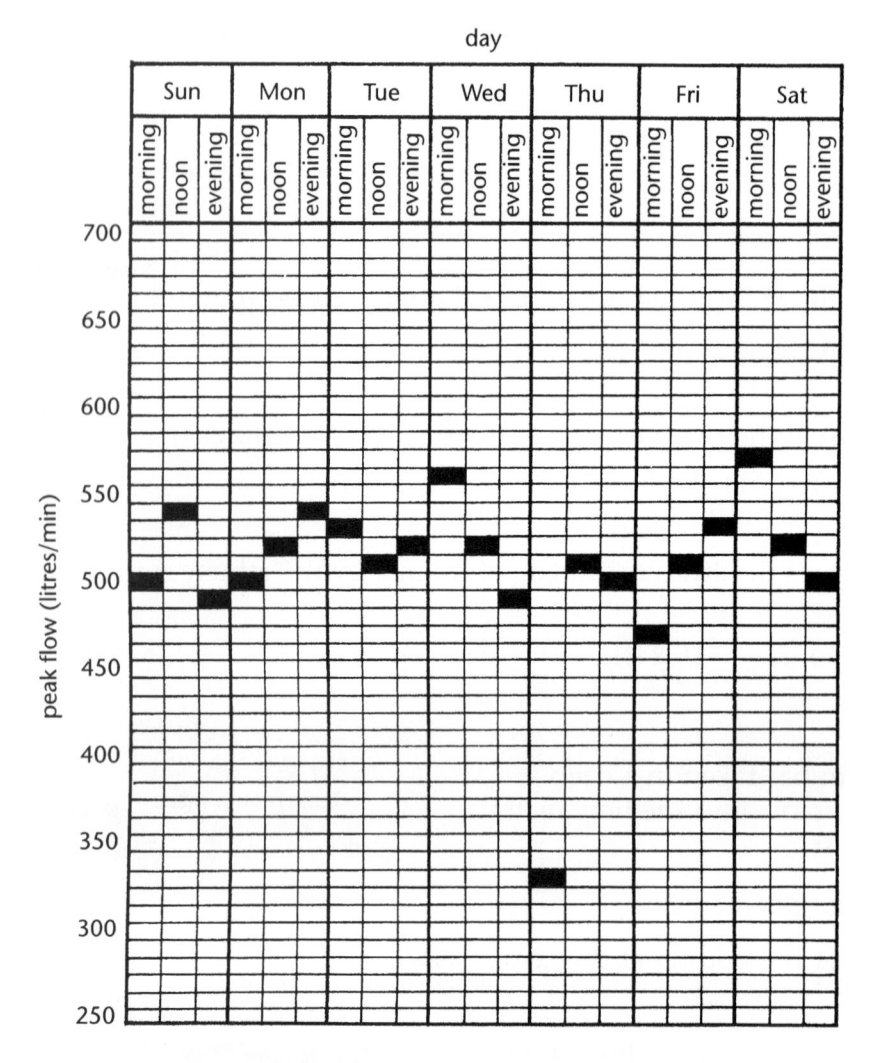

15 Each entry on the chart is the highest of three blows. How many times did the person use their peak flow meter each day?

A 3.   B 9.   C 21.   D 63.

16 On which day did the person suffer a wheezing chest and have to use their bronchodilator to relieve an asthma attack?

A Wednesday.   B Thursday.   C Friday.   D Saturday.

Multiple Choice Test 2 continued

Chapter 3 **Healthy Lungs**

Questions 17 and 18 refer to the diagram. It shows an experiment set up to investigate if tips on cigarettes reduce the tar content of inhaled smoke.

17 The one variable factor in this experiment should be

A mass of filter wool in the U-tubes.

B brand of tobacco present in the cigarettes.

C presence or absence of tips on the cigarettes.

D rate of flow of water passing through the pumps.

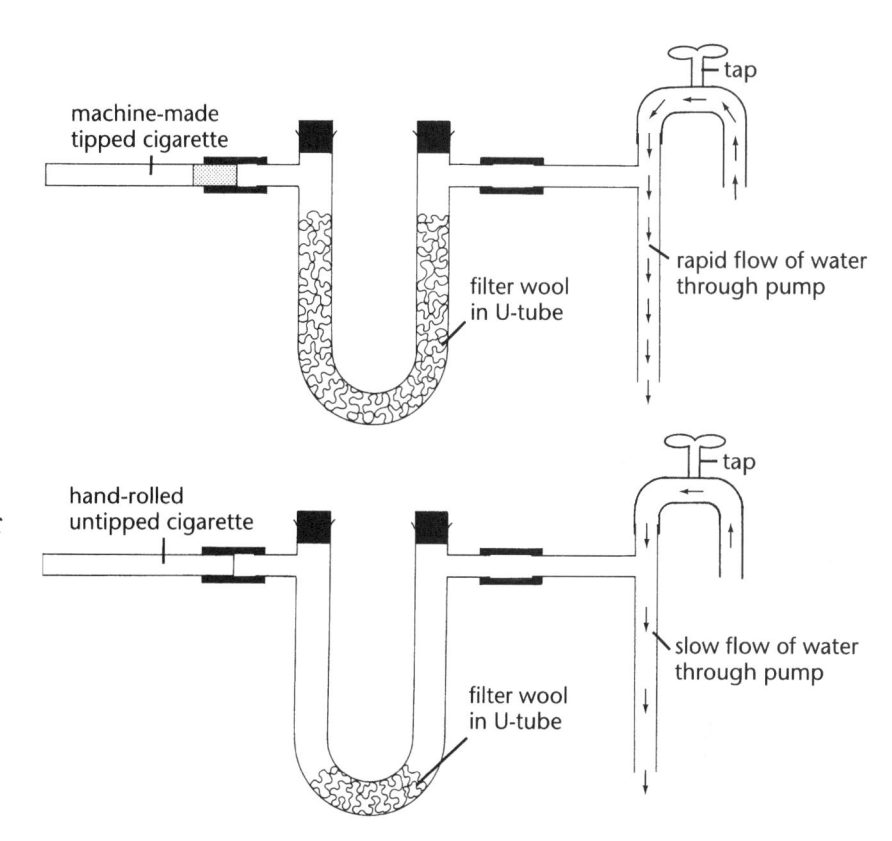

18 Which line in the following table is correct?

	suggested improvement to design	reason for carrying out the improvement
A	the mass of filter wool used each time should be equal	so that a control experiment is included
B	the procedure should be repeated several times	so that the experiment is fair
C	the water passing through the pumps should flow at the same rate	so that the results are correct
D	the hand-rolled untipped cigarette should be replaced by a machine-made one without its tip	so that a valid comparison can be made

49

Unit 1 **Health and Technology**

Multiple Choice Test 2 continued

Questions 19, 20 and 21 refer to the bar chart. It is based on a survey of the number of cigarettes smoked daily and the death rates from coronary heart disease in British men.

19 The annual death rate per 100 000 from coronary heart disease for 40 year old men who smoke 20 cigarettes daily is

    A 70.   B 85.   C 100.   D 360.

20 An annual death rate of 400 per 100 000 from coronary heart disease is found for men aged

    A 45–54 who smoke 1–15 cigarettes daily.

    B 45–54 who smoke 16–25 cigarettes daily.

    C 45–54 who smoke 26+ cigarettes daily.

    D 55–64 who smoke 0 cigarettes daily.

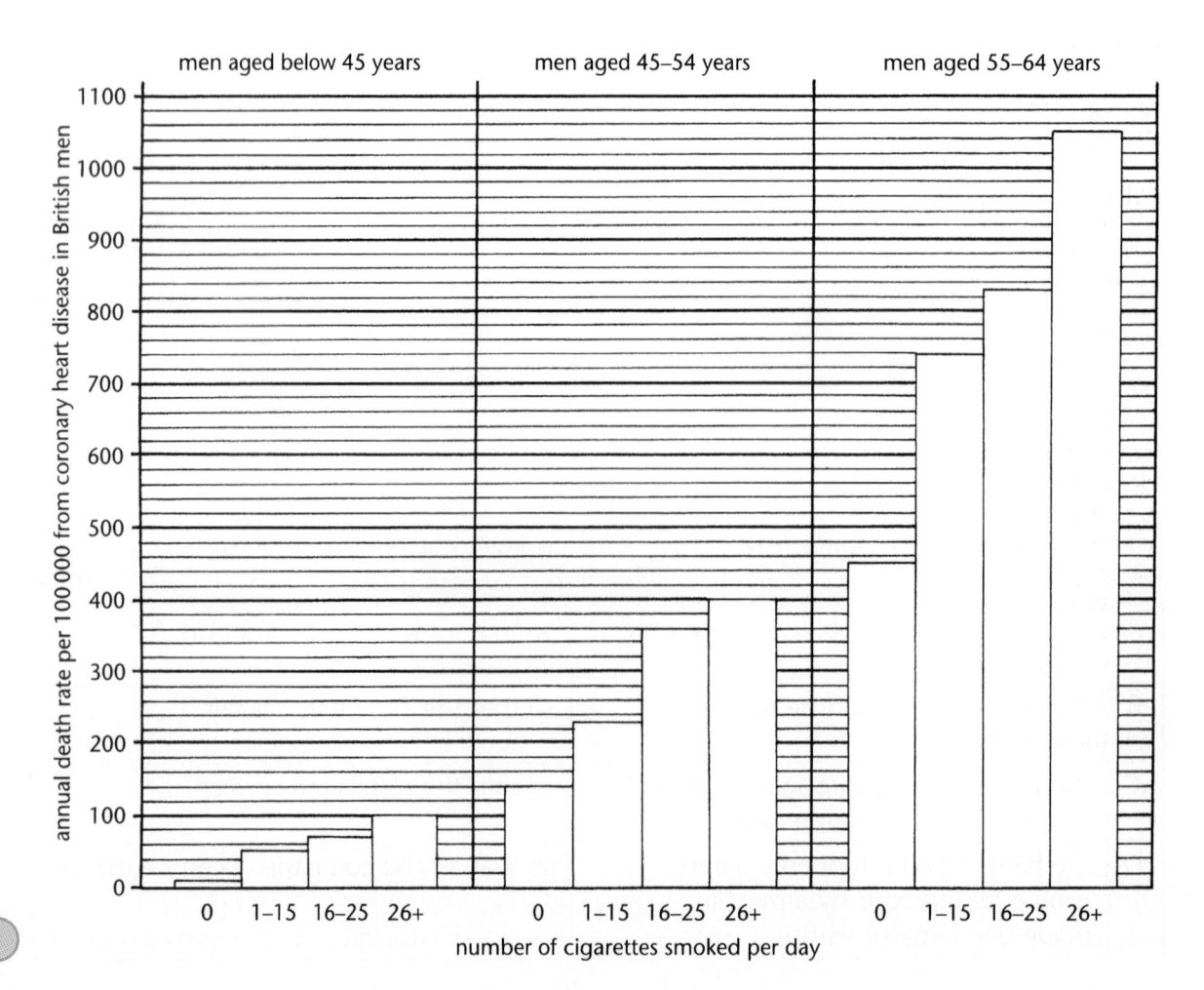

Multiple Choice Test 2 continued

21 Which of the following conclusions can be correctly drawn from the information in the bar chart?

  A Among men under the age of 45, only smokers die of coronary heart disease.

  B 60 year-old men who smoke 10 cigarettes daily are less likely to die of coronary heart disease than 50 year olds who smoke 20 cigarettes daily.

  C The chance of dying of coronary heart disease decreases for men who survive beyond the age of 55 and still continue to smoke 10 cigarettes daily.

  D Men who smoke 30 cigarettes daily are 4 times more likely to suffer coronary heart disease when they are 50 than when they are 25.

Questions 22, 23, 24 and 25 refer to the following passage.

SMOKERS BEWARE

When air is breathed in, oxygen in the inhaled air combines with a red substance in red blood cells called haemoglobin and forms oxyhaemoglobin. The oxygen is then carried in this form to all parts of the body where it is needed for energy release by living cells.

When a cigarette is smoked, hot smoke containing nicotine, oily tars and the poisonous gas carbon monoxide is inhaled on to the delicate lining of the lungs. Once it has been breathed in, the carbon monoxide combines with haemoglobin to form carboxyhaemoglobin. Haemoglobin affected in this way can no longer pick up oxygen and carry it to the body's cells. Up to 10 per cent of the oxygen-carrying capacity of a smoker's blood is lost in this way.

It is found that:

- endurance when exercising decreases as number of cigarettes smoked increases;
- improvement of fitness produced by training is less for smokers than non-smokers;
- time taken to complete an exercise programme decreases when the person stops smoking.

The early symptoms of mild carbon monoxide poisoning are headaches, nausea and tiredness. In addition heart rate increases because the heart has to work harder to deliver the poorer oxygen supply in the blood to the cells and tissues. So if you are a smoker, don't break your heart. Quit now and give your heart a break.

Multiple Choice Test 2 continued

22 Which equation represents the chemical reaction that takes place when non-smokers breathe fresh air into their lungs?

   A   carbon monoxide + haemoglobin ⟶ carboxyhaemoglobin.

   B   oxygen + haemoglobin ⟶ carboxyhaemoglobin.

   C   carbon monoxide + haemoglobin ⟶ oxyhaemoglobin.

   D   oxygen + haemoglobin ⟶ oxyhaemoglobin.

23 Which equation represents the chemical reaction that occurs when smokers inhale tobacco smoke?

   A   carbon monoxide + haemoglobin ⟶ carboxyhaemoglobin.

   B   carbon dioxide + haemoglobin ⟶ carboxyhaemoglobin.

   C   carbon monoxide + haemoglobin ⟶ oxyhaemoglobin.

   D   carbon dioxide + haemoglobin ⟶ oxyhaemoglobin.

24 Compared with non-smokers, people who smoke

   A   gain more benefit from training programmes.

   B   can continue doing a strenuous exercise for longer.

   C   can complete a demanding exercise programme more quickly.

   D   suffer a greater number of headaches and nausea.

25 Which line in the table gives two results of the body suffering poisoning by carbon monoxide?

	tiredness	heart rate
A	↑	↑
B	↑	↓
C	↓	↑
D	↓	↓

Key
↑ = increase   ↓ = decrease

Unit 1 · 4 Healthy Body

Matching Test 1

Match the words in list X with their descriptions in list Y.

List X	List Y
1) anorexia	a) unit used to measure energy
2) callipers	b) energy-rich food that contains double the energy present in the same mass of carbohydrate
3) carbohydrate	c) word that describes a person who is excessively overweight
4) fat	d) psychological disorder where an underweight person suffers a fear of becoming fat and refuses to eat
5) kilojoule (kJ)	e) chemical compound needed in tiny amounts to protect the body against deficiency diseases
6) liver	f) chemical element such as iron needed for good health
7) mineral	g) energy-rich food such as sugar or starch
8) obese	h) food needed for growth and tissue repair
9) protein	i) organ in the abdomen that is damaged by excessive intake of alcohol
10) vitamin	j) piece of equipment used to estimate the body's fat content

Unit 1 **Health and Technology**

Matching Test 2

Match the words in list X with their descriptions in list Y.

List X

1) alcohol
2) breathalyser
3) dynamometer
4) exercise
5) fatigue
6) hyperthermia
7) hypothermia
8) reaction time
9) relaxation
10) thermometer

List Y

a) condition suffered by muscles after strenuous exercise
b) interval of time between detecting a signal and responding to it
c) piece of equipment used to measure temperature
d) piece of equipment used to estimate the amount of alcohol in the breath
e) piece of equipment used to measure muscle strength
f) resting condition that relieves stress and muscle fatigue
g) intoxicating liquid that is harmful to the liver and brain when consumed to excess
h) physical exertion especially for the purpose of keeping fit
i) condition suffered by a person whose body temperature has dropped to a subnormal level
j) condition suffered by a person whose body temperature has risen to an abnormally high level

Chapter 4 **Healthy Body**

Multiple Choice Test 1

Choose the ONE correct answer to each of the following questions.

Questions 1, 2 and 3 refer to the accompanying diagram. It shows examples of the four groups of food that make up a balanced diet.

1 The foods shown in group 1 are all rich in
   A calcium.
   B protein.
   C carbohydrate.
   D vitamin C.

2 Which of the following diagrams shows the two foods missing from group 2 in the first diagram?

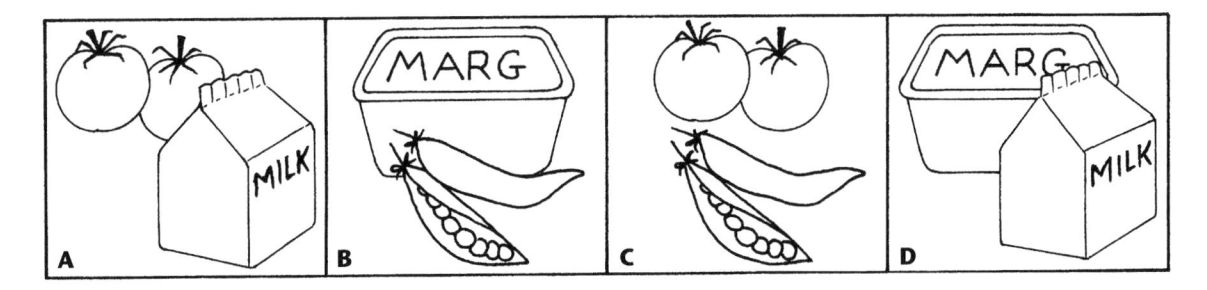

3 Which two groups contain foods that give the body most of its energy?
   A 1 and 2.
   B 1 and 4.
   C 2 and 3.
   D 3 and 4.

55

Unit 1 Health and Technology

Multiple Choice Test 1 continued

4. The following table gives information about the vitamin C content of four types of fruit.

fruit	average weight of one piece (g)	vitamin C content (mg/100g)
orange	200	50
grapefruit	300	40
banana	200	10
peach	100	40

A pregnant woman needs at least 80 mg of vitamin C every day. Which of the following would fail to supply her daily requirement of vitamin C?

   A 1 orange.   B 1 grapefruit.   C 2 bananas.   D 2 peaches.

Questions 5 and 6 refer to the data in the diagram below.

5. The result that should have been entered in box X in the wholemeal bread table is
   A 11.6.   B 42.0.   C 58.0.   D 862.0.

6. The simple whole number ratio of water in wholemeal bread to that of chocolate is
   A 1:20.   B 20:1.   C 42:1.   D 80:1.

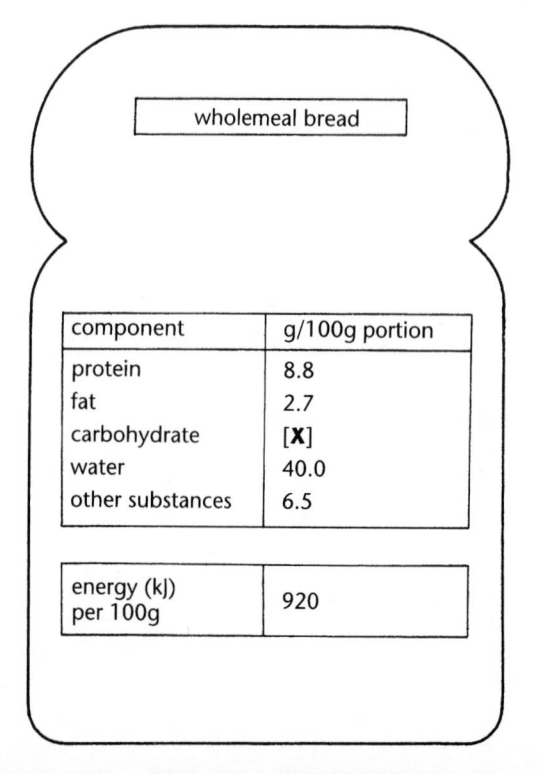

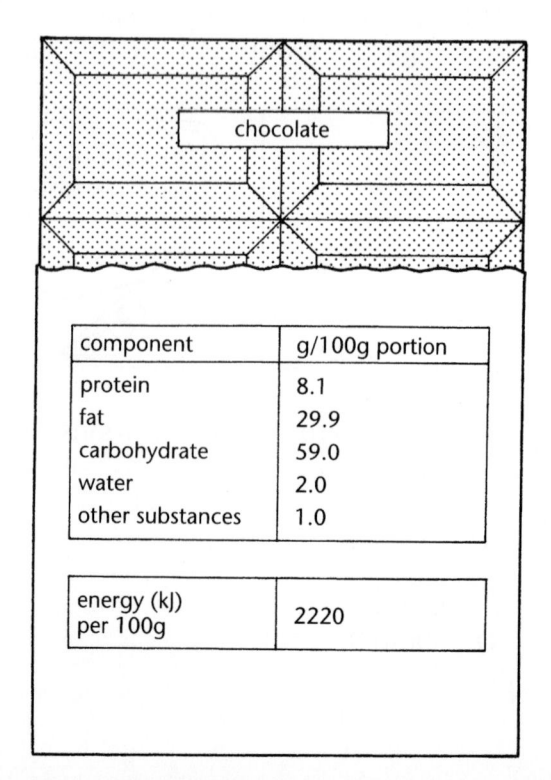

wholemeal bread

component	g/100g portion
protein	8.8
fat	2.7
carbohydrate	[X]
water	40.0
other substances	6.5

energy (kJ) per 100g	920

chocolate

component	g/100g portion
protein	8.1
fat	29.9
carbohydrate	59.0
water	2.0
other substances	1.0

energy (kJ) per 100g	2220

Multiple Choice Test 1 continued

Questions 7, 8 and 9 refer to the accompanying table which gives the energy used up by men of different weights when carrying out different activities.

activity	average energy used (kJ/min.)		
	body weight 60–69 kg 	body weight 70–79 kg 	body weight 80+ kg 
rowing	41	48	53
jogging	50	59	65
dancing	28	33	36
walking	23	26	29

7 Which activity uses up most energy?

    A rowing.   B jogging.   C dancing.   D walking.

8 From the data it can be concluded that as body weight increases, the amount of energy used for

    A all activities increases.   C rowing and jogging only, increases.

    B all activities decreases.   D dancing and walking only, decreases.

9 Which of the following histograms correctly represents the effect of increasing body weight on energy used up during rowing?

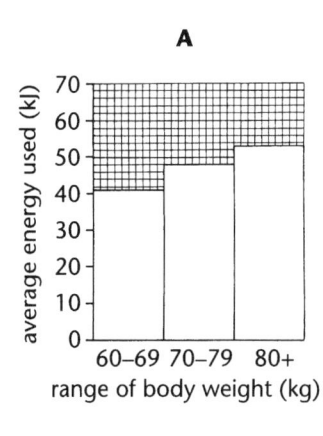

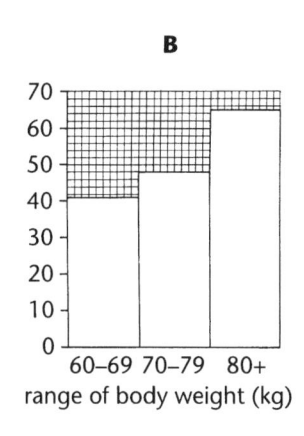

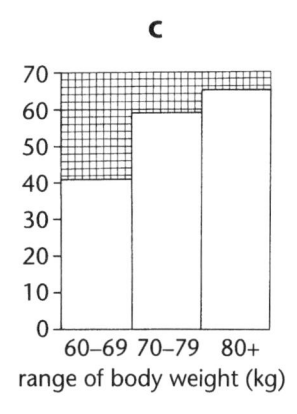

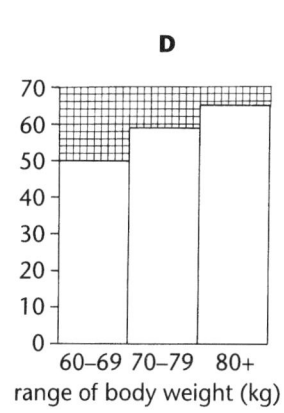

Unit 1 Health and Technology

Multiple Choice Test 1 continued

Questions 10, 11 and 12 refer to the data in the accompanying table.

group number	description of people in group age (years)	sex (♀=f, ♂=m)	type of work	average daily energy requirement (kJ)
1	35	♀	light	9500
2	35	♀	heavy	12000
3	35	♂	light	11500
4	35	♂	heavy	13000
5	50	♀	light	9500
6	50	♀	heavy	12000
7	50	♂	light	11500
8	50	♂	heavy	13000

10 How many kJ are needed each day by a 50 year-old woman who does heavy work?
   A 9500.   B 11500.   C 12000.   D 13000.

11 Which group of people should you compare with group 5 if you want to find out the effect of a person's sex on their average daily energy requirement?
   A 1.   B 3.   C 6.   D 7.

12 In this survey which factor did not affect the person's average daily energy requirement?
   A age.   B sex.   C build.   D type of work.

13 Being overweight can lead to increased risk of both
   A diabetes and hyperthermia.   C leukaemia and kidney failure.
   B hypothermia and arthritis.   D heart disease and diabetes.

14 Which of the four places shown in the diagram would be **least** useful for measuring body fat using a skinfold calliper?

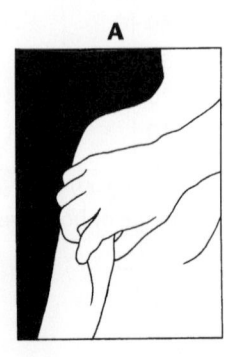

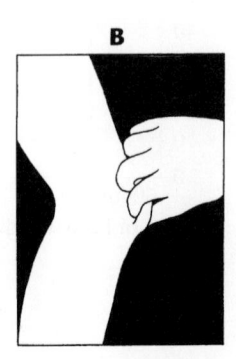

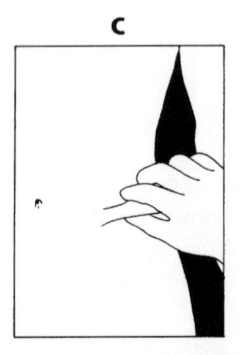

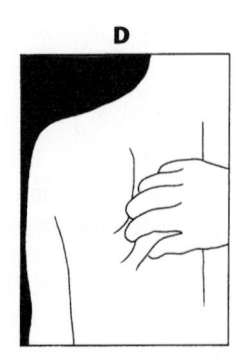

Chapter 4 **Healthy Body**

Multiple Choice Test 1 continued

Questions 15 and 16 refer to the accompanying graph. It shows the percentage of energy that Scottish people obtained from two classes of food over a period of 60 years.

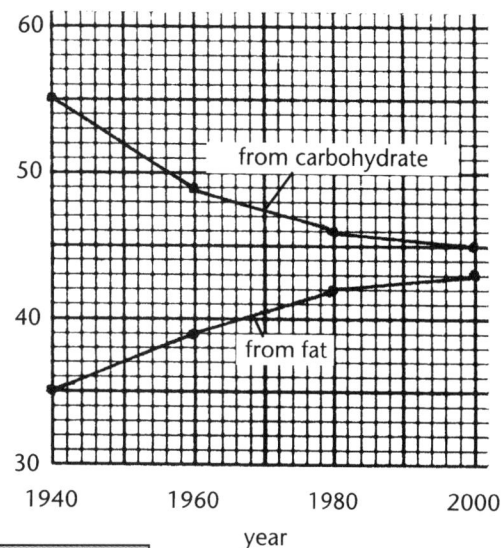

15 Which line in the following table is correct?

	year	energy (%)	
		from carbohydrate	from fat
A	1940	35	55
B	1960	39	49
C	1980	42	46
D	2000	45	43

16 The results from the graph suggest that compared with 60 years earlier, people in 2000 were eating

A more fat and less carbohydrate.
B more carbohydrate and less fat.
C a greater variety of certain foods.
D a greater variety of food generally.

17 The boy in the diagram is having his temperature taken using a liquid crystal strip thermometer.

The steps carried out during this procedure are listed below in the wrong order.

1 Allow 20 seconds for the reading to stabilise.
2 Clean the thermometer before using it.
3 Take the temperature reading by noting the number that remains most clearly visible for 10 seconds.
4 Have the person wear the thermometer like a headband.

The correct order of the steps is

A 2, 4, 1, 3.   B 2, 4, 3, 1.   C 4, 2, 1, 3.   D 4, 2, 3, 1.

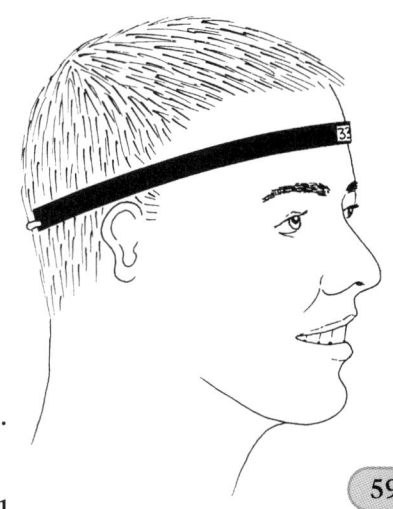

Unit 1 Health and Technology

Multiple Choice Test 1 continued

Questions 18 and 19 refer to the diagram which shows the effects on the body of temperatures that are above and below normal. The questions also refer to the diagram of four thermometers used to take the temperatures of four different hospital patients.

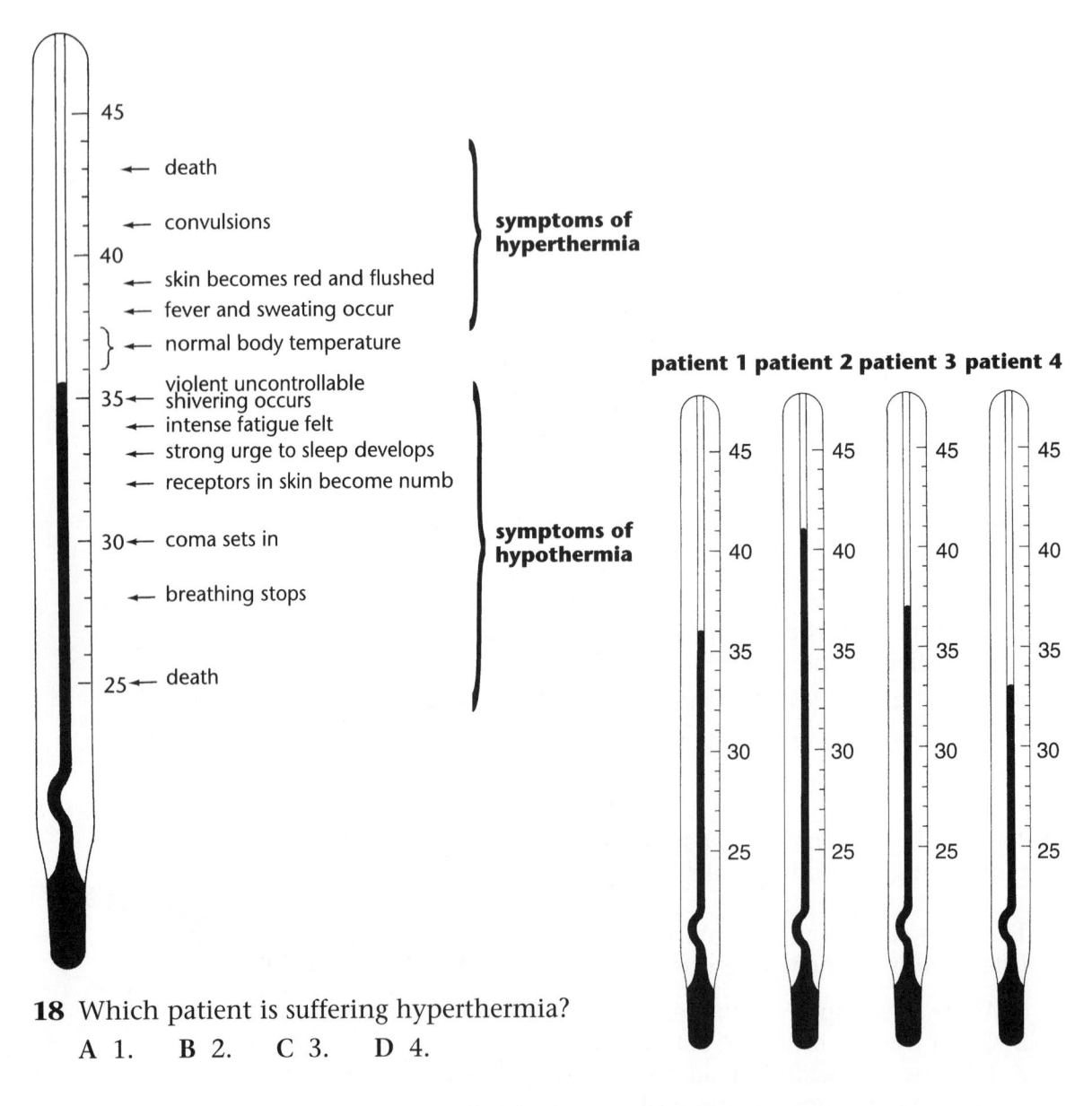

Main thermometer labels:
- 45 — death
- convulsions
- 40
- skin becomes red and flushed
- fever and sweating occur
- normal body temperature
- 35 — violent uncontrollable shivering occurs
- intense fatigue felt
- strong urge to sleep develops
- receptors in skin become numb
- 30 — coma sets in
- breathing stops
- 25 — death

symptoms of hyperthermia (above normal)
symptoms of hypothermia (below normal)

Patient thermometers (scale 25–45):
- patient 1: ~37
- patient 2: ~41
- patient 3: ~36
- patient 4: ~33

18 Which patient is suffering hyperthermia?

A 1. B 2. C 3. D 4.

19 Which of the following symptoms would be shown by patient 4?

A Coma has set in.
B Breathing has stopped.
C Strong urge to sleep has developed.
D Receptors in the skin have become numb.

Multiple Choice Test 1 continued

20 The diagram shows a piece of equipment being used to measure muscle strength.

It is called a

A pulsimeter.

B dynamometer.

C peak flow meter.

D sphygmomanometer.

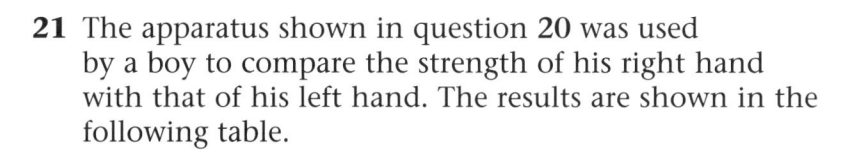

21 The apparatus shown in question 20 was used by a boy to compare the strength of his right hand with that of his left hand. The results are shown in the following table.

trial number	strength (units)	
	right hand	left hand
1	28	22
2	29	24
3	28	23

Which of the following conclusions can be correctly drawn from the results of this experiment alone?

A The boy's left hand is stronger than his right hand.

B The average strength of the boy's right hand is 28 units.

C The average strength of the boy's left hand is 23 units.

D Among the Scottish population, the right hand is stronger than the left.

Unit 1 Health and Technology

Multiple Choice Test 1 continued

22 The information in the line graph and table refers to an alert, sober driver having to make emergency stops at different speeds.

car speed (km/hour)	stopping distance (m)
32	12
48	22.5
64	[X]
80	52.5
96	[Y]
112	94.5

The readings (in metres) that should have been entered in the table at X and Y are

A X = 33, Y = 71.
B X = 33, Y = 72.
C X = 36, Y = 71.
D X = 36, Y = 72.

23 Drinking excessively large quantities of alcohol over a period of years increases the chance of a person suffering

A diabetes and leukaemia.
B anorexia and kidney failure.
C bronchitis and hyperthermia.
D brain damage and liver disease.

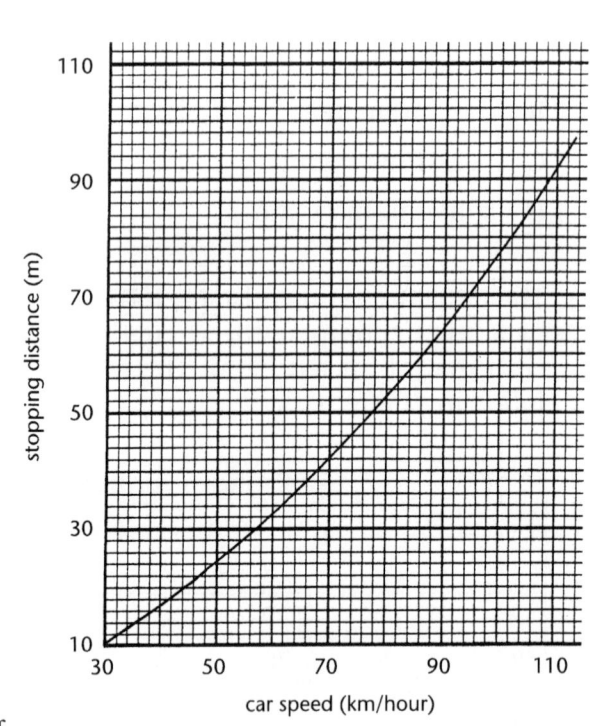

Multiple Choice Test 1 continued

Questions 24 and 25 refer to the graph. It shows the quantity of alcohol present in a woman's blood after she had drunk several glasses of wine at a party which finished at 02.00.

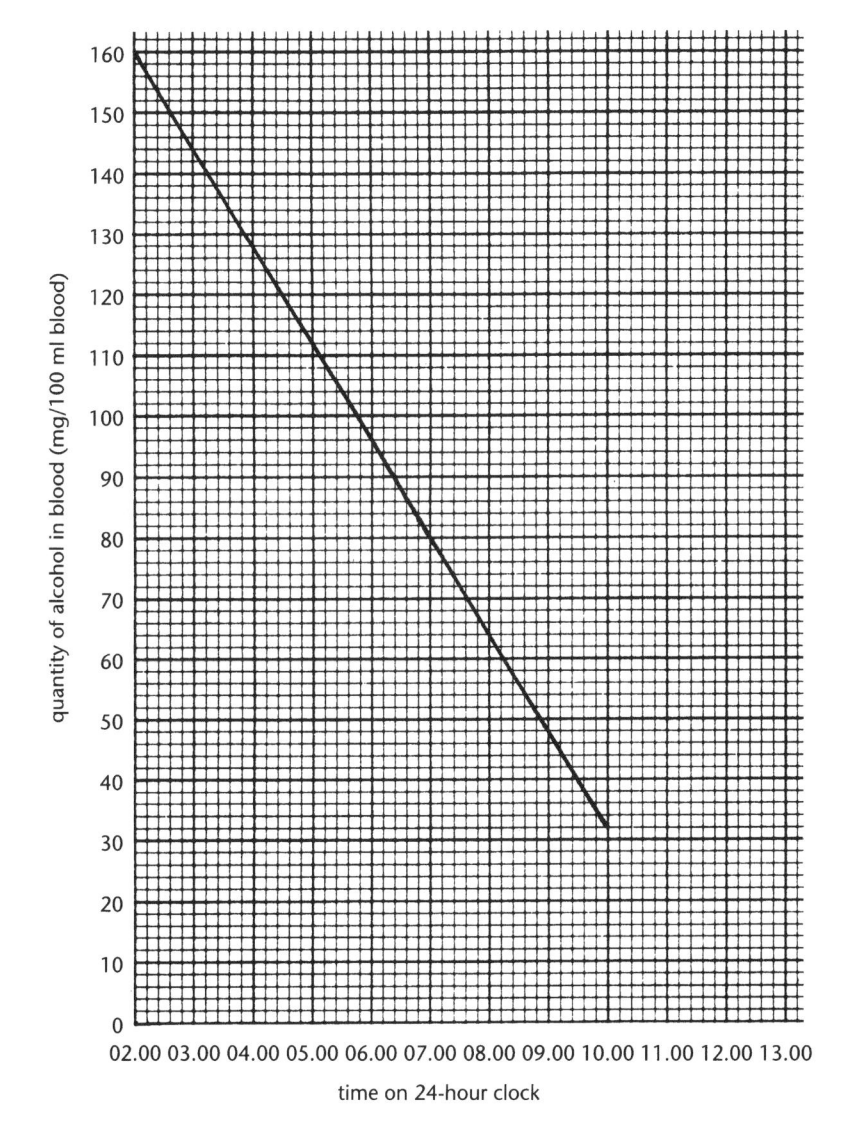

24 It is illegal to drive a car when the alcohol level in the blood is above 80 mg/100 ml blood. What is the earliest time at which the woman could drive legally?

A 07.00.   B 08.00.   C 10.00.   D 12.00.

25 If the trend in the graph continues, what time would it be when the quantity of alcohol in the woman's blood reaches zero?

A 10.00.   B 11.00.   C 12.00.   D 13.00.

Unit 1 **Health and Technology**

Multiple Choice Test 2

Choose the ONE correct answer to each of the following questions.

Questions 1, 2 and 3 refer to the following diagram which shows an analysis of 10 foods.

1 Which line in the following table correctly describes stewing steak?

	protein	fat	carbohydrate
A	high	medium	low/zero
B	low/zero	medium	high
C	medium	high	low/zero
D	high	low/zero	medium

food			
cheddar cheese	●	■	⬡
chocolate	⊖	■	⬢
eggs	●	▭	⬡
ice-cream	○	▭	⬢
oranges	○	□	⬢
peanut	●	■	⬡
potato chips	○	▭	⬢
rice	○	□	⬢
stewing steak	●	▭	⬡
wholemeal bread	⊖	□	⬢

KEY ○ = protein   ■ = high content
     □ = fat   ▭ = medium content
     ⬡ = carbohydrate   □ = low or zero content

2 Three foods with a high fat content are
   A peanut, eggs and chocolate.
   B eggs, stewing steak and ice-cream.
   C ice-cream, chocolate and potato chips.
   D peanut, chocolate and cheddar cheese.

3 Which two foods contain little protein and little fat but a high quantity of carbohydrate?
   A rice and oranges.   C oranges and potato chips.
   B ice-cream and rice.   D potato chips and ice-cream.

4 The following table shows the fibre content per 100 g portion of some breakfast cereals.

cereal	fibre content (g/100 g portion)
muesli	7
bran flakes	14
bran buds	26
all-bran	28

The whole number ratio of fibre in all-bran to that in muesli is
A 2:1.   B 4:1.   C 7:1.   D 28:1.

Multiple Choice Test 2 continued

5 The diagram contains two pie charts. They show the proportions of the three main classes of food that Scottish people, on average, actually eat and what experts say that they should eat.

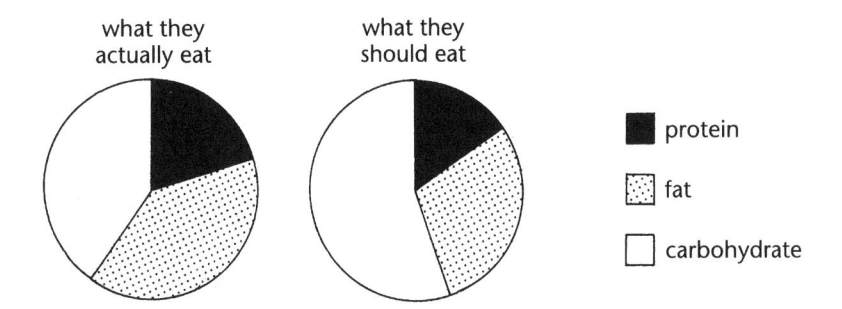

what they actually eat   what they should eat

■ protein
▨ fat
☐ carbohydrate

Which line in the following table shows the eating habits that Scottish people should adopt to improve their diet?

	protein	fat	carbohydrate
A	↓	↓	↑
B	↑	↑	↓
C	↓	↑	↓
D	↑	↓	↑

Key
↓ = reduce intake   ↑ = increase intake

6 What is the average protein content (in g/kg) of the foods shown in the accompanying table?

A 11.3.   B 12.6.
C 14.7.   D 88.2.

food	protein content (g/kg)
beans	5.1
beef	18.2
cheese	25.5
milk	3.3
peanuts	28.2
peas	5.8
potatoes	2.1

Unit 1 **Health and Technology**

Multiple Choice Test 2 continued

Questions 7, 8 and 9 refer to the bar chart below. It shows the amount of energy needed each day to do four different types of job.

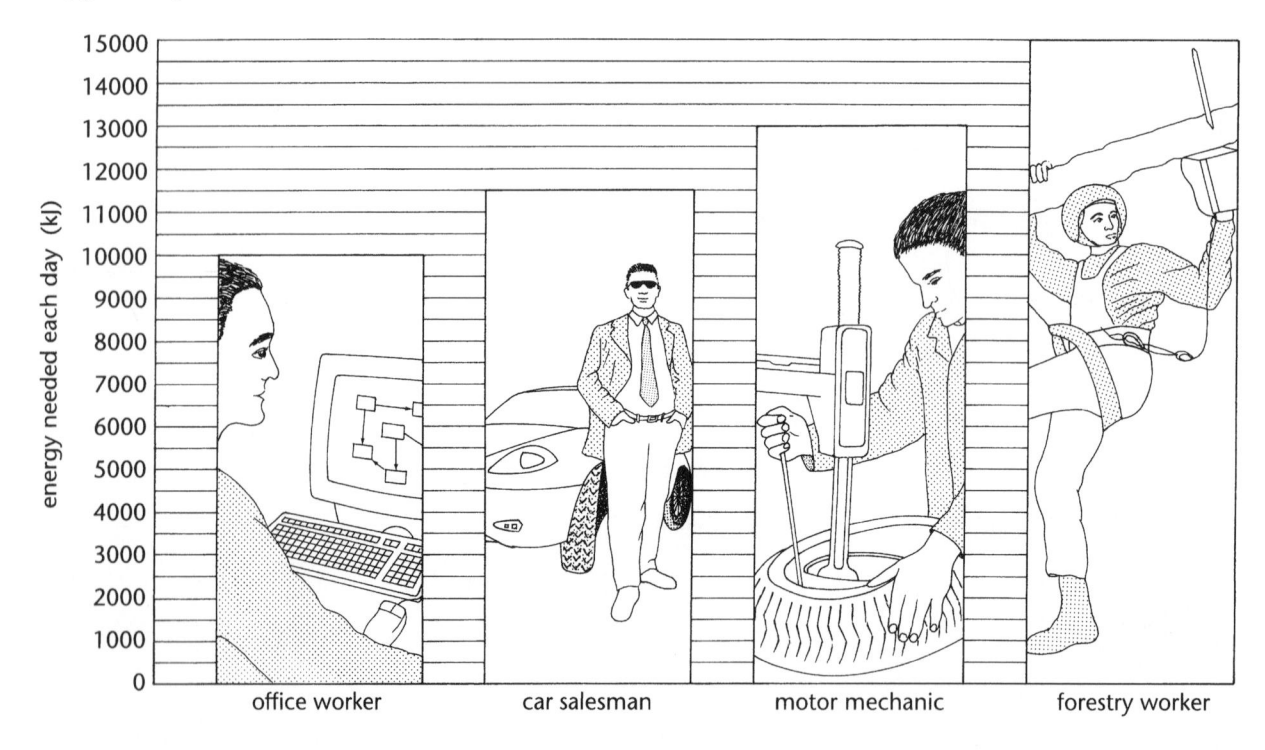

[Bar chart: energy needed each day (kJ) for office worker (~10000), car salesman (~8500), motor mechanic (~11500), forestry worker (~13500)]

7 Which job uses up 11500 kJ of energy daily?

   A   office worker.   C   motor mechanic.
   B   car salesman.   D   forestry worker.

8 How many more kilojoules (kJ) are used per day by a forestry worker compared with a car salesman?

   A   1500.   B   2000.   C   3500.   D   5000.

9 Imagine that the office worker changes his job and becomes a motor mechanic. What would be the percentage increase in the amount of energy that he would need each day?

   A   15.   B   20.   C   30.   D   50.

Multiple Choice Test 2 continued

Questions 10 and 11 refer to the following two tables. The first shows a set of results for five people ages 18 years using skinfold callipers. The second shows percentage fat content of the body for different skinfold thicknesses.

location tested	average skinfold thickness (mm) using skinfold callipers				
	Marion	Callum	Iyesha	Steven	Kirsty
side of waist	21	12	18	25	15
back of upper arm	19	10	15	22	13
front of upper arm	10	6	8	12	7
back below shoulder blade	20	12	19	21	15
total for 4 locations	70	40	60	80	50

total skinfold thickness for 4 locations (mm)	fat content of body (%)	
	women aged 16–20	men aged 16–20
20	14.0	8.0
30	19.5	13.0
40	23.5	16.5
50	26.5	19.0
60	29.0	21.0
70	31.0	23.0
80	33.0	25.0

10 What is the percentage fat content of Kirsty's body?

    A 19.0.   B 26.5.   C 29.0.   D 50.0.

11 Whose body contains 25 per cent fat?

    A Marion.   B Callum.   C Iyesha.   D Steven.

Unit 1 Health and Technology

Multiple Choice Test 2 continued

Questions 12, 13, 14 and 15 refer to the graph. It can be used to find out if a person's body weight is correct for his or her height.

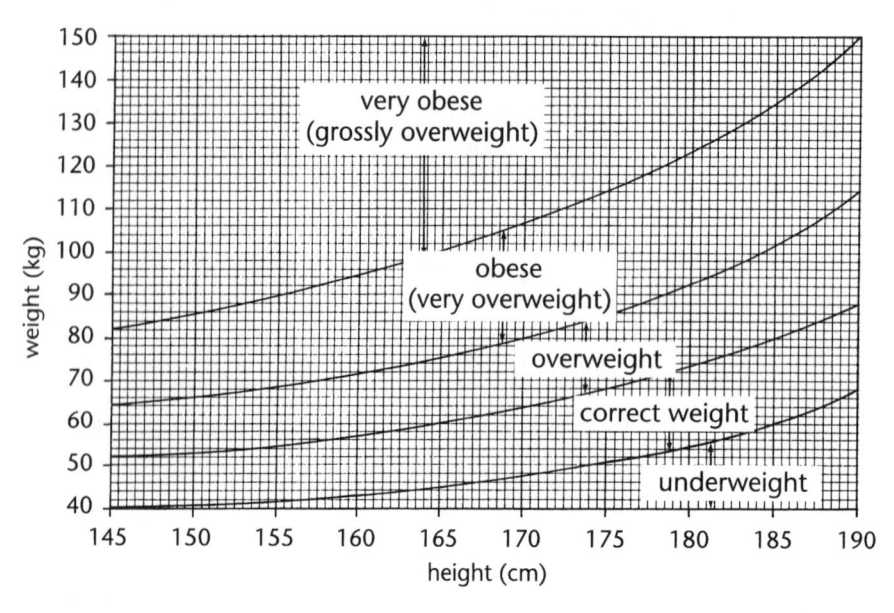

12 If a woman weighs 50 kg and is 180 cm in height, then she would be described as being
   A underweight.   B at her correct weight.   C overweight.   D obese.

13 Which of the following men is obese?

man	height (cm)	weight (kg)
A	170	70
B	175	95
C	180	70
D	185	95

14 If a man is 170 cm in height and he is overweight (but not obese), what could his weight (in kg) be?
   A 45.   B 60.   C 75.   D 90.

15 What is the minimum correct weight (in kg) for a person of height 185 cm?
   A 40.   B 60.   C 80.   D 100.

Chapter 4 **Healthy Body**

Multiple Choice Test 2 continued

16 The diagram shows a type of digital thermometer. The steps carried out during its use are given in the following list in a mixed-up order.

1 Press the thermometer's function key once.
2 Clean the thermometer's sensor using alcohol.
3 Press the function key again to turn off the digital display.
4 Place the sensor under the person's tongue.
5 Read the thermometer once the reading has stabilised for 10 seconds.

function key
display panel
sensor

The correct order is
A 4, 2, 1, 3, 5.   B 4, 3, 5, 1, 2.   C 2, 1, 4, 3, 5.   D 2, 4, 1, 5, 3.

17 The table opposite shows the body temperature readings for a hospital patient over a period of five days. Which of the following graphs represents these results correctly?

day	time	temperature (°C)
1	6 am	39.0
	6 pm	39.8
2	6 am	40.0
	6 pm	40.3
3	6 am	39.5
	6 pm	39.9
4	6 am	39.2
	6 pm	39.6
5	6 am	38.4
	6 pm	37.1

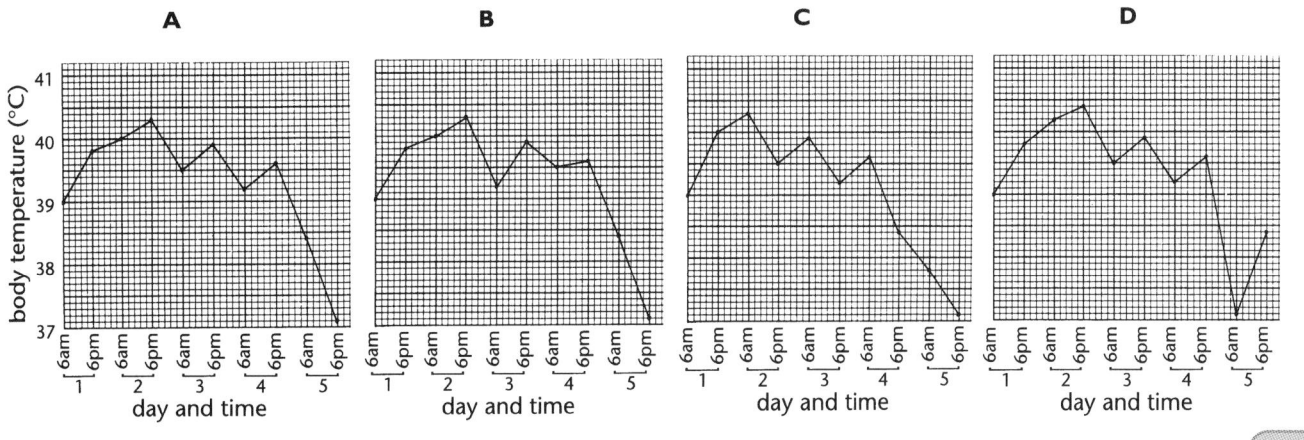

A   B   C   D

69

Unit 1 Health and Technology

Multiple Choice Test 2 continued

18 Which of the following statements is untrue? A regularly exercised muscle
   - A   increases in strength.
   - B   becomes more efficient.
   - C   develops a better blood supply.
   - D   decreases in muscle mass.

19 The diagram shows a set of bathroom scales.

They were used to measure the force that a boy's two hands could apply when gripping them as tightly as possible. He did this 10 times and drew this graph of his results.

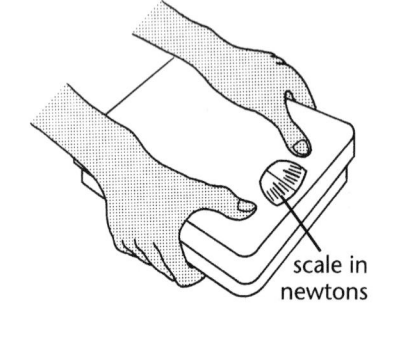

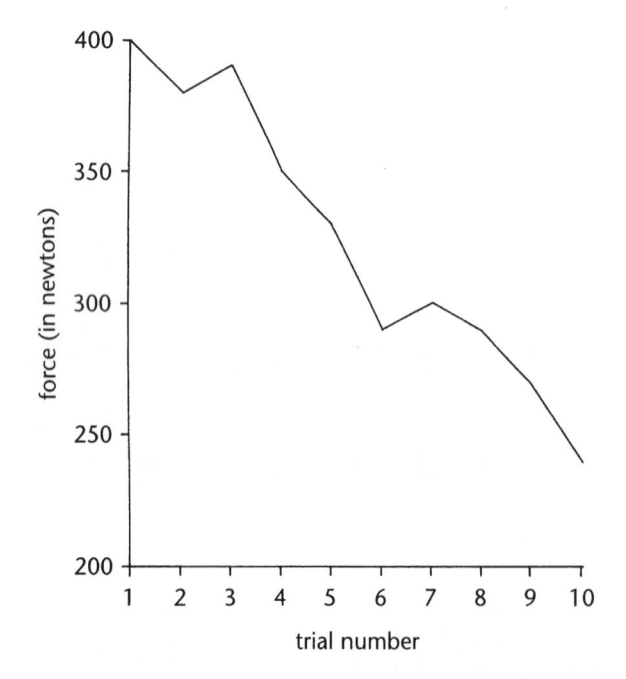

From the graph it can be concluded that
   - A   the boy was not as strong as other boys in the class.
   - B   the force that the boy applied increased over the ten trials.
   - C   the boy's muscles were showing signs of fatigue by trial number ten.
   - D   The boy's right hand was stronger than his left hand.

Chapter 4 **Healthy Body**

Multiple Choice Test 2 continued

Questions 20 and 21 refer to the diagram which shows a girl measuring her reaction time.

She was responding to a signal on the screen by pressing the space bar as quickly as she could. After ten trials she drew the bar chart of her results.

20 The biggest decrease in the girl's reaction time took place between trial numbers

    A 1 and 2.   **B** 3 and 4.

    C 7 and 8.   **D** 9 and 10.

21 The results show that practice

    A has no overall effect on reaction time.

    B makes the reaction time increase over the ten trials.

    C makes the reaction time decrease over the ten trials.

    D makes the reaction time increase at trial 2 and level off by trial 7.

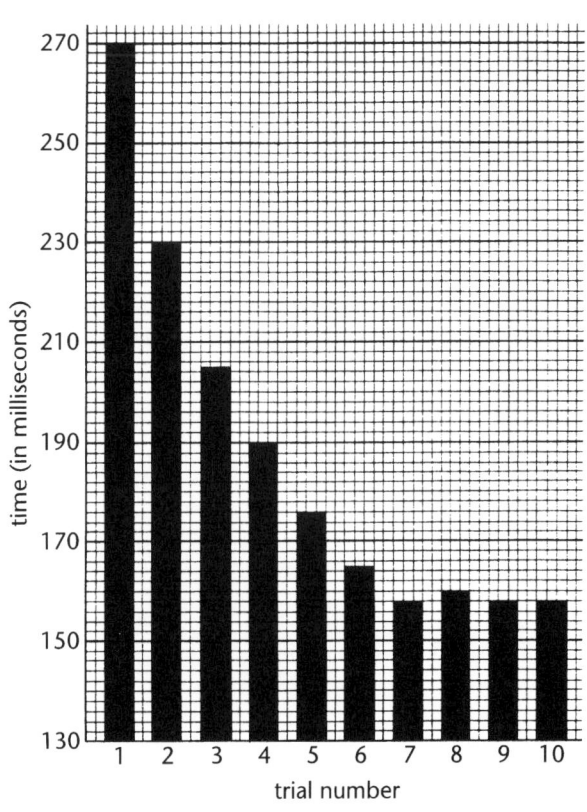

Unit 1 Health and Technology

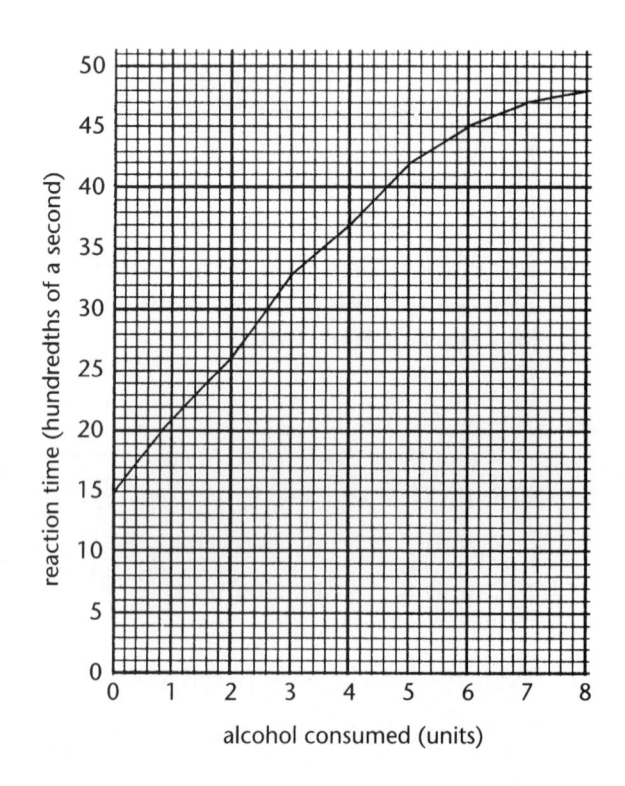

Multiple Choice Test 2 continued

22 Drinking alcohol can lead to

    A increased awareness of surroundings.

    B improved judgement of distance.

    C shorter reaction time.

    D poorer muscular control.

Questions 23, 24 and 25 refer to the line graph. It shows the effect of alcohol on a man's reaction time.

23 What was the man's reaction time (in hundredths of a second) after he had drunk two pints of beer each containing two units of alcohol?

    A 25.1.   B 26.0.

    C 35.2.   D 37.0.

24 What was the increase in length of his reaction time (in hundredths of a second) when the alcohol that he consumed rose from 1 unit to 8 units?

    A 22.   B 27.   C 33.   D 48.

25 What was the percentage increase in length of his reaction time when the alcohol that he consumed rose from 1 unit to 5 units?

    A 42.   B 50.   C 100.   D 200.

Unit 2
Biotechnological Industries

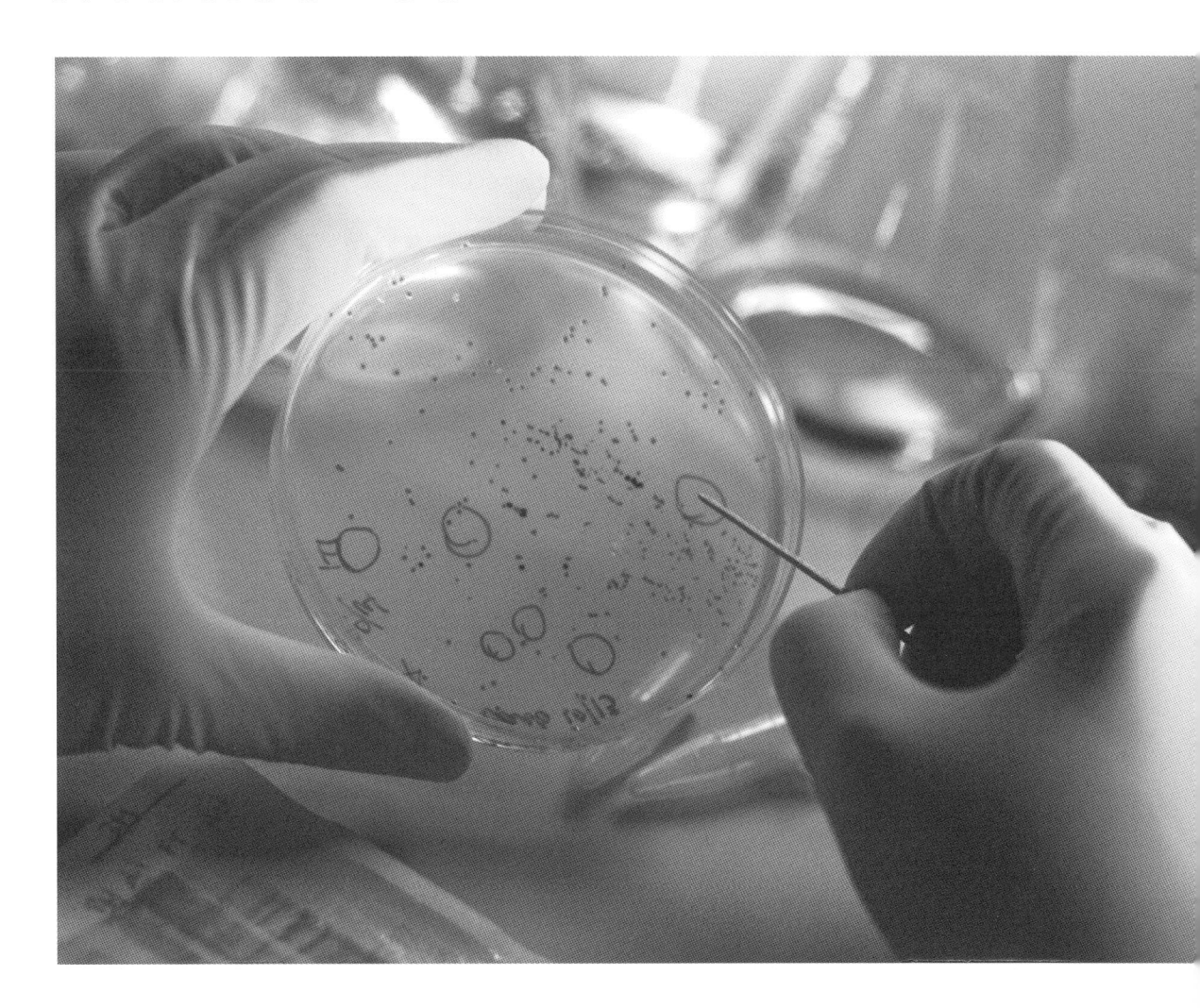

Unit 2 — 5 Dairy Industries

Matching Test 1

Match the words in list X with their descriptions in list Y.

List X

1) evaporated
2) milk
3) pasteurised
4) semi-skimmed
5) skimmed
6) UHT

List Y

a) first food for mammals that contains sugar, fat, protein, vitamins and minerals

b) word describing milk that has been heated to 72°C for 15 seconds

c) group of letters referring to milk that has been heated to 140°C for 5 seconds

d) word describing milk that has had half of its water content removed

e) word describing milk that has had half of its fat content removed

f) word describing milk that has had almost all of its fat content removed

Chapter 5 **Dairy Industries**

Matching Test 2

Match the words in list X with their descriptions in list Y.

List X

1) bacteria
2) curds
3) lactic acid
4) rennet
5) resazurin
6) upgrading
7) whey
8) yoghurt

List Y

a) process where a waste material is changed into a useful product

b) chemical substance originally from calves' stomachs used to make milk clot

c) unicellular micro-organisms used to make cheese and yoghurt

d) liquid substance that separates out from curds when milk is made to clot during cheese-making

e) solid substance formed when milk is made to clot by the action of rennet during cheese-making

f) food produced from milk by the action of lactic acid-forming bacteria

g) chemical reagent used to test the bacterial content of milk

h) chemical substance made by the action of certain bacteria on milk

Multiple Choice Test 1

Choose the ONE correct answer to each of the following questions.

Questions 1, 2 and 3 refer to the diagram about milk.

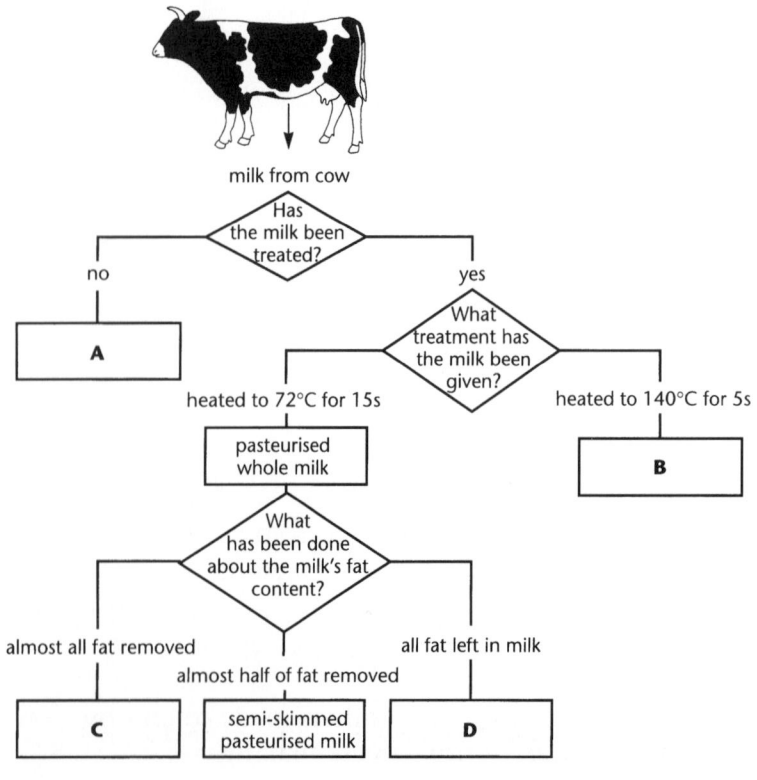

```
                    milk from cow
                          ↓
                    ╱ Has    ╲
                   ╱ the milk been ╲
                   ╲   treated?    ╱
                    ╲            ╱
              no    ╱            ╲   yes
                                    ╱ What         ╲
                                   ╱ treatment has  ╲
            ┌───┐                  ╲ the milk been  ╱
            │ A │                   ╲   given?     ╱
            └───┘                    ╲           ╱
                     heated to 72°C for 15s    heated to 140°C for 5s
                         ┌──────────┐
                         │pasteurised│                 ┌───┐
                         │whole milk │                 │ B │
                         └──────────┘                 └───┘
                        ╱ What         ╲
                       ╱ has been done  ╲
                       ╲ about the milk's fat ╱
                        ╲   content?    ╱
        almost all fat removed    all fat left in milk
                   almost half of fat removed
            ┌───┐    ┌──────────┐      ┌───┐
            │ C │    │semi-skimmed│    │ D │
            └───┘    │pasteurised milk│  └───┘
                     └──────────┘
```

1 Which letter represents UHT whole milk?

2 Which letter represents raw whole milk which must not be sold to the public?

3 Which letter represents skimmed pasteurised milk?

Questions 4 and 5 refer to the possible answers in the following table.

	chemical reagent	treatment	positive result
A	Biuret	heat	orange
B	Biuret	no heat	pale lilac
C	Benedict's	heat	orange
D	Benedict's	no heat	pale lilac

4 Which line in the table refers correctly to the test for simple sugar?

5 Which line in the table refers correctly to the test for protein?

Chapter 5 Dairy Industries

Multiple Choice Test 1 continued

Questions 6, 7, 8, 9 and 10 refer to the diagram of four cartons of milk.

6 Which type of milk is richest in calcium?
   A whole.   B semi-skimmed.   C skimmed.   D evaporated.

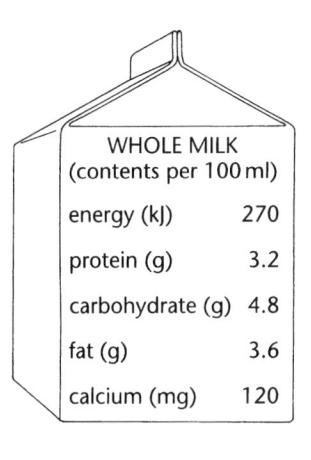

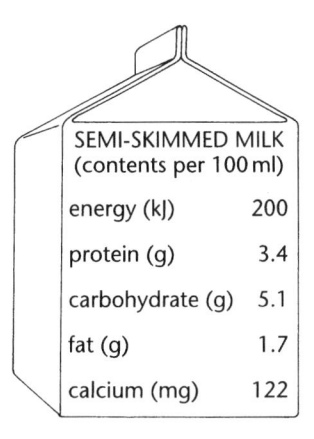

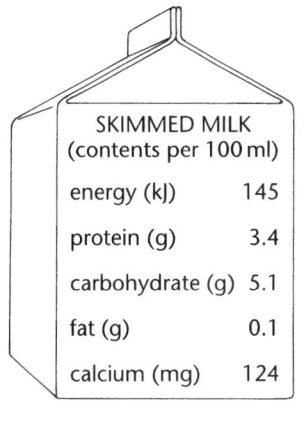

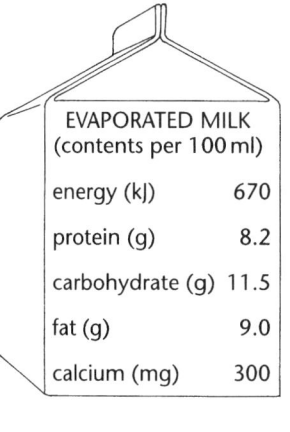

WHOLE MILK (contents per 100 ml)		SEMI-SKIMMED MILK (contents per 100 ml)		SKIMMED MILK (contents per 100 ml)		EVAPORATED MILK (contents per 100 ml)	
energy (kJ)	270	energy (kJ)	200	energy (kJ)	145	energy (kJ)	670
protein (g)	3.2	protein (g)	3.4	protein (g)	3.4	protein (g)	8.2
carbohydrate (g)	4.8	carbohydrate (g)	5.1	carbohydrate (g)	5.1	carbohydrate (g)	11.5
fat (g)	3.6	fat (g)	1.7	fat (g)	0.1	fat (g)	9.0
calcium (mg)	120	calcium (mg)	122	calcium (mg)	124	calcium (mg)	300

7 Compared with whole milk, evaporated milk contains
   A less carbohydrate and less fat.   C less carbohydrate and more fat.
   B more carbohydrate and less fat.   D more carbohydrate and more fat.

8 Which of the bar graphs in the diagram correctly represents the energy content of the four types of milk?

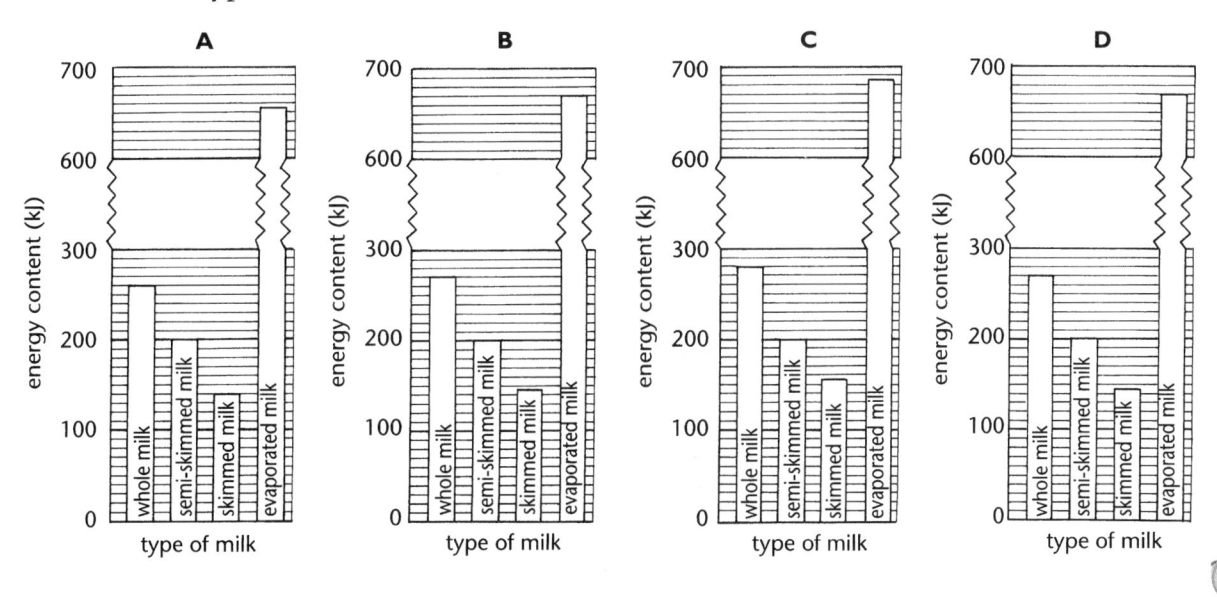

Unit 2 Biotechnological Industries

Multiple Choice Test 1 continued

9 Compared with skimmed milk, the quantity of fat in semi-skimmed milk is greater by a factor of
   A 1.7 times.   B 3.6 times.   C 17.0 times.   D 36.0 times.

10 In semi-skimmed milk, what is the ratio of protein to carbohydrate to fat?
   A 2:3:1.   B 3:4:3.   C 3:5:1.   D 34:51:1.

11 The human body needs 800 mg of calcium every day. 100 ml of whole milk contains 120 mg of calcium. What percentage of the calcium requirement is gained by drinking 100 ml of whole milk?
   A 15.   B 40.   C 68.   D 96.

Questions 12, 13 and 14 refer to the following information. Samples of whole milk from four farms were tested using resazurin dye. The following table shows the results.

time (min)	colour of milk sample containing resazurin dye			
	farm 1	farm 2	farm 3	farm 4
0	purple	purple	purple	purple
5	purple	purple	mauve	[box X]
10	purple	mauve	pink	purple
15	purple	mauve	pink	mauve
20	purple	pink	white	mauve

12 What colour should have been given in box X?
   A white.   B pink.   C mauve.   D purple.

13 According to these results, one of the milk samples was unfit for human consumption. Which farm did it come from?
   A 1.   B 2.   C 3.   D 4.

14 What should scientists do to improve the reliability of the results?
   A Run the test for 40 minutes instead of 20 minutes.
   B Repeat the tests using more samples from the four farms.
   C Carry out a separate series of tests using Benedict's reagent.
   D Boil the milk samples and then repeat the resazurin test.

Multiple Choice Test 1 continued

15 During the production of yoghurt from milk, yoghurt bacteria
  A change milk sugar in milk to lactic acid.
  B make milk sugar molecules clot together.
  C turn whole pasteurised milk into UHT milk.
  D change the pH of the milk from acidic to neutral.

Questions 16, 17, 18 and 19 refer to the diagram. The five cartons represent the steps involved in the production of a popular brand of yoghurt.

1	2	3	4	5
milk cooled to 44°C	yoghurt stored at 4°C	milk kept at 44°C for 4 hours	milk heated to 95°C for 20 minutes	yoghurt-making bacteria added to milk

16 The correct order in which the steps would be carried out is
  A 1, 4, 5, 2, 3.   B 1, 4, 5, 3, 2.   C 4, 1, 2, 5, 3.   D 4, 1, 5, 3, 2.

17 Which step is carried out to make the milk virtually sterile before it is made into yoghurt?
  A 1.   B 2.   C 3.   D 4.

18 Which stage gives the bacteria ideal conditions to grow and change the milk into yoghurt?
  A 1.   B 2.   C 3.   D 4.

19 Which stage is carried out to slow down the action of the yoghurt-forming bacteria?
  A 1.   B 2.   C 3.   D 4.

20 Which of the following is the original, natural source of rennet?
  A sour pasteurised milk.   C genetically modified bacteria.
  B stomach wall of calves.   D fermented strains of brewer's yeast.

Unit 2 Biotechnological Industries

Multiple Choice Test 1 continued

21 The first of the diagrams shows a test tube. It is part of an experiment set up to investigate the effect of rennet on pasteurised milk.

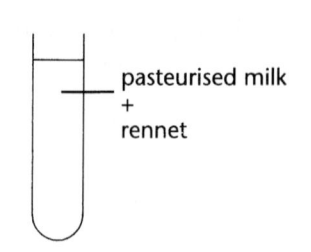

pasteurised milk + rennet

Which test tube in the second diagram would make the best control for this experiment?

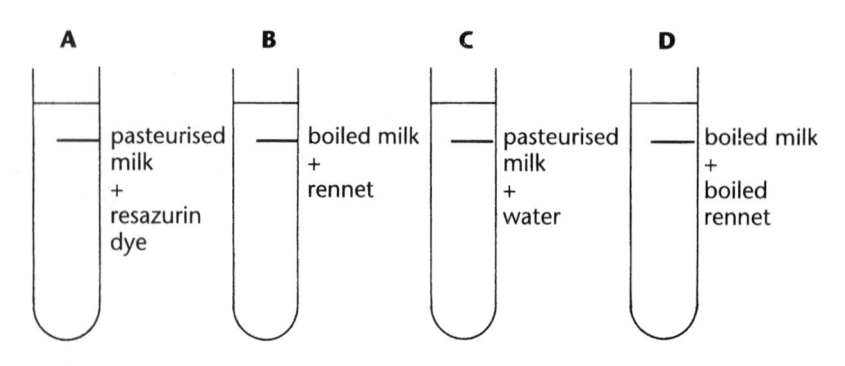

A pasteurised milk + resazurin dye

B boiled milk + rennet

C pasteurised milk + water

D boiled milk + boiled rennet

22 The five measuring cylinders in the diagram show an experiment set up to separate milk into curds and whey.

What was the average volume of curds produced per 100 ml of milk?

A 14.   B 18.
C 70.   D 86.

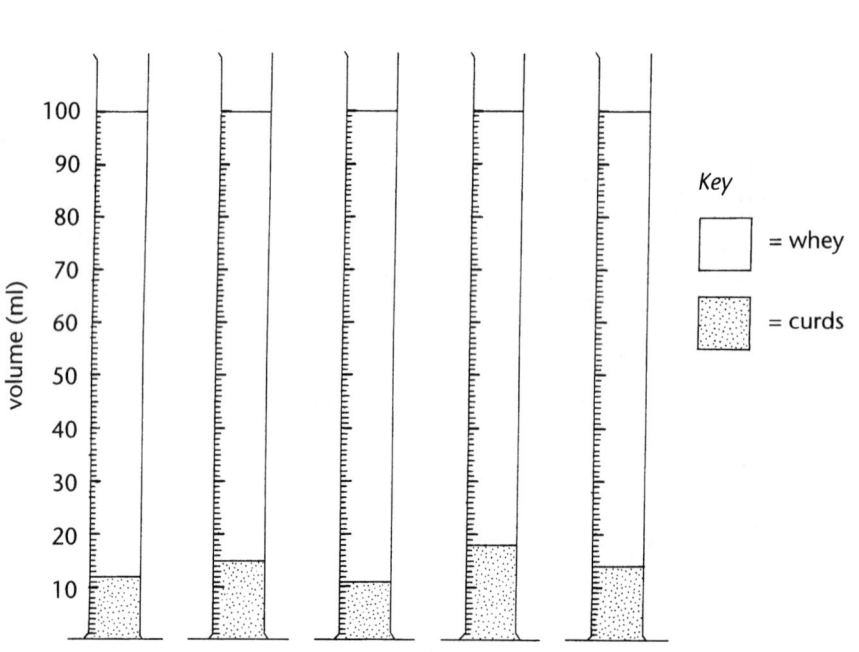

Key
☐ = whey
▨ = curds

23 Which of the following is true about fungal rennet?
   A   Its production depends on the mass production of genetically modified yeast cells.
   B   The calves that produce it must be fed a diet rich in mushrooms.
   C   It is the most expensive form of rennet used in cheese making.
   D   The fungus that produces it is grown on a large scale in a fermenter.

Chapter 5 **Dairy Industries**

Multiple Choice Test 1 continued

24 Whey was accidentally discharged into a river. The table opposite shows data about the oxygen content of the river. The information was collected at different distances downstream from the discharge point.

distance downstream from discharge point (m)	oxygen concentration (units)
0	10
500	2
1000	5
1500	10
2000	20
3000	45
4000	60
5000	65

Which part of the diagram below correctly represents this data as a line graph?

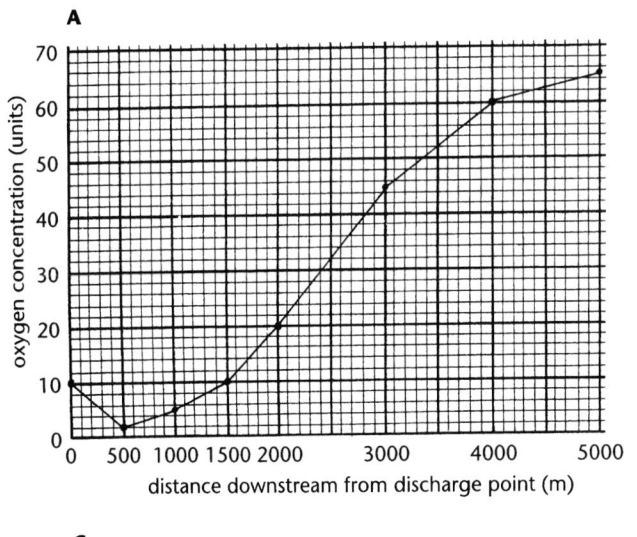

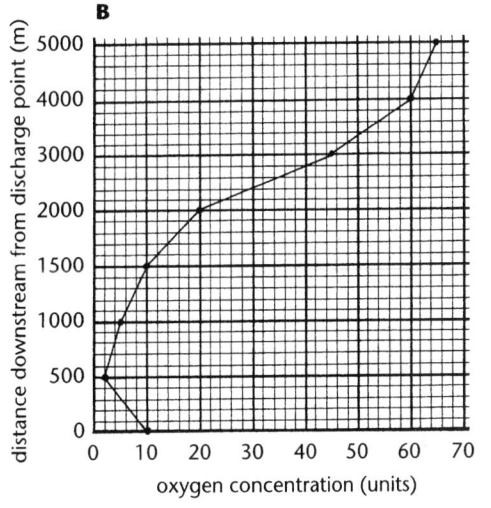

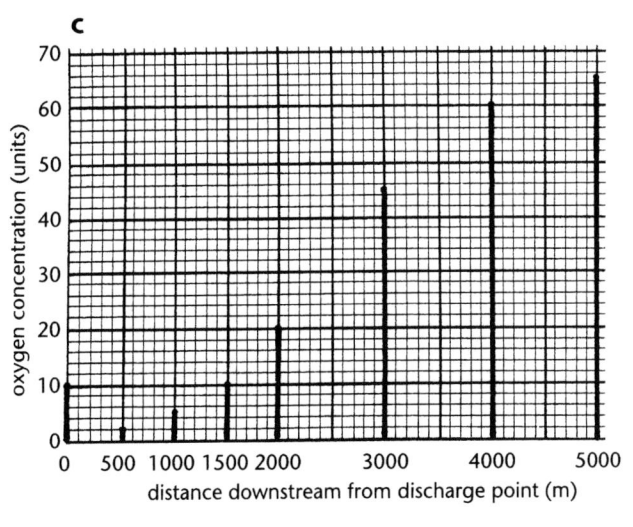

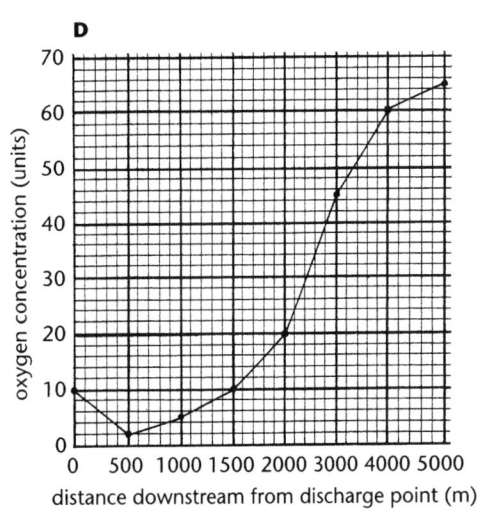

A

B

C

D

Unit 2 Biotechnological Industries

Multiple Choice Test 1 continued

25 The diagram shows a river being polluted by whey from a cheese making factory.

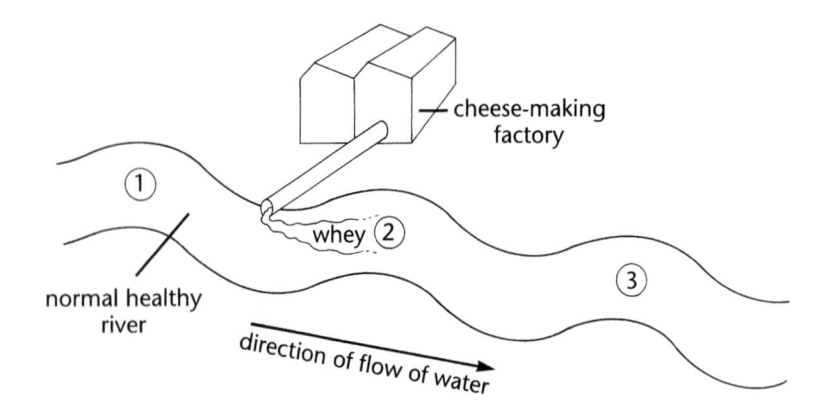

1, 2 and 3 are sites where water was sampled by scientists. Compared with the other two sites, water from site 2 would contain

A more dissolved oxygen and more bacteria.

B more dissolved oxygen and fewer bacteria.

C less dissolved oxygen and more bacteria.

D less dissolved oxygen and fewer bacteria.

Chapter 5 Dairy Industries

Multiple Choice Test 2

Choose the ONE correct answer to each of the following questions.

Questions 1, 2, 3, 4, 5 and 6 refer to the diagram about milk.

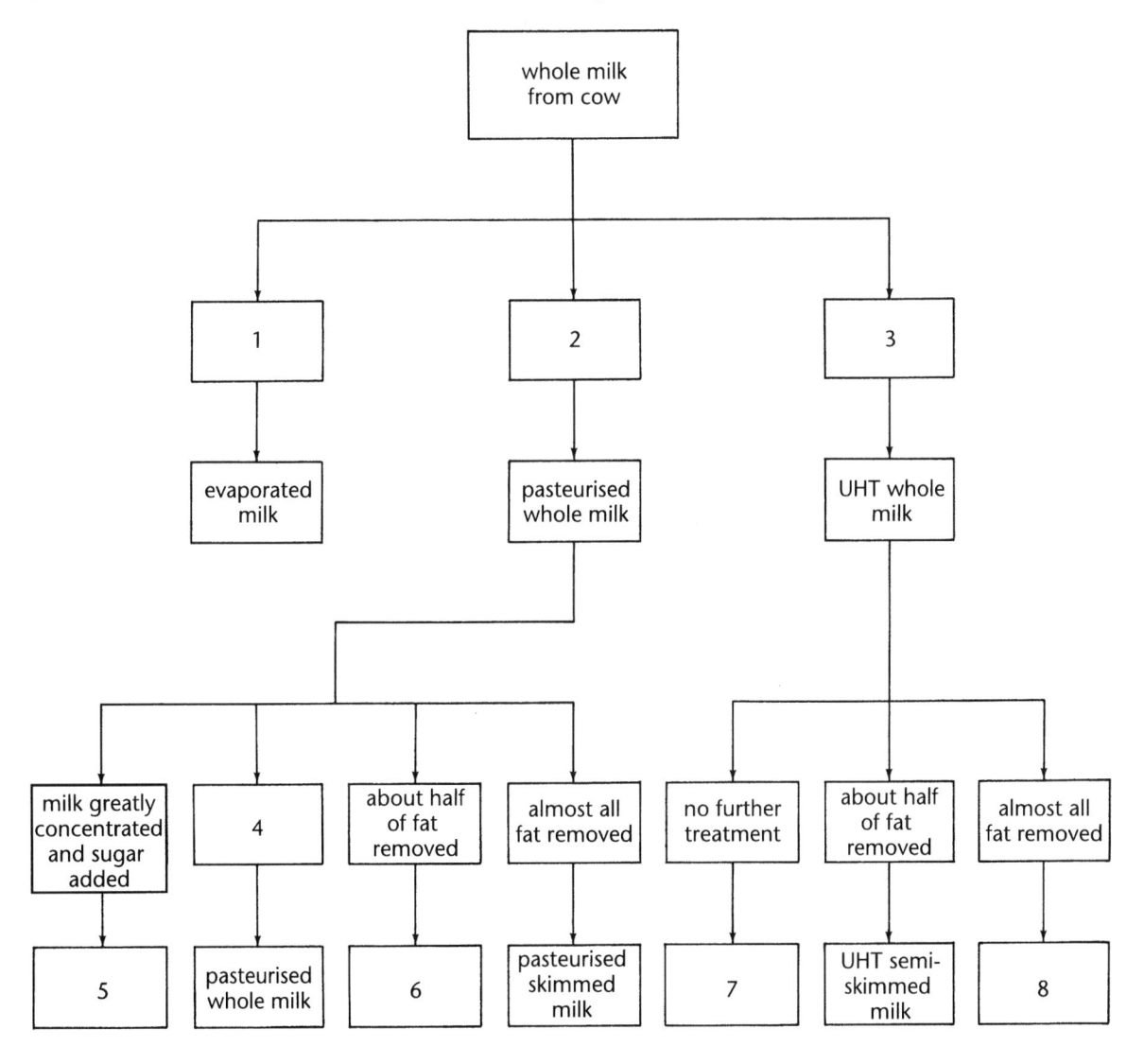

```
                    whole milk
                    from cow
        ┌───────────────┼───────────────┐
        ▼               ▼               ▼
       [1]             [2]             [3]
        │               │               │
        ▼               ▼               ▼
    evaporated    pasteurised       UHT whole
      milk        whole milk          milk
                      │                 │
   ┌──────┬───────┬───┴───┐       ┌─────┼──────┐
   ▼      ▼       ▼       ▼       ▼     ▼      ▼
milk    [4]   about    almost   no      about  almost
greatly       half of  all fat  further half   all fat
concen-       fat      removed  treat-  of fat removed
trated        removed           ment    removed
and sugar
added
   │      │       │       │       │     │      │
   ▼      ▼       ▼       ▼       ▼     ▼      ▼
  [5]  pasteurised [6]  pasteurised [7] UHT    [8]
       whole milk      skimmed         semi-
                        milk           skimmed
                                       milk
```

1 The statement 'milk heated to 72°C for 15 seconds' should have been put into box

 A 1.   B 2.   C 3.   D 4.

2 The statement 'milk heated to 140°C for 5 seconds' should have been put into box

 A 1.   B 2.   C 3.   D 4.

Unit 2 **Biotechnological Industries**

Multiple Choice Test 2 continued

3 The statement 'more than half of the water removed by a special heating process' should have been put into box
A 1.   B 2.   C 3.   D 4.

4 The words 'UHT whole milk' should have been put into box
A 5.   B 6.   C 7.   D 8.

5 The words 'pasteurised semi-skimmed milk' should have been put into box
A 5.   B 6.   C 7.   D 8.

6 The words 'condensed milk' should have been put into box
A 5.   B 6.   C 7.   D 8.

7 Which line in the table opposite refers correctly to the test for starch?

	chemical reagent	treatment	positive result
A	iodine solution	no heat	blue-black
B	Benedict's reagent	no heat	orange
C	iodine solution	heat	orange
D	Benedict's reagent	heat	blue-black

8 The following table shows the composition of condensed milk.

component	percentage
protein	8
carbohydrate	54
fat	9
water (and other substances)	29

Which pie chart in the diagram represents this information correctly?

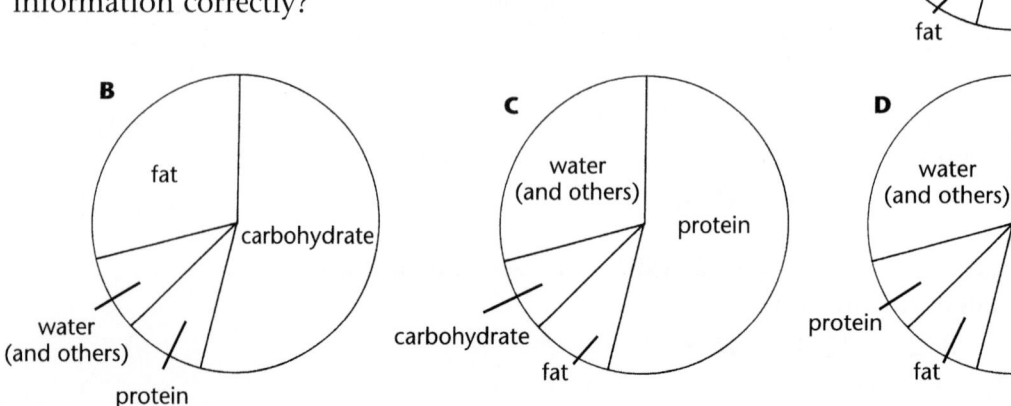

Multiple Choice Test 2 continued

9 The table opposite gives the vitamin A content of three types of dried milk.

type of dried milk	vitamin A content (units)
whole	248
half-cream	144
skimmed	4

This information shows that when whole milk is skimmed, its vitamin A content is reduced by

A 36 times.   B 62 times.   C 140 times.   D 244 times.

10 Evaporated milk contains vitamin B_{12}. 100 ml of evaporated milk contain 20 per cent of the body's daily requirement of this vitamin. What volume of evaporated milk (in ml) would a person have to drink to get their full daily requirement of vitamin B_{12}?

A 5.   B 100.   C 500.   D 5000.

11 Resazurin dye is used to test the quality of milk. Which of the following tables is correct?

A

colour of milk sample after 20 min.	quality of milk
white	good
purple	satisfactory
mauve	poor
pink	failed

B

colour of milk sample after 20 min.	quality of milk
purple	good
mauve	satisfactory
pink	poor
white	failed

C

colour of milk sample after 20 min.	quality of milk
purple	failed
mauve	poor
pink	satisfactory
white	good

D

colour of milk sample after 20 min.	quality of milk
white	failed
purple	poor
mauve	satisfactory
pink	good

Unit 2 **Biotechnological Industries**

Multiple Choice Test 2 continued

12 The test tube in the first diagram (opposite) was set up to investigate the action of yoghurt bacteria on the pH of milk.

Which test tube in the second diagram would act as a suitable control for this experiment?

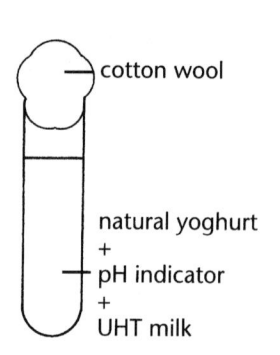

First diagram (opposite): cotton wool; natural yoghurt + pH indicator + UHT milk

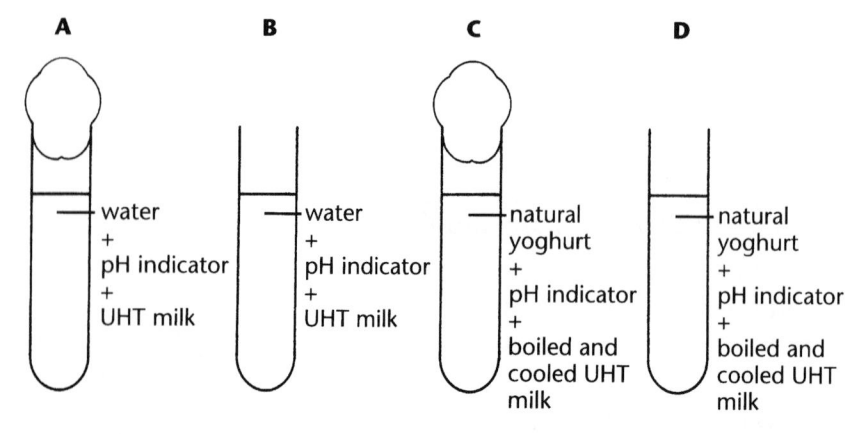

A water + pH indicator + UHT milk

B water + pH indicator + UHT milk

C natural yoghurt + pH indicator + boiled and cooled UHT milk

D natural yoghurt + pH indicator + boiled and cooled UHT milk

Questions 13, 14 and 15 refer to the diagram showing the six steps carried out in a science lab to make yoghurt.

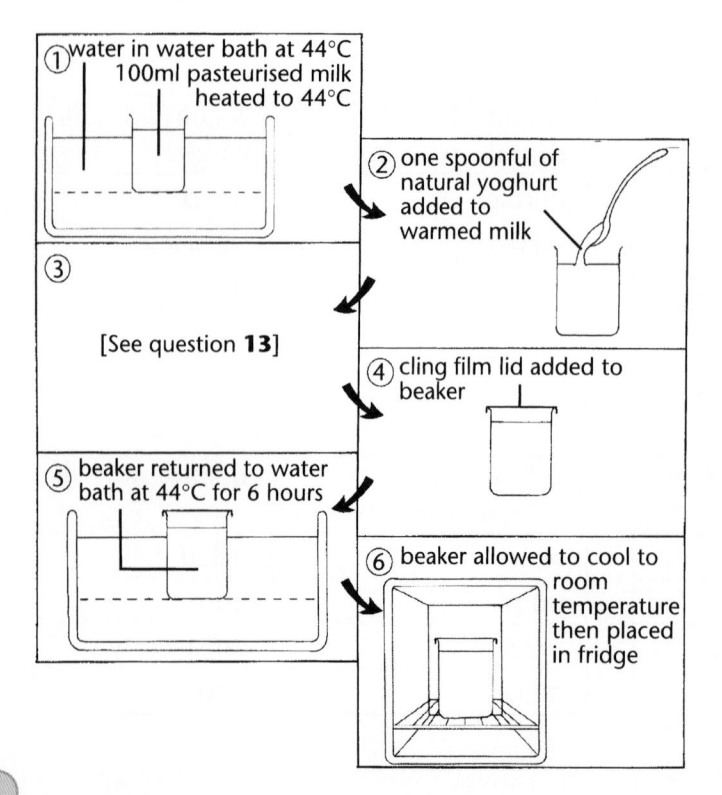

① water in water bath at 44°C
100ml pasteurised milk heated to 44°C

② one spoonful of natural yoghurt added to warmed milk

③ [See question 13]

④ cling film lid added to beaker

⑤ beaker returned to water bath at 44°C for 6 hours

⑥ beaker allowed to cool to room temperature then placed in fridge

13 Which part of the diagram below shows step 3 missing from the first diagram?

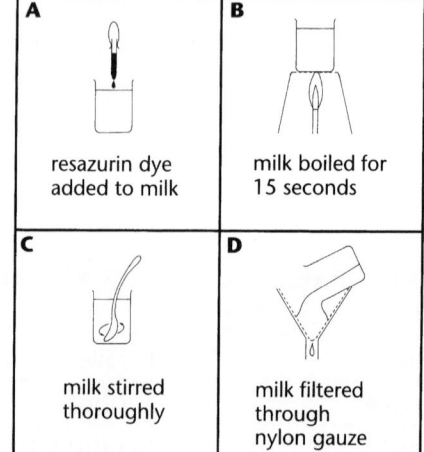

A resazurin dye added to milk

B milk boiled for 15 seconds

C milk stirred thoroughly

D milk filtered through nylon gauze

86

Chapter 5 **Dairy Industries**

Multiple Choice Test 2 continued

14 The reason for carrying out step 2 is to add
   A rennet.   B lactic acid.   C vanilla flavouring.   D yoghurt-forming bacteria.

15 During which stage would most lactic acid be formed from milk sugar?
   A 2.   B 4.   C 5.   D 6.

16 During yoghurt production, sugar in milk is changed by yoghurt-forming bacteria to lactic acid. Since other bacteria that make food go bad cannot grow in acidic conditions, lactic acid is described as a natural _____.
What is the missing word in the above paragraph?
   A bacterium.   B flavouring.   C micro-organism.   D preservative.

17 Rennet contains an enzyme used to make molecules of milk protein clot during cheese production. The table opposite shows the results of an investigation into the effect of temperature on the action of rennet.

Which line graph in the diagram represents these results accurately?

temperature (°C)	time taken for milk to clot (min.)
10	50
20	40
30	20
40	5
50	60

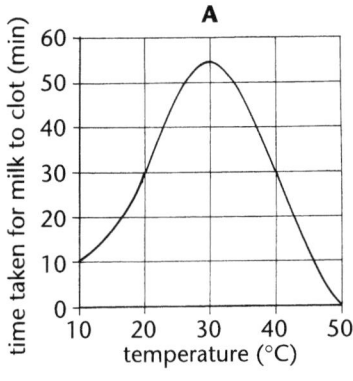

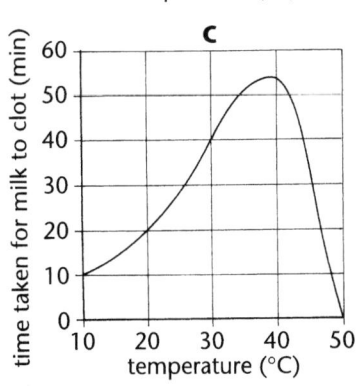

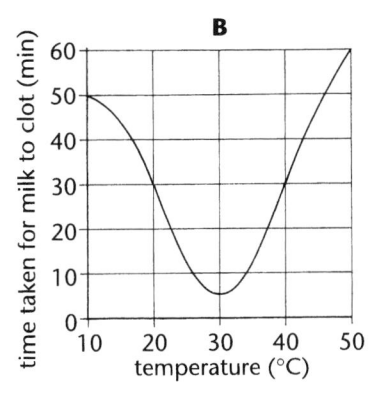

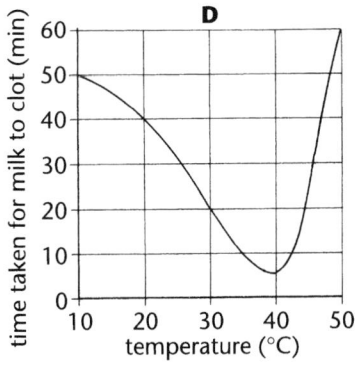

Multiple Choice Test 2 continued

Questions 18, 19 and 20 refer to the diagram opposite. It shows some of the stages involved in cheese-making.

18 What is being added to the pasteurised milk from the jug at stage 3?

  A cheese-flavouring chemicals.
  B yoghurt-forming bacteria.
  C alcohol-tolerant yeast.
  D cheese-forming bacteria.

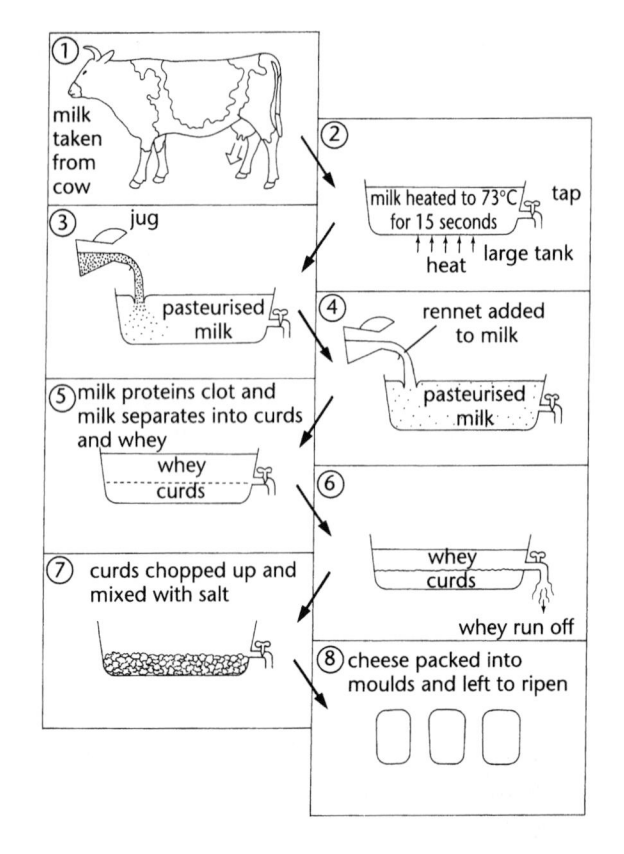

19 Which line in the table opposite describes the state of the curds and whey formed when rennet acts on milk?

	curds solid	curds liquid	whey solid	whey liquid
A	✔	✘	✘	✔
B	✔	✘	✔	✘
C	✘	✔	✘	✔
D	✘	✔	✔	✘

20 Which stage in the process is carried out deliberately to slow down the action of the cheese-making micro-organisms?

  A 2.   B 4.   C 6.   D 7.

21 Which of the following is true about rennet from genetically modified yeast?
  A It is cheaper to produce than fungal rennet.
  B It is a natural form of the enzyme that occurs in the wild.
  C It behaves the same way as calf rennet when added to milk.
  D It can be extracted from the stomach lining of young calves.

Multiple Choice Test 2 continued

Questions 22, 23 and 24 refer to the graph which shows the effect of pouring a large quantity of whey into a healthy river.

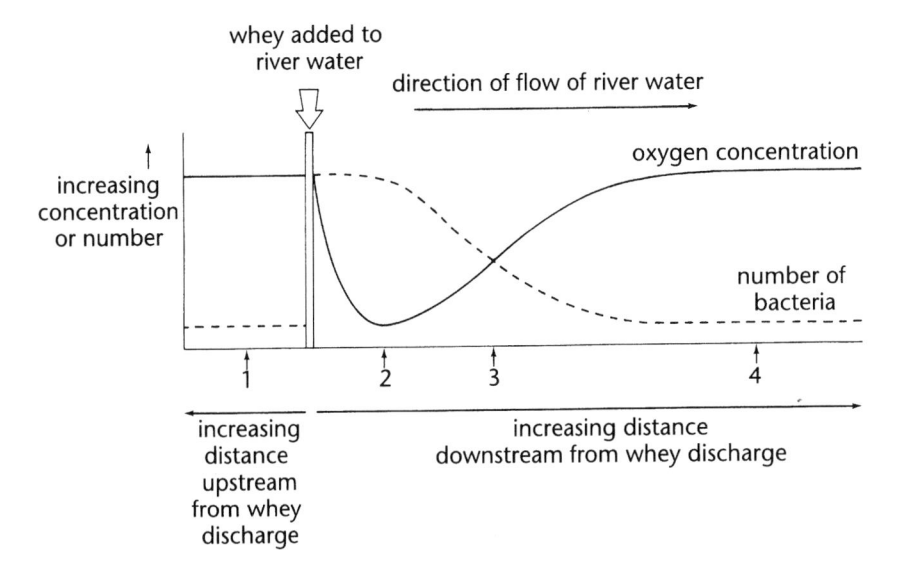

22 At which of the following points in the river was the number of bacteria greatest?
  A 1.   B 2.   C 3.   D 4.

23 At which point in the river was the oxygen concentration lowest?
  A 1.   B 2.   C 3.   D 4.

24 At which points in the river would most fish be found?
  A 1 and 2.   B 2 and 3.   C 1 and 4.   D 3 and 4.

25 Instead of being thrown away, whey can be upgraded by
  A using it as a food for growing yeast.
  B converting it into cheddar cheese.
  C making it into natural yoghurt.
  D using it to make more rennet.

Unit 2

6 Yeast-Based Industries

Matching Test 1

Match the words in list X with their descriptions in list Y.

List X

1) agar
2) beer
3) carbon dioxide
4) enzyme
5) fermenter
6) methylene blue
7) yeast

List Y

a) unicellular fungus used in brewing and baking
b) substance made by living cells that speeds up a biochemical reaction
c) jelly-like material on which micro-organisms are grown
d) chemical that indicates the oxygen content of water
e) alcoholic drink that varies in flavour and alcohol content
f) gas released by yeast cells that makes dough rise during bread making
g) container in which a fermentation process is brought about by a micro-organism

Chapter 6 **Yeast-Based Industries**

Matching Test 2

Match the words in list X with their descriptions in list Y.

List X

1) brewery-conditioned
2) cask-conditioned
3) colouring
4) fermented
5) flavouring
6) immobilised
7) upgrading

List Y

a) process by which waste material is changed into a useful product
b) word describing molecules or cells trapped in gel beads to allow them to be re-used
c) word describing a drink that contains alcohol
d) word describing beer that has been left to mature in wooden barrels
e) word describing beer that has been filtered and stored in metal kegs
f) chemical added to food to improve its taste
g) chemical added to food to alter its appearance

Unit 2 **Biotechnological Industries**

Multiple Choice Test 1

Choose the ONE correct answer to each of the following questions.

Question 1, 2, 3 and 4 refer to the diagram opposite. It shows an experiment set up to investigate the effect of live yeast cells on the raising of dough.

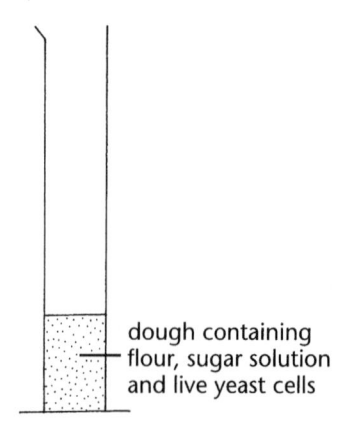

dough containing flour, sugar solution and live yeast cells

The following table shows the results from this experiment.

time (hours)	0	1	2	3	4	5
volume of dough (cm^3)	30	33	42	54	60	60

1 Which line graph in the diagram below correctly represents the results in the table?

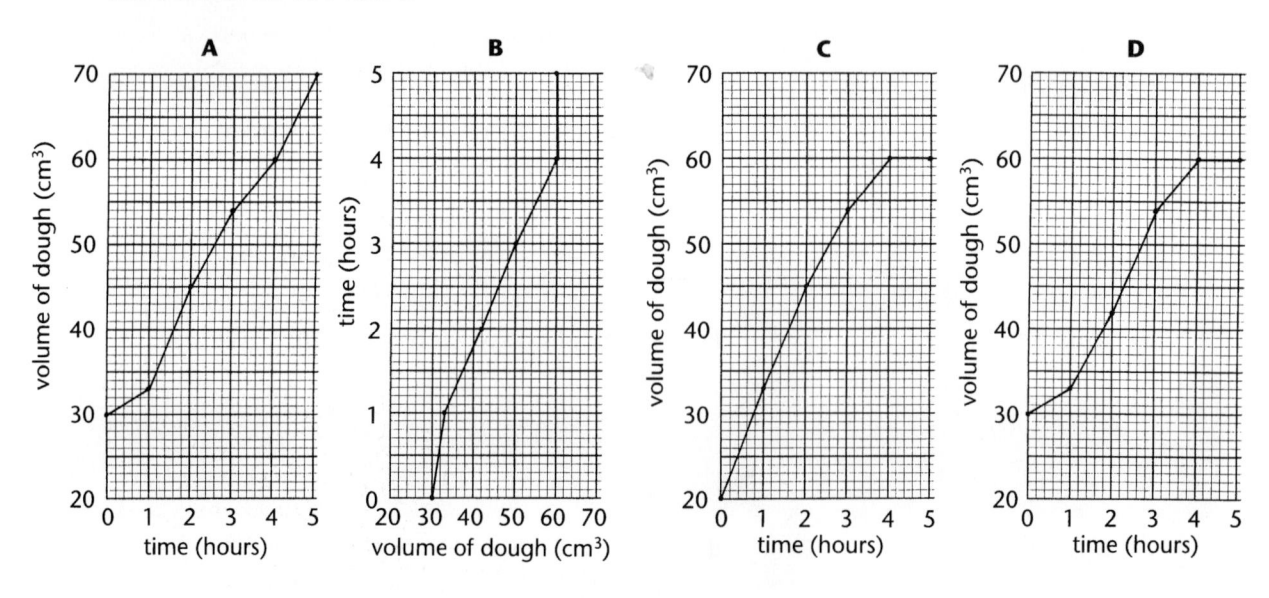

A   B   C   D

92

Chapter 6 Yeast-Based Industries

Multiple Choice Test 1 continued

2 The greatest increase in volume of dough occurred between hours

   A 0 and 1.   B 1 and 2.   C 2 and 3.   D 3 and 4.

3 If the experiment had been left for a further hour, what would the volume (in cm^3) of dough have been?

   A 30.   B 54.   C 60.   D 66.

4 Which of the following would make the best control for this experiment?

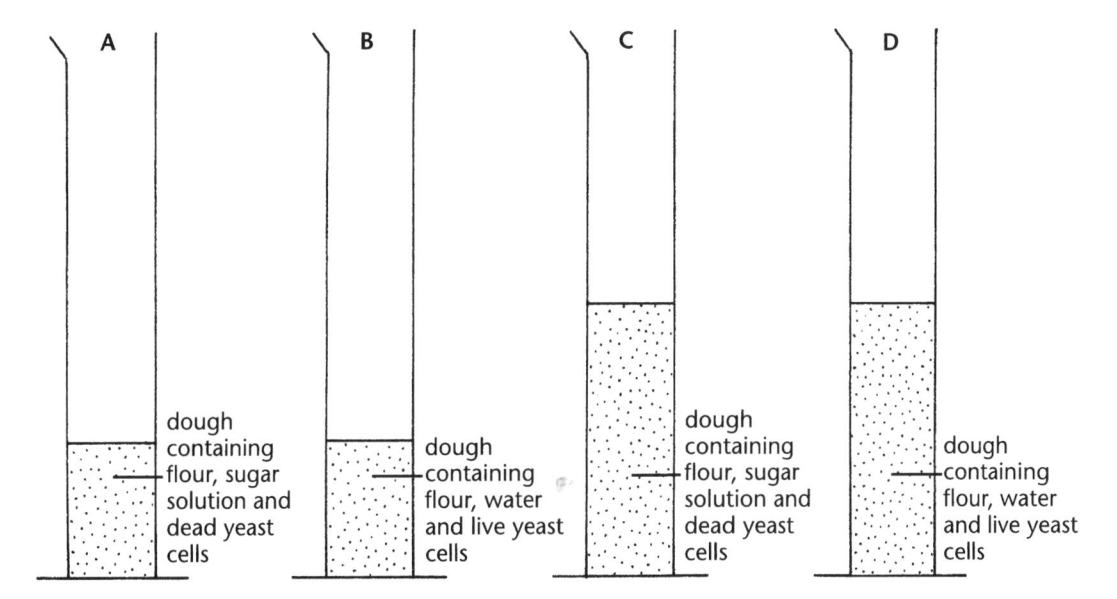

A: dough containing flour, sugar solution and dead yeast cells

B: dough containing flour, water and live yeast cells

C: dough containing flour, sugar solution and dead yeast cells

D: dough containing flour, water and live yeast cells

5 Under ideal growing conditions, yeast takes 2 hours to double its mass. How many hours would it take 5 g of yeast to become 40 g under such conditions?

   A 6.   B 8.   C 10.   D 14.

93

Unit 2 Biotechnological Industries

Multiple Choice Test 1 continued

Questions 6, 7 and 8 refer to the accompanying diagram. It shows ways in which a microbiologist tries to prevent unwanted micro-organisms in the air from getting into the experiment.

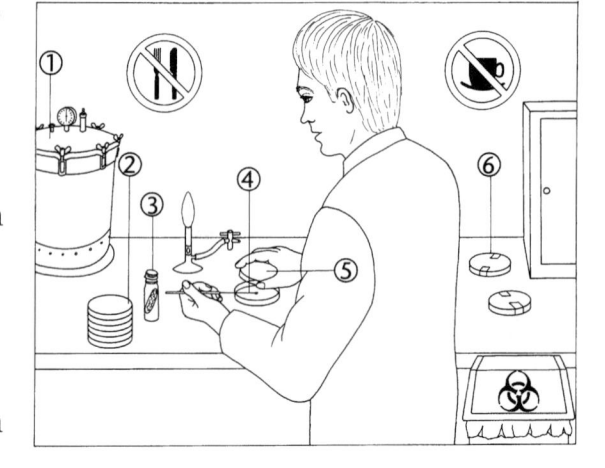

6 Which number in the diagram matches the description 'dishes of sterile nutrient agar jelly closed until needed'?

A 1.   B 2.   C 3.   D 4.

7 Which number matches the description 'wire loop has been flamed before use to destroy unwanted micro-organisms'?

A 1.   B 3.   C 4.   D 5.

8 Which number matches the description 'dish sealed with tape to prevent entry and exit of micro-organisms'?

A 2.   B 3.   C 5.   D 6.

9 The diagram shows five of the steps carried out at a bakery to make bread.

The correct order of these steps is

A 2, 1, 5, 3, 4.   B 2, 5, 1, 4, 3.   C 5, 2, 1, 4, 3.   D 5, 2, 4, 1, 3.

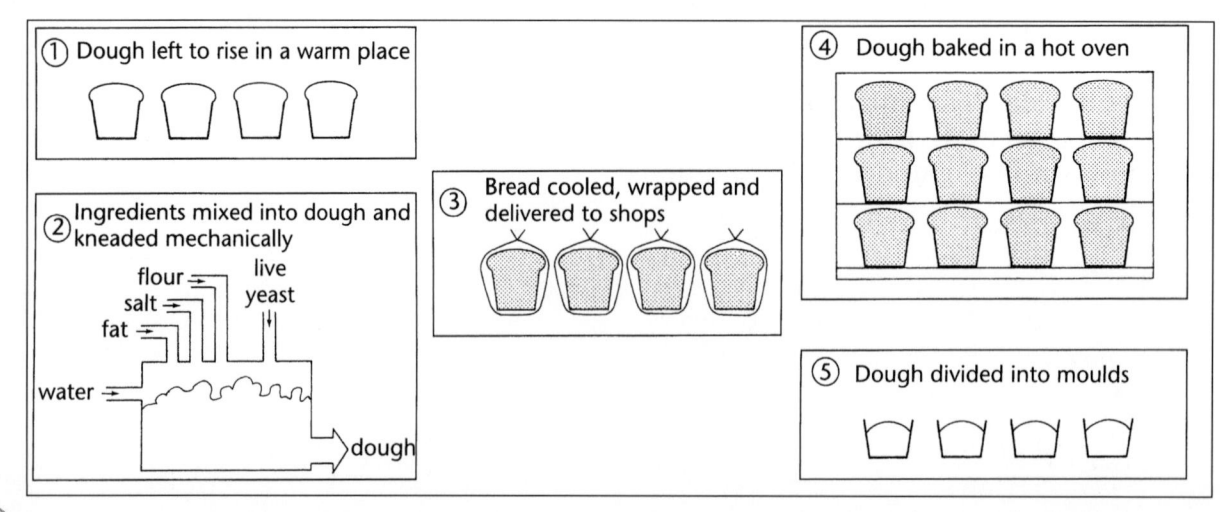

① Dough left to rise in a warm place

② Ingredients mixed into dough and kneaded mechanically
flour, salt, fat, live yeast, water → dough

③ Bread cooled, wrapped and delivered to shops

④ Dough baked in a hot oven

⑤ Dough divided into moulds

Chapter 6 **Yeast-Based Industries**

Multiple Choice Test 1 continued

10 The column on the left side of the accompanying diagram shows test tubes 1, 2, 3 and 4 set up to investigate the growth of yeast cells in glucose solution. When yeast cells respire and grow they release CO_2 gas which inflates the balloon attached to the top of the test tube. Which column in the diagram shows the results after 3 days?

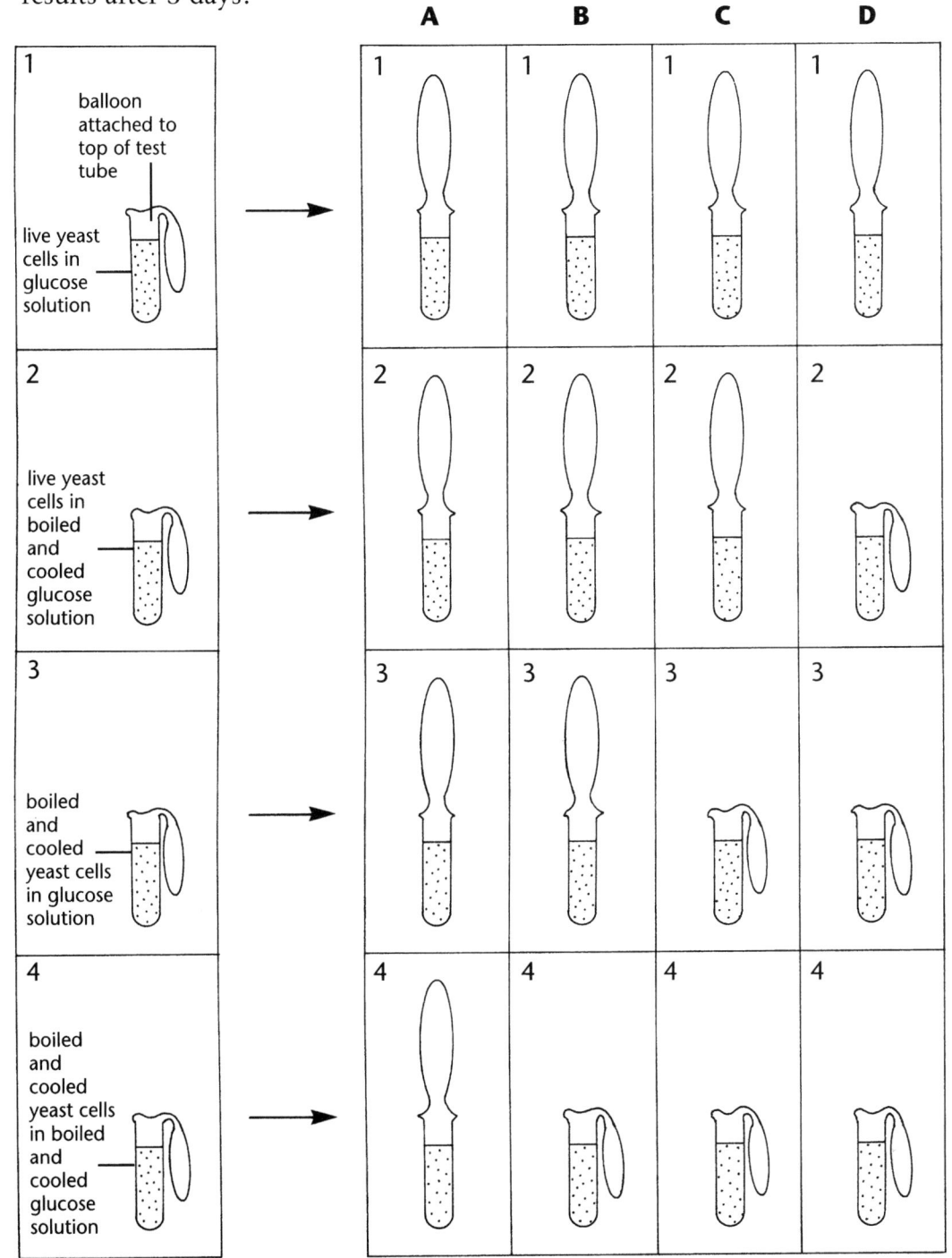

Unit 2 **Biotechnological Industries**

Multiple Choice Test 1 continued

Questions 11 and 12 refer to the accompanying flow chart.
It shows how two types of beer are made.

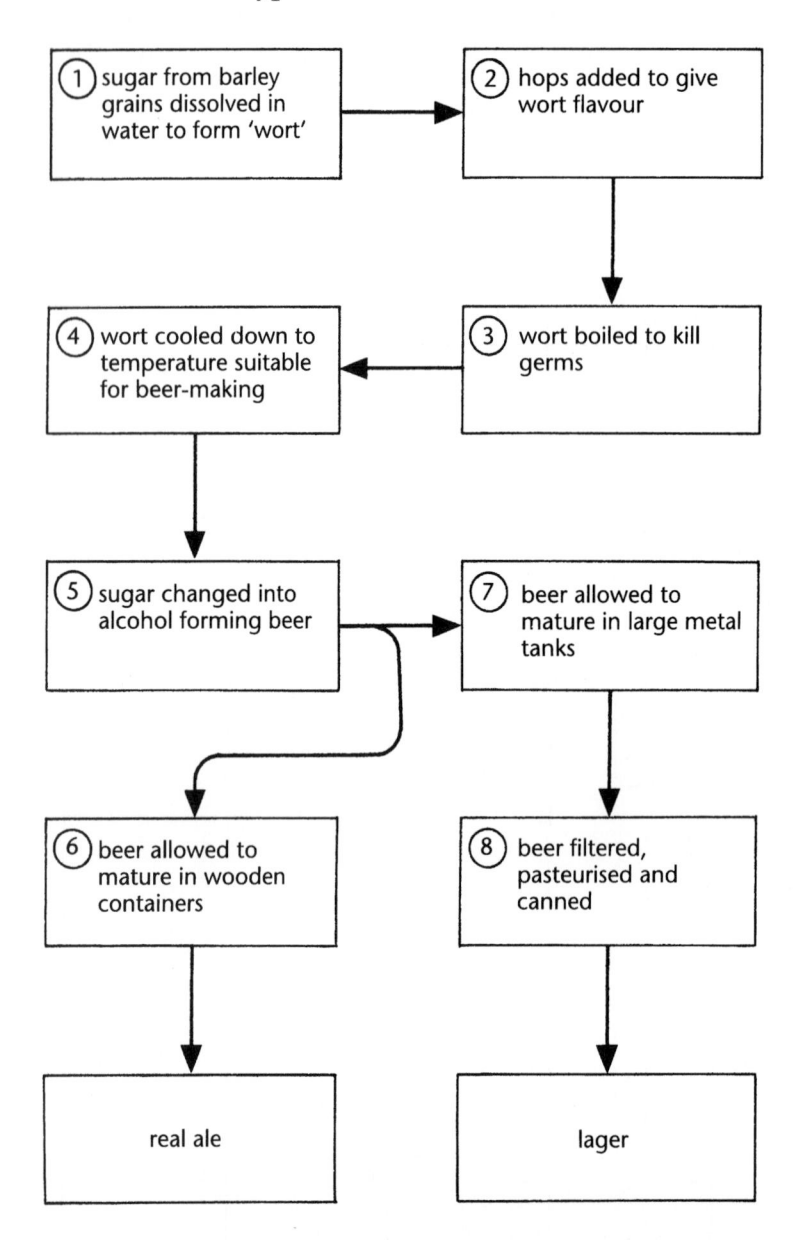

```
┌─────────────────────────┐      ┌─────────────────────────┐
│ ① sugar from barley     │      │ ② hops added to give    │
│   grains dissolved in   │ ───▶ │   wort flavour          │
│   water to form 'wort'  │      │                         │
└─────────────────────────┘      └─────────────────────────┘
                                              │
                                              ▼
┌─────────────────────────┐      ┌─────────────────────────┐
│ ④ wort cooled down to   │      │ ③ wort boiled to kill   │
│   temperature suitable  │ ◀─── │   germs                 │
│   for beer-making       │      │                         │
└─────────────────────────┘      └─────────────────────────┘
           │
           ▼
┌─────────────────────────┐      ┌─────────────────────────┐
│ ⑤ sugar changed into    │      │ ⑦ beer allowed to       │
│   alcohol forming beer  │ ───▶ │   mature in large metal │
│                         │      │   tanks                 │
└─────────────────────────┘      └─────────────────────────┘
           │                                  │
           ▼                                  ▼
┌─────────────────────────┐      ┌─────────────────────────┐
│ ⑥ beer allowed to       │      │ ⑧ beer filtered,        │
│   mature in wooden      │      │   pasteurised and       │
│   containers            │      │   canned                │
└─────────────────────────┘      └─────────────────────────┘
           │                                  │
           ▼                                  ▼
        real ale                           lager
```

11 At which stage is brewer's yeast most active in the process?
   A 1.   B 2.   C 4.   D 5.

12 At which stage is beer allowed to 'condition' in casks?
   A 2.   B 4.   C 6.   D 8.

Multiple Choice Test 1 continued

Chapter 6 Yeast-Based Industries

Questions 13, 14 and 15 refer to the accompanying graph. It shows the change in number of yeast cells grown in glucose solution.

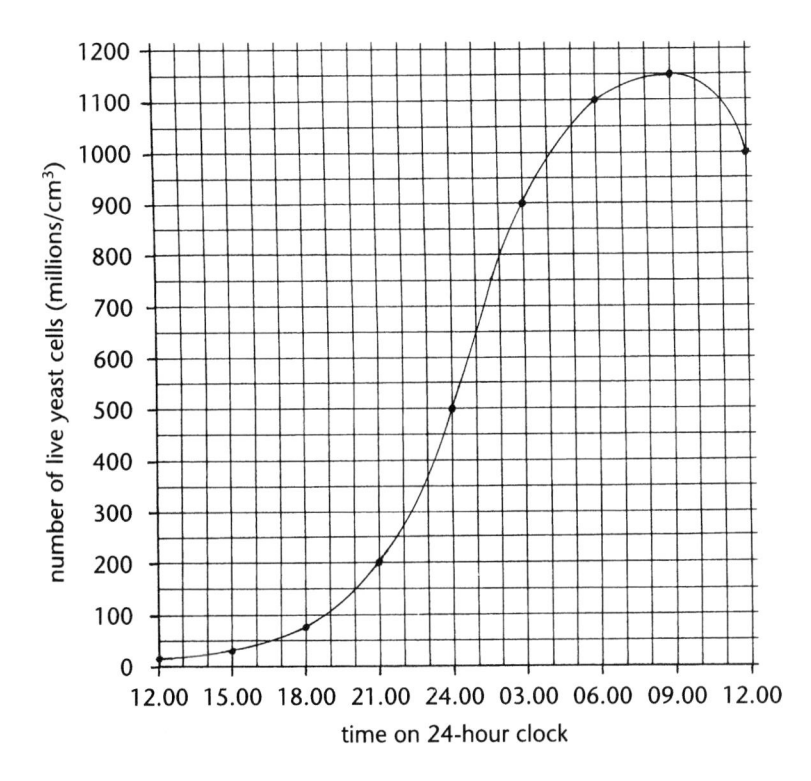

13 For how many hours was the experiment run?

A 8.   B 12.   C 18.   D 24.

14 Between which times did the number of yeast cells show the biggest increase?

A   21.00 and 24.00.   B   24.00 and 03.00.
C   03.00 and 06.00.   D   06.00 and 09.00.

15 At 21.00 hours there were 200 million yeast cells per cm^3 of culture liquid. At what time on the 24-hour clock had this number increased to 4 times its size?

A 01.00.   B 02.00.   C 03.00.   D 04.00.

Questions 16 and 17 refer to the following table which gives the steps carried out when an enzyme is being immobilised.

1	Place a sample of enzyme solution and sodium alginate solution in a beaker.
2	Stir the mixture with a stirring rod.
3	Place calcium chloride solution in a second beaker.
4	[see question 16]
5	Add the enzyme-alginate mixture to the calcium chloride solution one drop at a time from a syringe.
6	Leave the newly formed beads in the calcium chloride solution for a few minutes.
7	Rinse the beads with water and collect them in a sieve ready for use.

16 The step that should have been given at 4 in the table is

    A Collect the enzyme-alginate mixture in a syringe.

    B Pour the enzyme-alginate mixture through a strainer.

    C Collect the calcium chloride solution in a syringe.

    D Pour the calcium chloride solution through a strainer.

17 During which stage does the enzyme become immobilised in beads of gel?

    A 1.   B 2.   C 5.   D 7.

Chapter 6 **Yeast-Based Industries**

Multiple Choice Test 1 continued

18 The first of the following diagrams shows an experiment set up to show that both yeast and an enzyme are needed to change a mixture of milk and yoghurt into a fermented drink.

Which part of the second diagram would make the best control for this experiment?

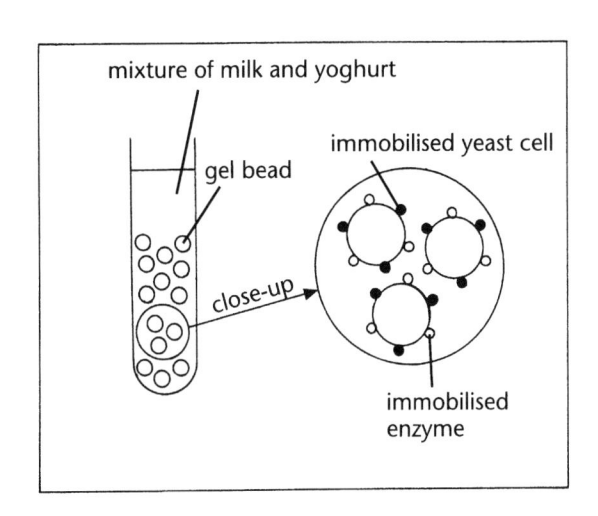

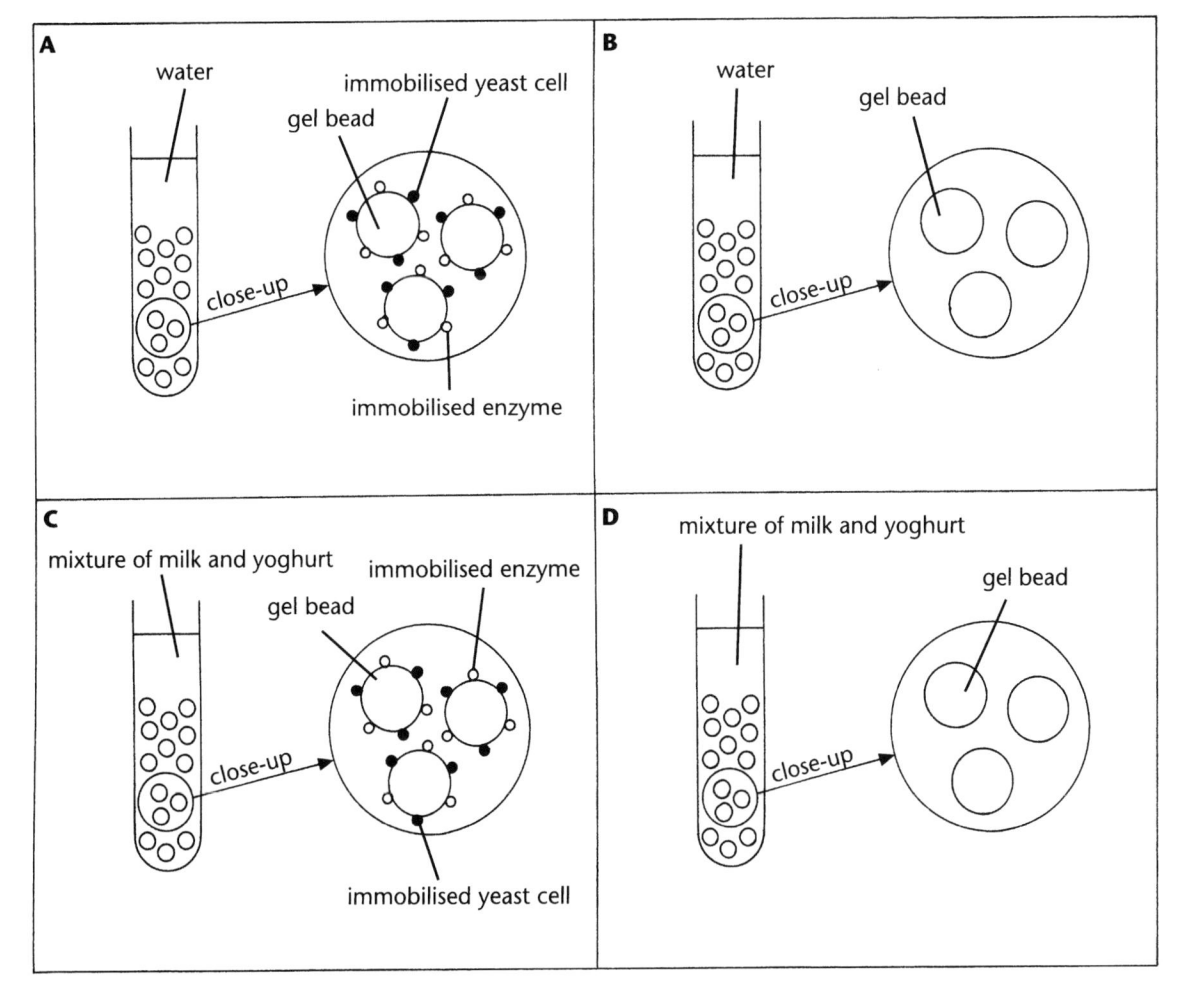

A water; immobilised yeast cell, gel bead, immobilised enzyme

B water; gel bead only

C mixture of milk and yoghurt; immobilised enzyme, gel bead, immobilised yeast cell

D mixture of milk and yoghurt; gel bead only

Unit 2 Biotechnological Industries

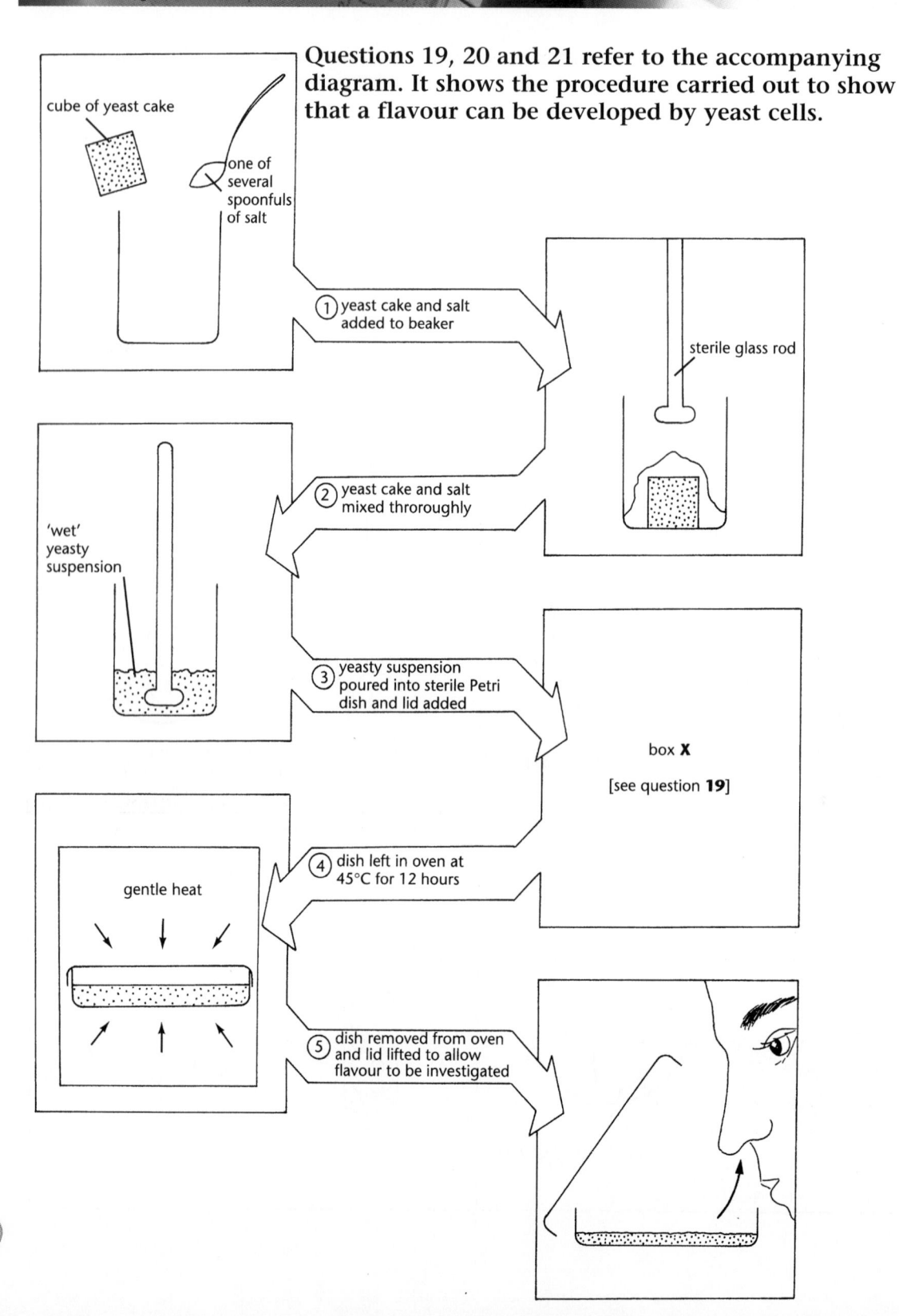

Multiple Choice Test 1 continued

Questions 19, 20 and 21 refer to the accompanying diagram. It shows the procedure carried out to show that a flavour can be developed by yeast cells.

- cube of yeast cake
- one of several spoonfuls of salt

1. yeast cake and salt added to beaker

   sterile glass rod

2. yeast cake and salt mixed throroughly

   'wet' yeasty suspension

3. yeasty suspension poured into sterile Petri dish and lid added

   box **X**

   [see question **19**]

4. dish left in oven at 45°C for 12 hours

   gentle heat

5. dish removed from oven and lid lifted to allow flavour to be investigated

Multiple Choice Test 1 continued

19 Which part of the diagram below shows the missing contents of box X in the first diagram?

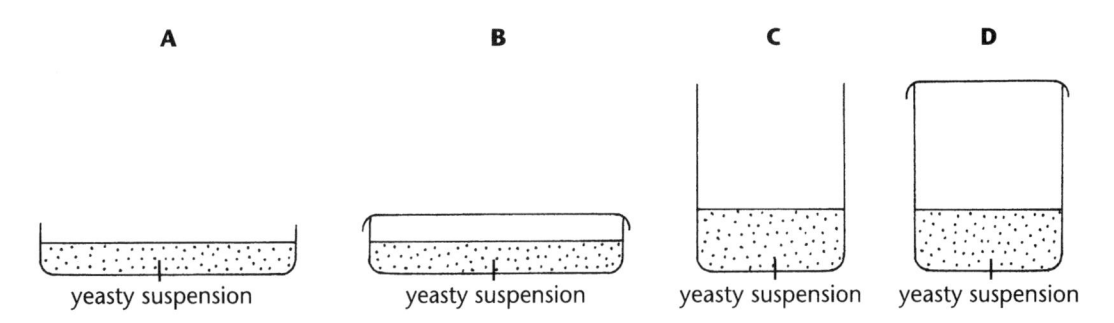

A   B   C   D

yeasty suspension   yeasty suspension   yeasty suspension   yeasty suspension

20 During which numbered stage does salt act on most of the yeast cells and force them to release much of their water?

A 1.   B 2.   C 3.   D 4.

21 During which numbered stage does most of the flavour develop?

A 2.   B 3.   C 4.   D 5.

22 The following table refers to two strains of yeast, one 'pink' and the other 'white'. Which line in the table is correct?

	colour of yeast	growth at 5°C	growth at 20°C	growth at 30°C	growth at 50°C
A	pink	good	very good	very poor	none
B	white	poor	good	very good	excellent
C	pink	poor	good	very good	excellent
D	white	good	very good	very poor	none

23 Methylene blue is a chemical used to test treated waste water from yeast industries to see if it is safe to put into the local river. If the water is safe, the methylene blue

  A   remains blue in colour.
  B   changes quickly to pink.
  C   changes slowly to mauve.
  D   goes colourless rapidly.

Unit 2 **Biotechnological Industries**

Multiple Choice Test 1 continued

Questions 24 and 25 refer to the flow diagram. It shows how waste materials can be upgraded into a useful substance instead of being thrown away.

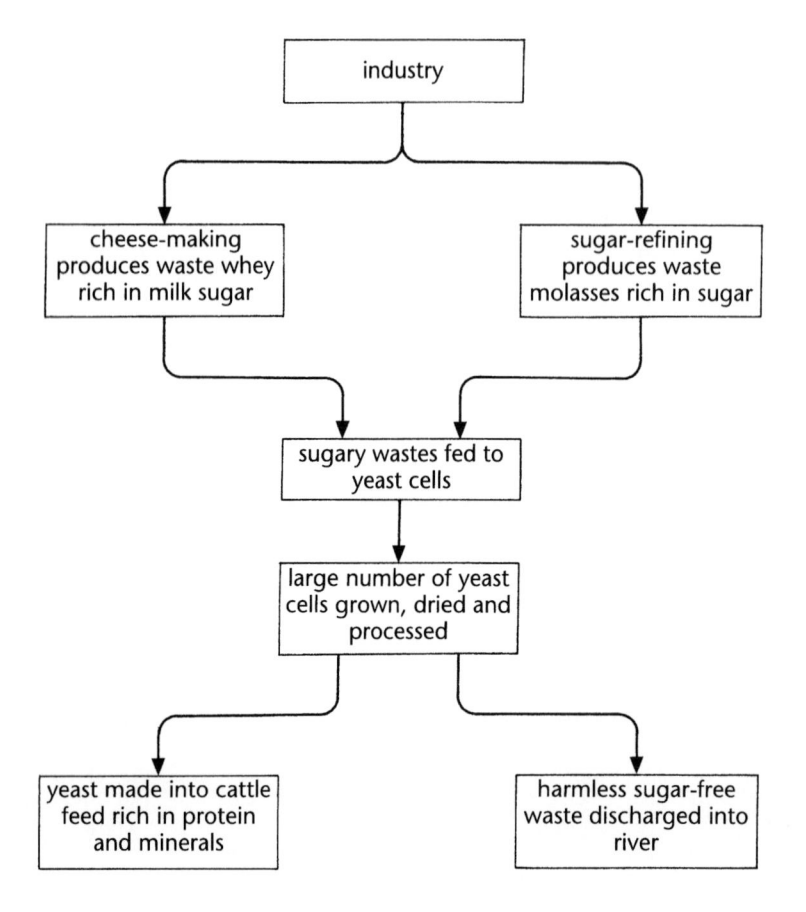

```
                    industry
                   /        \
      cheese-making          sugar-refining
      produces waste whey    produces waste
      rich in milk sugar     molasses rich in sugar
                   \        /
              sugary wastes fed to
                   yeast cells
                       |
              large number of yeast
              cells grown, dried and
                    processed
                   /        \
      yeast made into cattle   harmless sugar-free
      feed rich in protein     waste discharged into
         and minerals                river
```

24 What is the useful substance formed as a result of this process?

A whey. B molasses.
C milk sugar. D cattle feed.

25 If the untreated sugary wastes were discharged directly into the local river

A the bacterial numbers in the river water would increase.
B the yeast numbers in the river water would decrease.
C the oxygen concentration of the river water would increase.
D the carbon dioxide concentration of the river water would decrease.

Chapter 6 Yeast-Based Industries

Multiple Choice Test 2

Choose the ONE correct answer to each of the following questions.

Questions 1, 2 and 3 refer to the accompanying diagram. It shows an experiment set up to investigate the raising of dough by yeast.

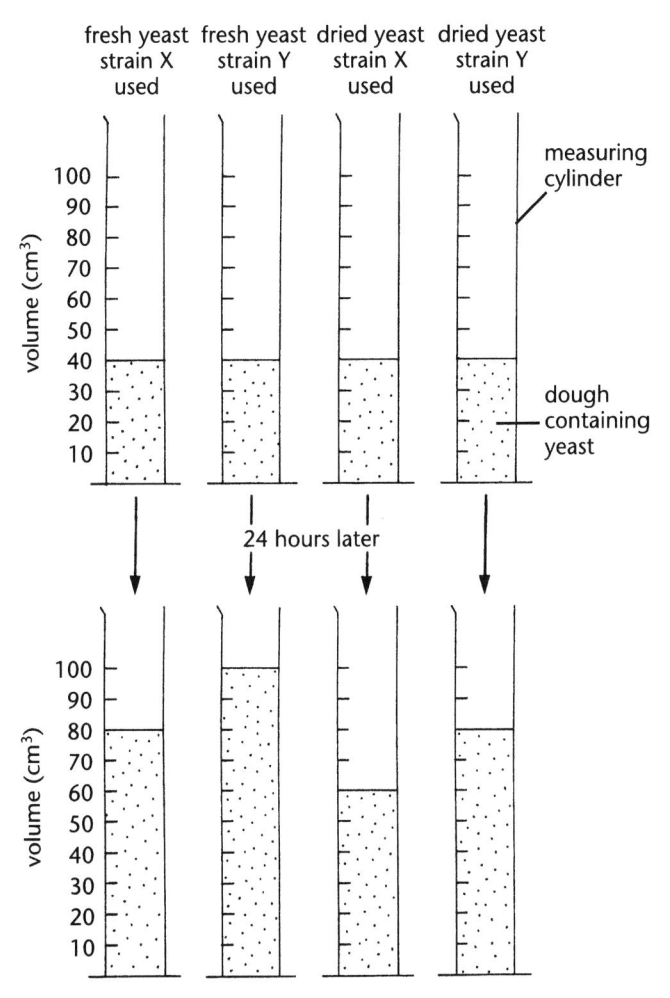

1 What substance released by yeast makes dough rise?

    A carbon dioxide.   B carbon monoxide.   C alcohol.   D air.

2 It can be concluded from this experiment that

    A   fresh yeast strain X is faster-acting than fresh yeast strain Y.

    B   fresh yeast strain X is faster-acting than dried yeast strain Y.

    C   dried yeast strain Y is faster-acting than dried yeast strain X.

    D   dried yeast strain Y is faster-acting than fresh yeast strain X.

103

Unit 2 Biotechnological Industries

Multiple Choice Test 2 continued

3 What is the percentage increase in volume shown by dried yeast strain X?

A 20. B 40. C 50. D 60.

4 Under ideal growing conditions, yeast takes 2 hours to double its mass. Starting with 10 g of yeast, what mass (in g) would be present after 8 hours of ideal growing conditions?

A 50. B 60. C 80. D 160.

5 The diagram shows four steps carried out to grow a culture of yeast cells on nutrient agar jelly. What is the correct order of the four steps?

A 3, 1, 2, 4. B 3, 1, 4, 2. C 1, 3, 2, 4. D 1, 3, 4, 2.

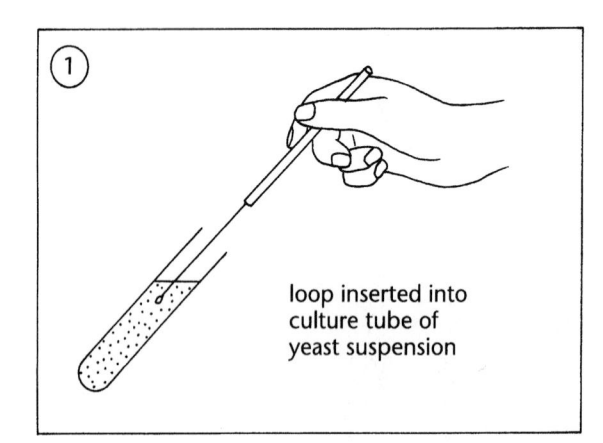

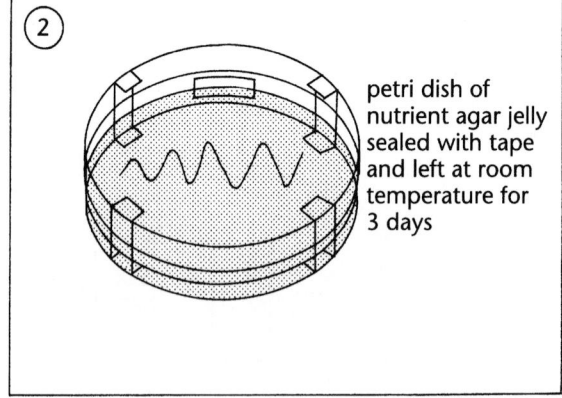

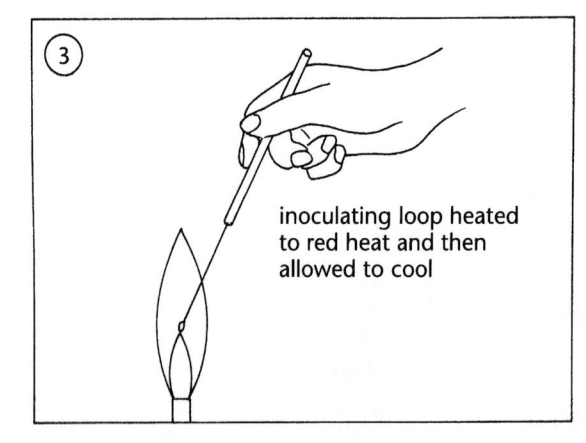

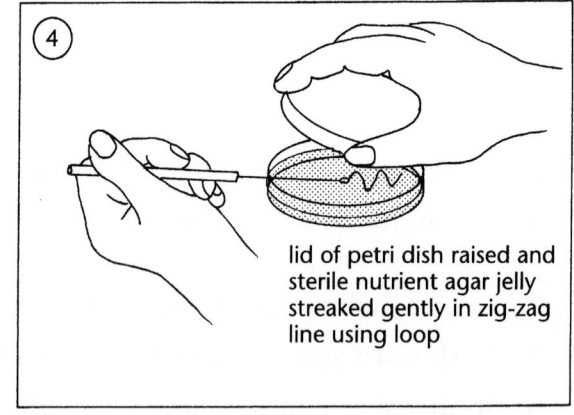

① loop inserted into culture tube of yeast suspension

② petri dish of nutrient agar jelly sealed with tape and left at room temperature for 3 days

③ inoculating loop heated to red heat and then allowed to cool

④ lid of petri dish raised and sterile nutrient agar jelly streaked gently in zig-zag line using loop

Multiple Choice Test 2 continued

Questions 6 and 7 refer to the following table which lists the ingredients needed for bread making.

ingredient	parts (by volume)
salt	1
sugar	1
yeast	5
water	60
flour	100

6 If a baker decides to make loaves each containing 300 cm^3 of flour, then the volume of water (in cm^3) needed for each loaf would be

   A 20.

   B 30.

   C 160.

   D 180.

7 In each loaf, what is the ratio of water to yeast by volume?

   A 5:1.

   B 12:1.

   C 60:1.

   D 300:1.

Unit 2 Biotechnological Industries

Multiple Choice Test 2 continued

Questions 8, 9 and 10 on the next page refer to the diagram of a simple fermenter.

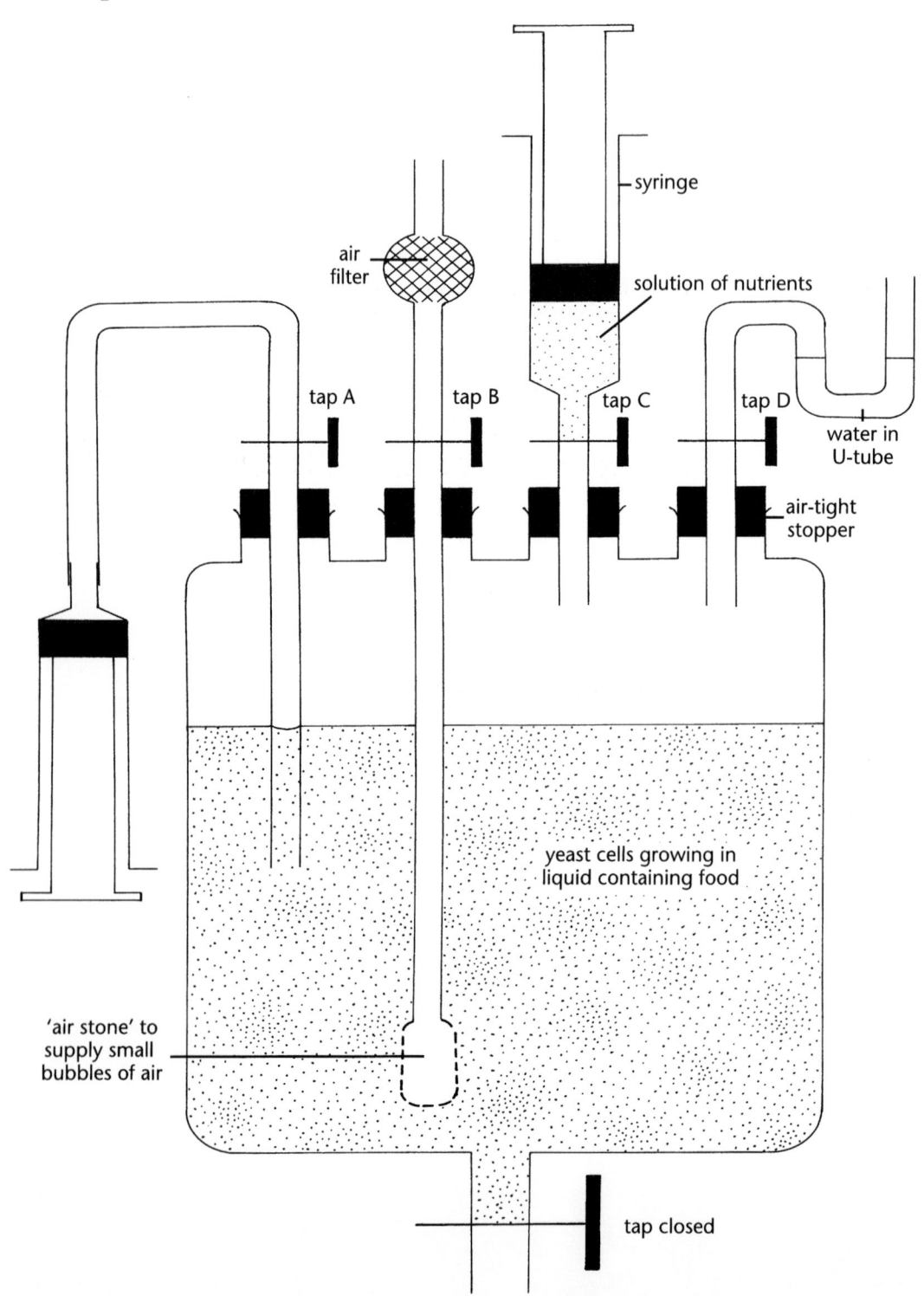

- syringe
- air filter
- solution of nutrients
- tap A
- tap B
- tap C
- tap D
- water in U-tube
- air-tight stopper
- yeast cells growing in liquid containing food
- 'air stone' to supply small bubbles of air
- tap closed

Multiple Choice Test 2 continued

8 Which tap should be opened to supply the yeast cells with extra nutrients?

9 Which tap should be opened to allow carbon dioxide gas to escape?

10 Which tap should be opened to allow a small sample of the yeast cells to be removed from the fermenter?

Questions 11, 12 and 13 refer to the following table. It contains information about two strains of yeast used to brew beer.

	length of time taken by yeast to grow (days)	temperature range needed by yeast (°C)	place in fermentation container where yeast cells gather
A	6	8–14	top
B	6	14–20	top
C	20	8–14	bottom
D	20	14–20	bottom

11 Which line in the table refers to a lager yeast?

12 Which line in the table refers to an ale yeast?

13 At which temperature (in °C) would both of these strains of yeast grow?

　　A　8.

　　B　10.

　　C　14.

　　D　18.

Unit 2 Biotechnological Industries

Multiple Choice Test 2 continued

Questions 14 and 15 refer to the accompanying graph. It shows the results of an experiment set up to follow the use of sugar by yeast cells during beer making over a period of four days.

14 During which day did the greatest decrease in sugar concentration occur?
   A Monday.
   B Tuesday.
   C Wednesday.
   D Thursday.

15 The sugar concentration decreases because
   A yeast feeds on it and makes alcohol.
   B the alcohol formed burns up the sugar.
   C yeast uses alcohol as an energy source.
   D the alcohol and sugar undergo a chemical reaction.

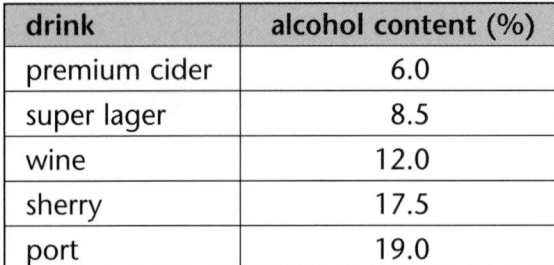

16 The following table lists the alcohol content of some drinks.

drink	alcohol content (%)
premium cider	6.0
super lager	8.5
wine	12.0
sherry	17.5
port	19.0

Which of the following is **drink X** in the accompanying bar chart?
   A premium cider.
   B super lager.
   C wine.
   D sherry.

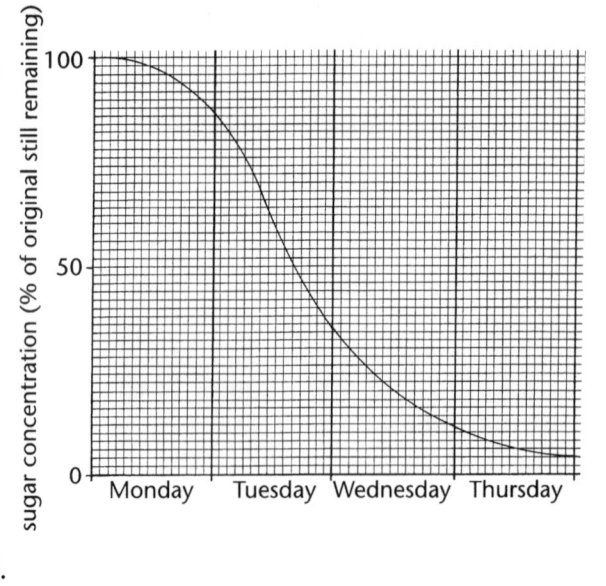

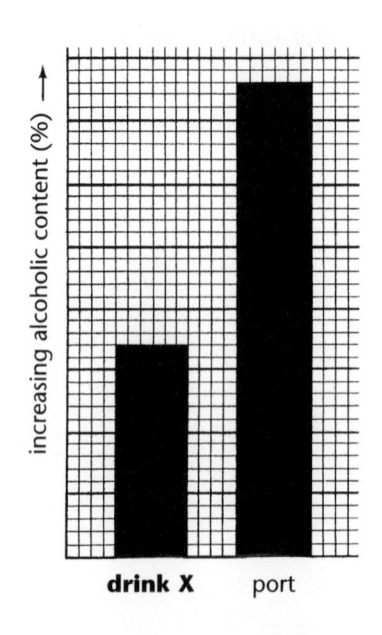

Chapter 6 Yeast-Based Industries

Multiple Choice Test 2 continued

17 The diagram shows four steps carried out during the preparation of gel beads containing immobilised enzyme.

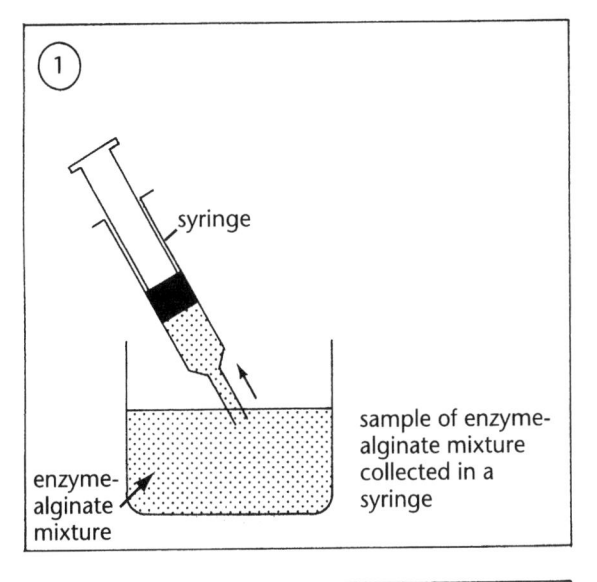

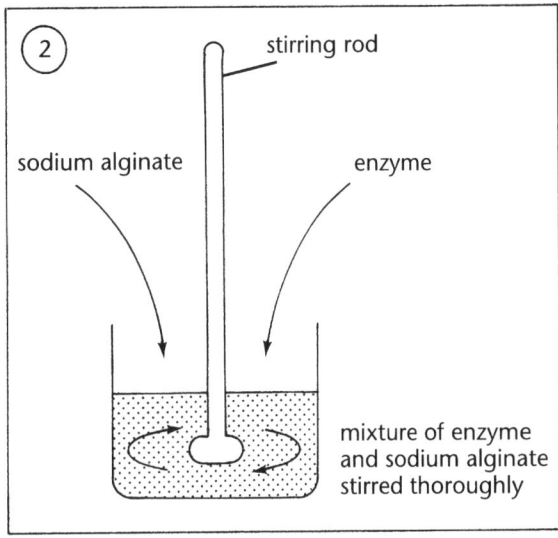

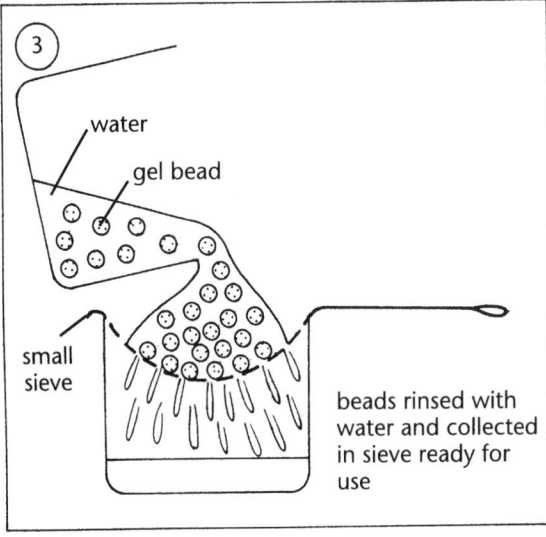

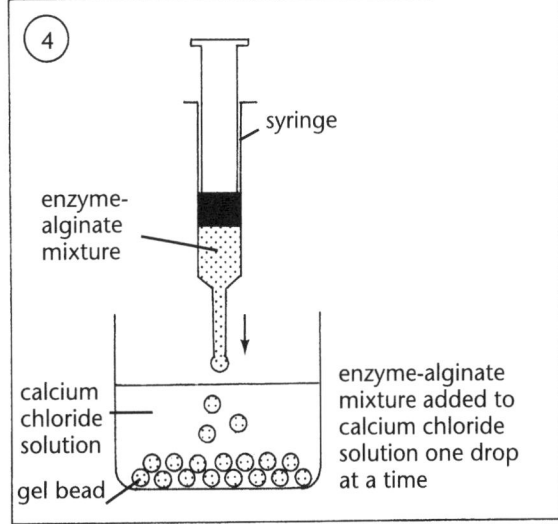

① syringe — enzyme-alginate mixture — sample of enzyme-alginate mixture collected in a syringe

② stirring rod — sodium alginate — enzyme — mixture of enzyme and sodium alginate stirred thoroughly

③ water — gel bead — small sieve — beads rinsed with water and collected in sieve ready for use

④ syringe — enzyme-alginate mixture — calcium chloride solution — gel bead — enzyme-alginate mixture added to calcium chloride solution one drop at a time

The correct order would be

    A 1, 2, 4, 3.

    B 2, 1, 4, 3.

    C 2, 1, 3, 4.

    D 2, 4, 1, 3.

Unit 2 **Biotechnological Industries**

Multiple Choice Test 2 continued

18 The diagram opposite shows gel beads with enzyme molecules and yeast cells immobilised on their surfaces. They are being used to change a mixture of milk and yoghurt into a fermented drink.

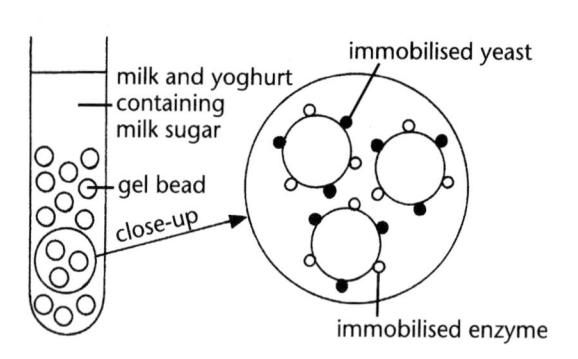

Which of the following represents the chemical reactions that take place during this process?

A milk sugar $\xrightarrow{\text{immobilised enzyme}}$ simple sugar $\xrightarrow{\text{immobilised yeast}}$ alcohol.

B milk sugar $\xrightarrow{\text{immobilised yeast}}$ simple sugar $\xrightarrow{\text{immobilised enzyme}}$ alcohol.

C simple sugar $\xrightarrow{\text{immobilised enzyme}}$ milk sugar $\xrightarrow{\text{immobilised yeast}}$ alcohol.

D simple sugar $\xrightarrow{\text{immobilised yeast}}$ milk sugar $\xrightarrow{\text{immobilised enzyme}}$ alcohol.

19 The following list gives the steps carried out to show that yeast can be used to develop flavourings for food. They are in a mixed-up order.

1	Petri dish left in oven at 45°C for 12 hours.
2	Yeast cake and salt mixed thoroughly using sterile glass rod.
3	Petri dish removed from oven, lid lifted and flavour from yeast sampled by smelling it.
4	Yeasty suspension poured into sterile glass Petri dish.

The correct order of these steps is

    A 1, 2, 4, 3.   B 2, 4, 3, 1.   C 1, 3, 2, 4.   D 2, 4, 1, 3.

Chapter 6 Yeast-Based Industries

Multiple Choice Test 2 continued

Questions 20, 21 and 22 refer to the accompanying diagram. It shows the use of yeast in the salmon industry.

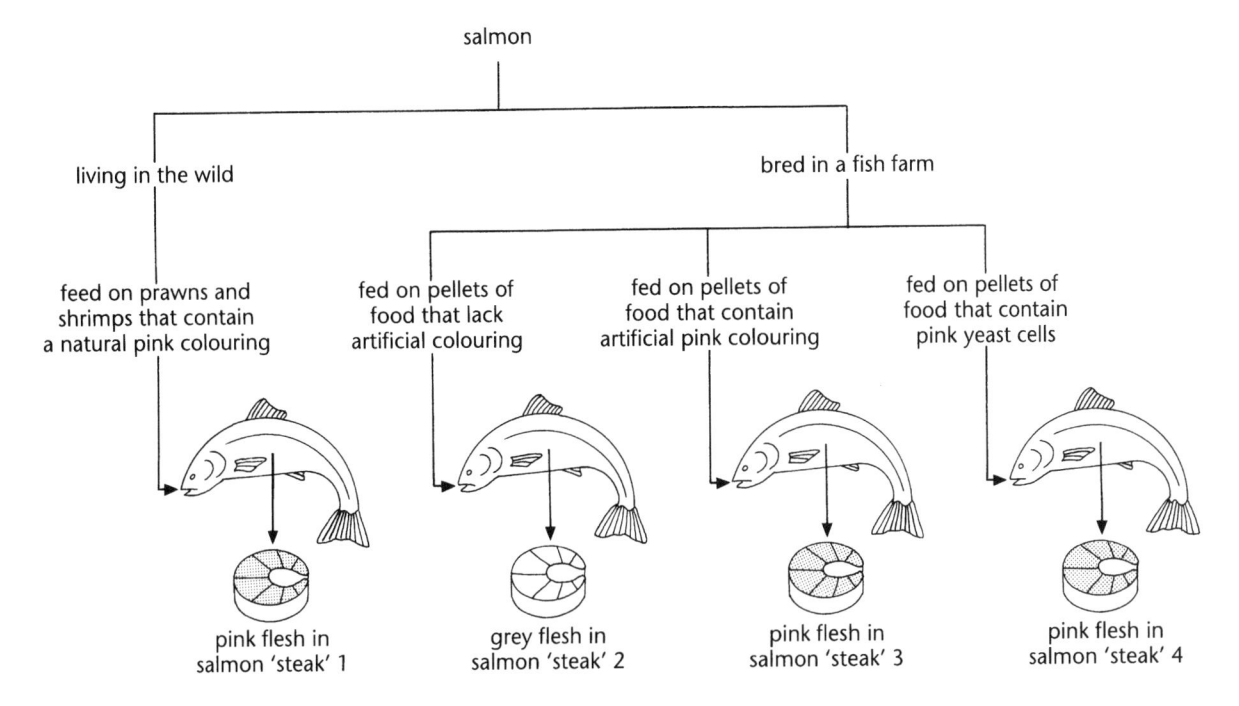

salmon
- living in the wild
  - feed on prawns and shrimps that contain a natural pink colouring → pink flesh in salmon 'steak' 1
- bred in a fish farm
  - fed on pellets of food that lack artificial colouring → grey flesh in salmon 'steak' 2
  - fed on pellets of food that contain artificial pink colouring → pink flesh in salmon 'steak' 3
  - fed on pellets of food that contain pink yeast cells → pink flesh in salmon 'steak' 4

20 If a salmon has grey flesh, it has lived its life
   A in the wild and has fed on shrimps and prawns.
   B in the wild and has fed on pink yeast cells.
   C in a fish farm and has been fed colourless food pellets.
   D in a fish farm and has been fed coloured food pellets.

21 Of the four types of salmon 'steak' shown in the diagram, which one is the most natural food?
   A 1.   B 2.   C 3.   D 4.

22 Of the types of salmon bred in a fish farm, the more natural of the types with pink flesh has been fed food pellets containing
   A prawns and shrimps.
   B colourless yeast cells.
   C artificial pink colouring.
   D pink yeast cells.

Unit 2 Biotechnological Industries

Multiple Choice Test 2 continued

23 In the diagram of a river, four pipes (A, B, C and D) are discharging liquid into the river. The water in the river has been sampled at points 1, 2, 3, 4 and 5 for oxygen concentration and bacterial number. The bar chart part of the diagram shows the results. Which pipe is releasing untreated yeast waste into the river?

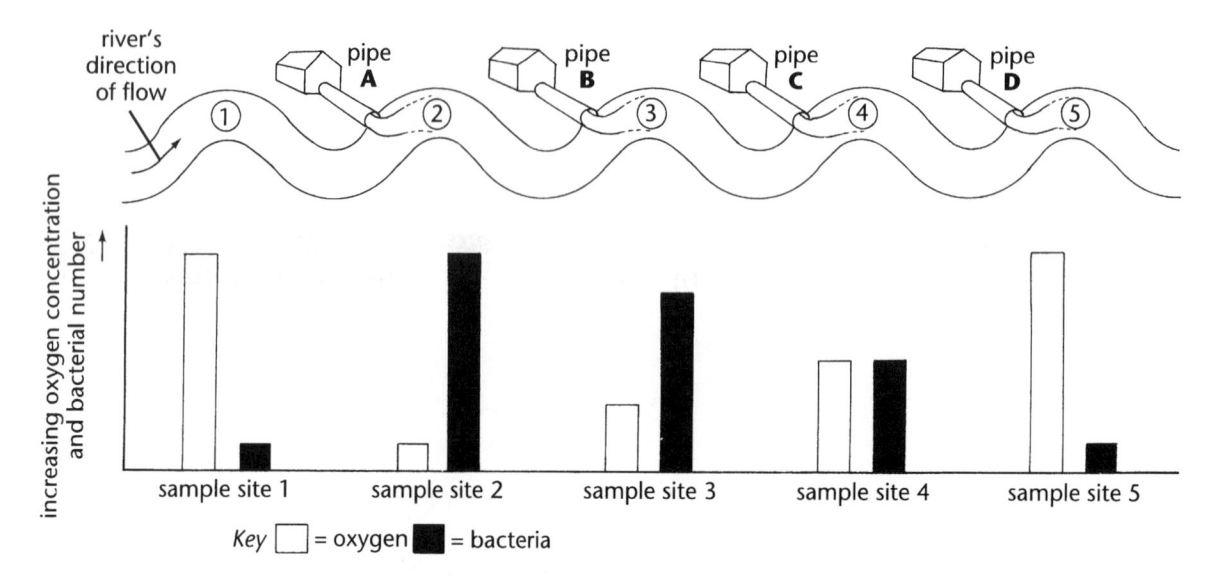

Key ☐ = oxygen ■ = bacteria

Questions 24 and 25 refer to the diagram opposite. It shows waste water samples from yeast factories P, Q, R and S being tested with methylene blue over a period of 5 days.

24 Which factory's waste water would be the most dangerous to put into the river?

A P.   B Q.   C R.   D S.

25 Which water needs further treatment before being put into the local river?

A P only.   C Q and S.
B S only.   D P, Q and R.

Key ■ = blue ☐ = colourless

Unit 2 — 7 Detergent Industries

Matching Test 1

Match the words in list X with their descriptions in list Y.

List X
1) allergic reaction
2) asthma
3) bacteria
4) biological washing powder
5) detergent
6) enzyme
7) fermenter
8) non-biological washing powder
9) protein
10) toxic

List Y
a) cleansing agent such as soap powder
b) substance made by bacteria that digests stains
c) container in which a fermentation process is brought about by micro-organisms
d) excessive response by the defence system to a harmless substance
e) class of food that forms a stain removed by biological washing powder
f) word describing a chemical that is poisonous
g) micro-organisms that make the enzymes used in biological detergents
h) allergic reaction involving wheezing and difficulty in breathing
i) type of detergent that contains a stain-digesting enzyme produced by bacteria
j) type of detergent that lacks stain-digesting enzymes

Unit 2 Biotechnological Industries

Multiple Choice Test 1

Choose the ONE correct answer to each of the following questions.

1. All of the following are detergents except
   - A soap.
   - B washing powder.
   - C washing-up liquid.
   - D disinfectant.

2. Why are enzymes in biological detergents enclosed in a waxy coating?
   - A It prevents the detergent from causing allergic reactions.
   - B It immobilises the molecules allowing them to be re-used.
   - C It stops the detergent interfering with sewage treatment.
   - D It speeds up the removal of greasy stains from clothes.

Questions 3, 4 and 5 refer to the accompanying diagram. It shows a simple version of an industrial fermenter used to culture the bacteria that make a useful enzyme.

3. Which tube is used to introduce air into the system?
   - A 1. B 2. C 3. D 4.

4. Which tube is used to drain the product from the fermenter once the bacteria have grown?
   - A 1. B 2. C 3. D 4.

5. Which lettered structure is the motor that operates the rotating paddles?
   - A P. B Q. C R. D S.

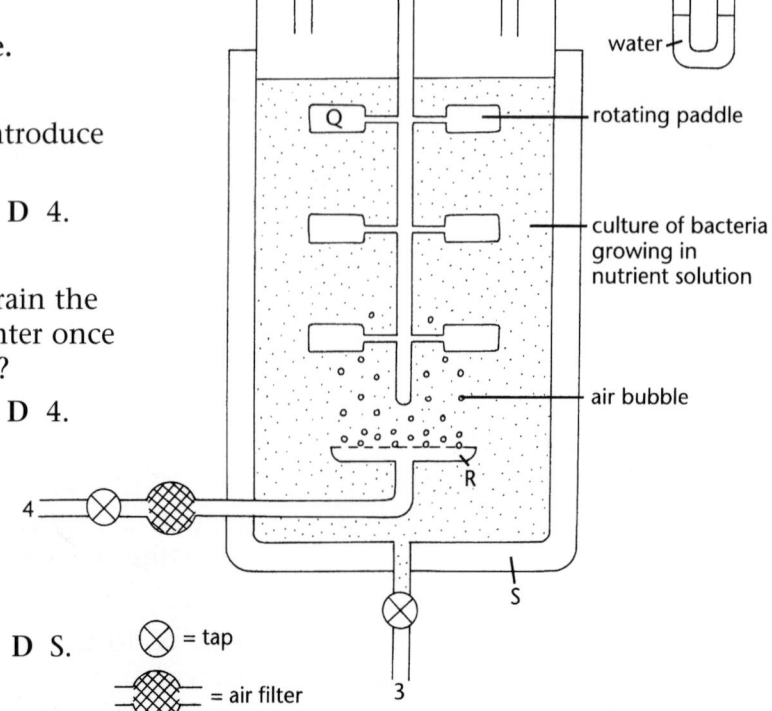

114

Chapter 7 **Detergent Industries**

Multiple Choice Test 1 continued

Questions 6, 7 and 8 refer to the following information. Amylase is an enzyme present in some biological detergents. The accompanying graph shows the effect of pH on the production of amylase in an industrial fermenter.

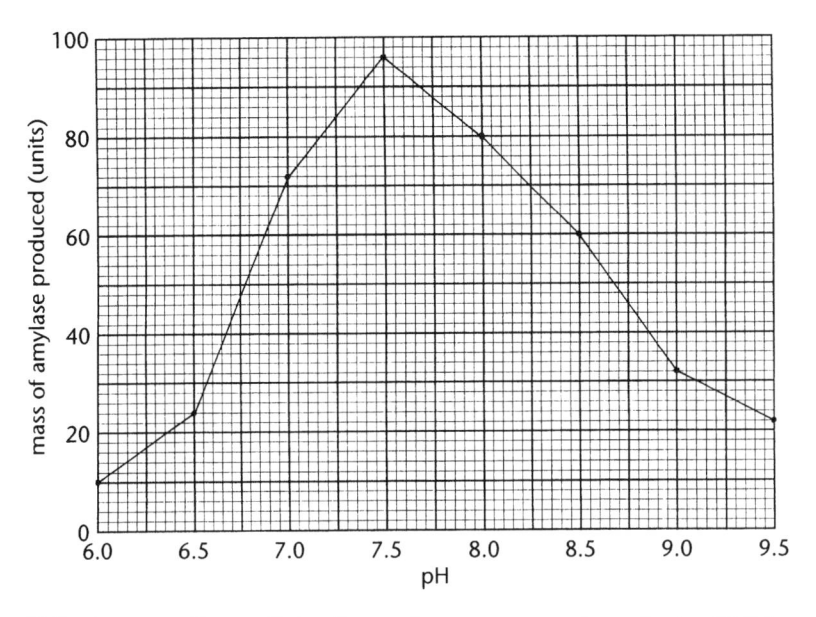

6 What mass (in units) of amylase was produced at pH 7?
   A 66.   B 71.   C 72.   D 76.

7 By how many times was the mass of amylase produced at pH 7.5 greater than that produced at pH 6.5?
   A 3.   B 4.   C 72.   D 96.

8 What is the ratio of mass of amylase produced at pH 7.5 compared with that produced at pH 9?
   A 2:1.   B 3:1.   C 4:1.   D 5:1.

9 The diagram below shows how protein glue makes the black chemical stick to photographic film.

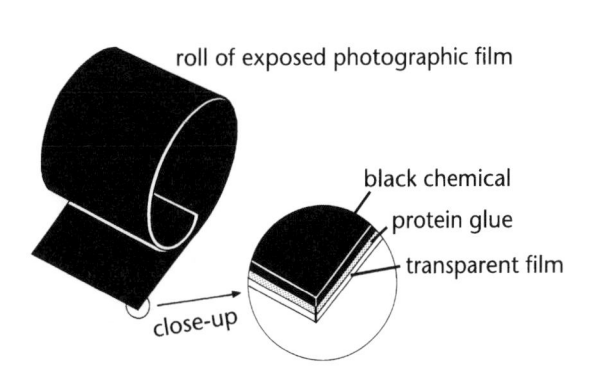

Unit 2 Biotechnological Industries

Multiple Choice Test 1 continued

The second diagram shows an experiment set up to investigate the effect of concentration of biological detergent on the film.

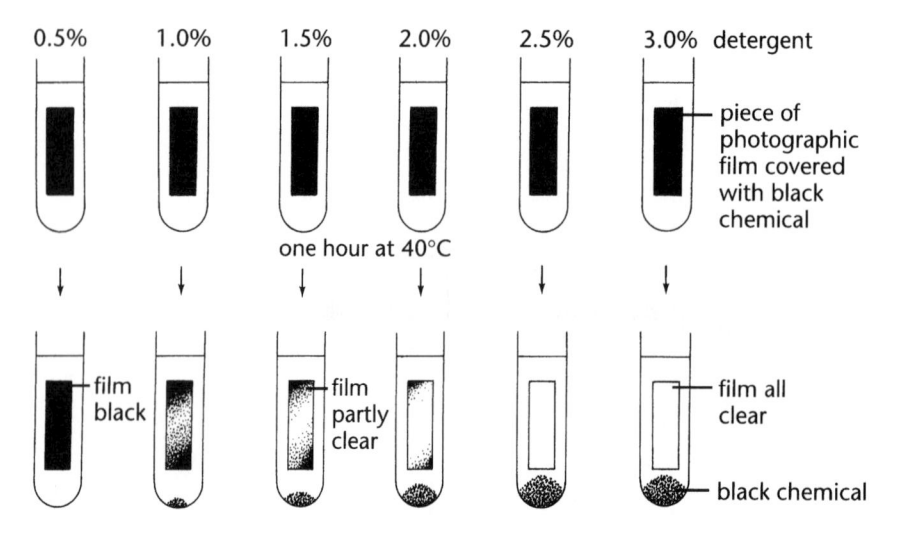

0.5%   1.0%   1.5%   2.0%   2.5%   3.0% detergent

piece of photographic film covered with black chemical

one hour at 40°C

film black   film partly clear   film all clear

black chemical

What is the lowest percentage concentration of detergent that has the maximum effect?

A 0.5.   B 1.5.   C 2.5.   D 3.0.

10 A protease is a type of enzyme that digests protein. When the protein in egg white is mixed with agar jelly, it makes it go cloudy. The diagram opposite shows one of four Petri dishes being set up to test the effect of pH on the activity of protease on egg white protein.

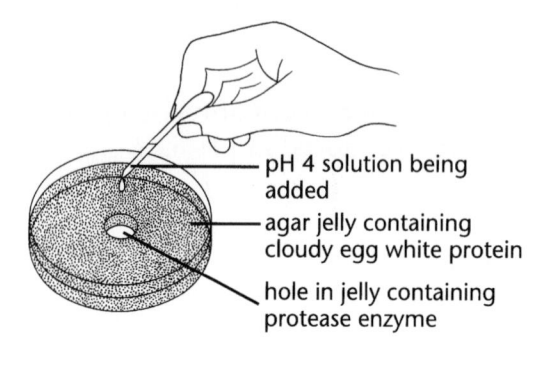

pH 4 solution being added
agar jelly containing cloudy egg white protein
hole in jelly containing protease enzyme

The second diagram shows the results after 4 hours at 35°C.

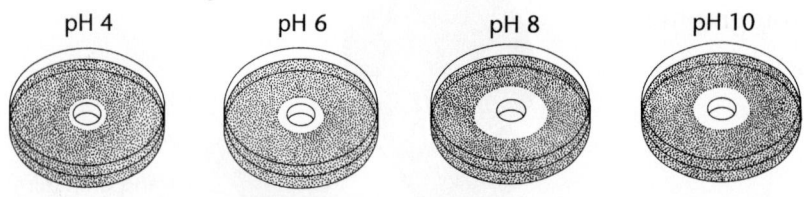

pH 4   pH 6   pH 8   pH 10

At which pH does protease digest egg white protein best?

A 4.   B 6.   C 8.   D 10.

Chapter 7 Detergent Industries

Multiple Choice Test 1 continued

Questions 11, 12 and 13 refer to the accompanying diagram. It shows an experiment set up to investigate the effect of a non-biological and a biological detergent at two different temperatures.

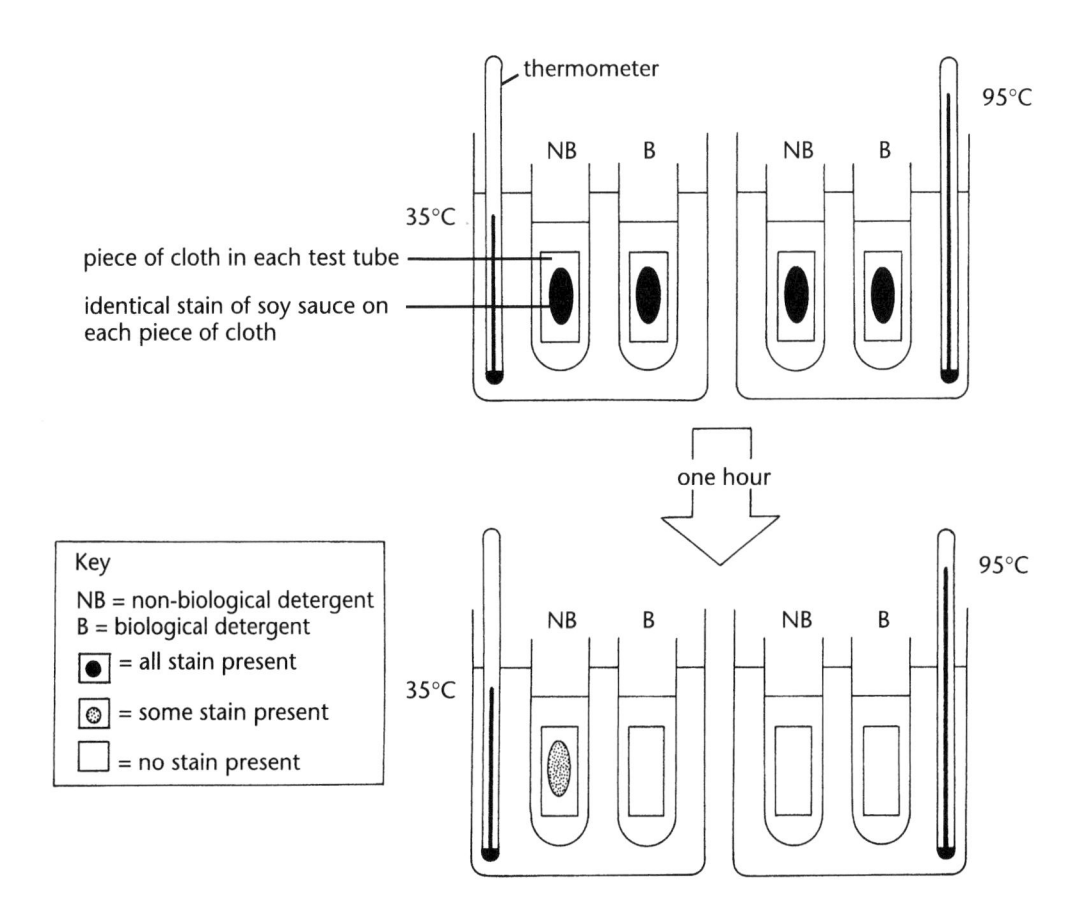

Key
NB = non-biological detergent
B = biological detergent
■ = all stain present
▨ = some stain present
□ = no stain present

11 A variable factor being investigated in this experiment was
  A concentration of non-biological detergent.
  B volume of biological detergent.
  C temperature at which the detergent works.
  D type of stain that the detergent digests.

Unit 2 Biotechnological Industries

Multiple Choice Test 1 continued

12 What conclusion can be correctly drawn from the results?
  A Biological detergent works better than non-biological detergent at 35°C.
  B Non-biological detergent works better than biological detergent at 35°C.
  C Biological detergent works better than non-biological detergent at 95°C.
  D Non-biological detergent works better than biological detergent at 95°C.

13 Which of the pairs shown in the diagram should be used as the control tubes in this experiment?

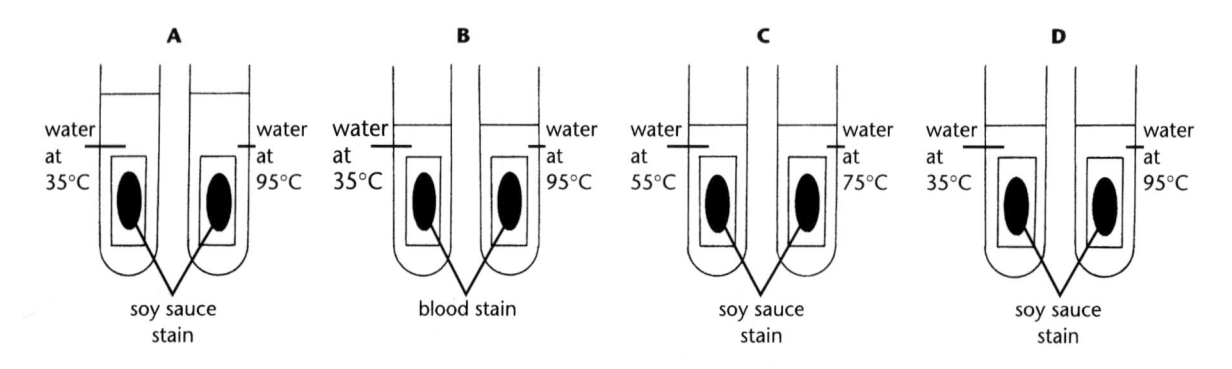

A	B	C	D
water at 35°C / water at 95°C	water at 35°C / water at 95°C	water at 55°C / water at 75°C	water at 35°C / water at 95°C
soy sauce stain	blood stain	soy sauce stain	soy sauce stain

14 The diagram shows the same type of soap powder packaged by four different supermarket chains. Which pack is the best value for money?

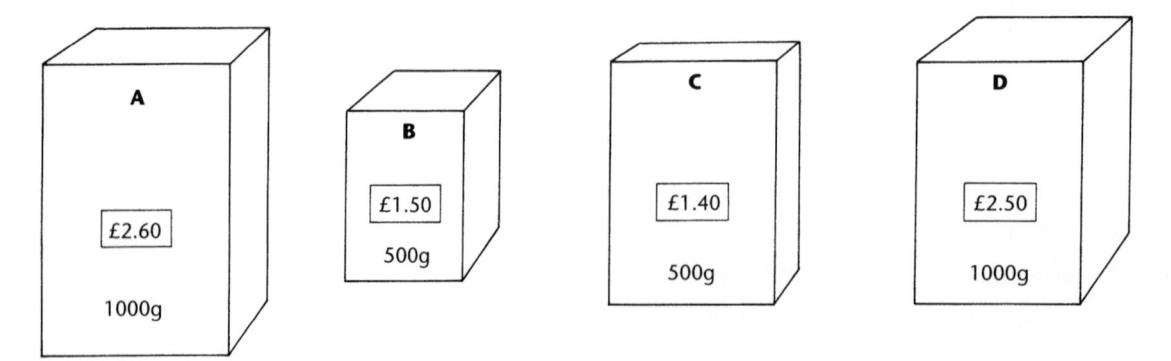

A £2.60 1000g
B £1.50 500g
C £1.40 500g
D £2.50 1000g

Chapter 7 Detergent Industries

Multiple Choice Test 1 continued

Questions 15, 16, 17 and 18 refer to the accompanying graph. It shows the results from an experiment where the action of two detergents on mud stains was compared at different temperatures.

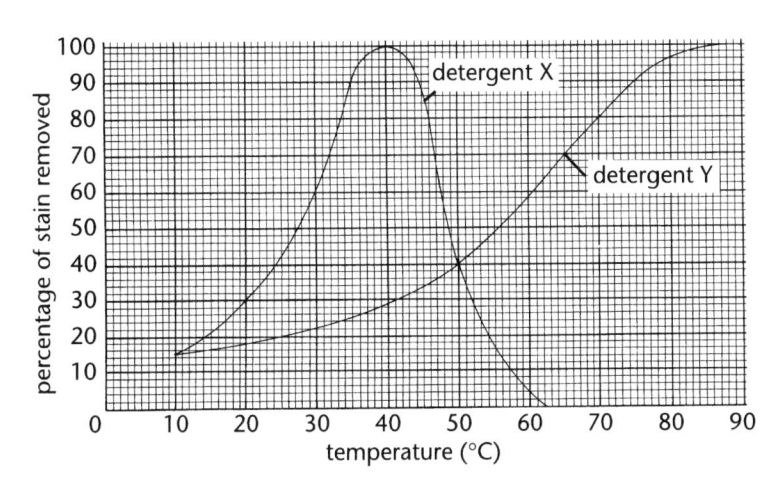

15 Which line in the following table draws a correct conclusion from the graph?

	\multicolumn{2}{c|}{detergent X}	\multicolumn{2}{c|}{detergent Y}
	type	best temperature (°C)	type	best temperature (°C)
A	biological	90	non-biological	40
B	non-biological	40	biological	90
C	biological	40	non-biological	90
D	non-biological	90	biological	40

16 At which two temperatures (°C) was the action of detergent X equal to that of Y?
   A 10 and 40.   B 10 and 50.   C 40 and 50.   D 40 and 90.

17 At what temperature (°C) did detergent Y remove 80 per cent of the stain?
   A 70.   B 80.   C 90.   D 97.

18 By how many times was the percentage of stain removed by detergent X at 35°C greater than that removed by X at 20°C?
   A 3.   B 4.   C 20.   D 35.

Unit 2 Biotechnological Industries

Multiple Choice Test 1 continued

19 A backpacker touring Europe went into a launderette and found that it would cost 1.5 euros to wash his clothes at 40°C. He also found that it would cost 0.25 euros more for each 10°C rise in temperature of the washing machine. He chose a non-biological wash at 80°C. How much did it cost in euros?

A 2.0.   B 2.5.   C 3.0.   D 3.5.

Questions 20, 21, 22, 23, 24 and 25 refer to the following magazine article.

DETERMINED TO DETER DETERGENTS!

Detergents for cleaning dishes and laundering clothes in washing machines have been widely available for about the last fifty years. Over that time their use has increased year after year. Much of this detergent is not really needed and ends up passing down waste pipes. If this soapy water reaches a river, it uses up the oxygen in the river water and it gets whipped up into large masses of foam. When fish and other river animals breathe in this soapy water lacking oxygen, they often die.

If waste water rich in detergent ends up at a sewage works, it may also get whipped up into a froth. The soapy foam kills off many of the useful micro-organisms that treat the sewage and make it harmless. This means that the liquid waste leaving the sewage works has not been treated properly and it will pollute the river.

Detergents are rich in chemicals that act as fertiliser. This encourages river plants such as slimy green algae to grow. Once a mat of algae has formed at the river's surface, it cuts out light and the river plants below the surface die.

Many of these harmful effects to wildlife could be greatly reduced by people using less detergent when washing dishes and clothes. So be determined to deter excessive use of detergent!

Chapter 7 Detergent Industries

Multiple Choice Test 1 continued

20 Approximately when during the last century did detergents become popular in British households?
- A 1930s.
- B 1950s.
- C 1970s.
- D 1990s.

21 Large quantities of detergent may arrive at a sewage works if people are using
- A powder instead of liquid detergent in their homes.
- B a low temperature wash to do their laundry.
- C biological detergent instead of a non-biological brand.
- D too much detergent for washing dishes and clothes.

22 Which of the following living things benefits from detergent being poured into a river?
- A bacteria at a sewage works.
- B freshwater fish.
- C human beings.
- D green algae.

23 Which number in the picture indicates a mass of harmful foam whipped up in the river by wind and wave action?
- A 1.
- B 2.
- C 4.
- D 6.

24 Which number indicates a mass of harmful foam whipped up at a sewage works?
- A 1.
- B 2.
- C 3.
- D 6.

25 Which number indicates sewage which has definitely not been properly treated?
- A 3.   B 4.   C 5.   D 6.

Unit 2 Biotechnological Industries

Multiple Choice Test 2

Choose the ONE correct answer to each of the following questions.

1. Which of the following is always present in biological powder but never present in non-biological powder?
   A enzyme. B detergent. C disinfectant. D bleach.

Questions 2, 3 and 4 refer to the graph, showing the results from an experiment. This was set up to investigate the effect of the quality of food supply on the growth of a type of bacterium that makes a useful enzyme.

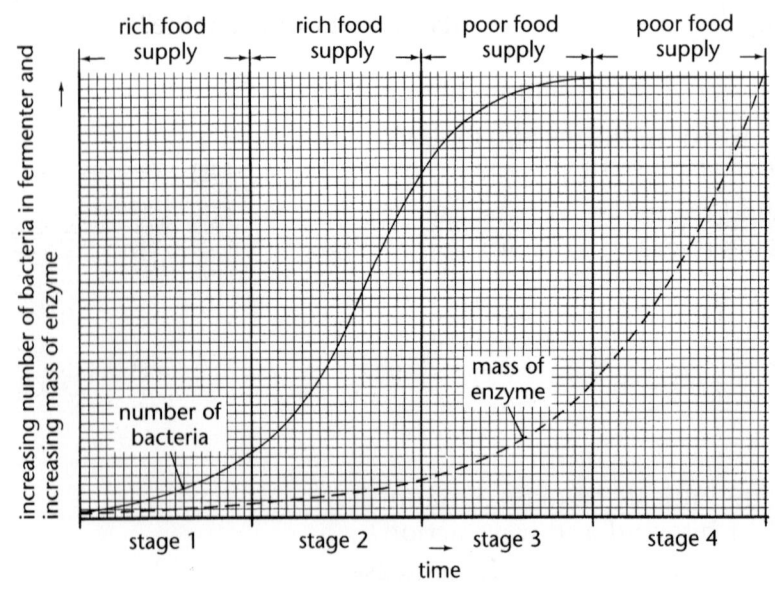

2. During which stage did the number of bacteria show the greatest increase in number?
   A 1. B 2. C 3. D 4.

3. During which stage was the greatest mass of enzyme produced?
   A 1. B 2. C 3. D 4.

4. Which combination of conditions leads to the highest production of enzyme?

	number of bacteria	state of food supply
A	low	poor
B	low	rich
C	high	poor
D	high	rich

Multiple Choice Test 2 continued

Questions 5, 6, 7, 8 and 9 refer to the following table which shows a company's annual production of four types of enzyme.

type of enzyme	substance digested by enzyme action	annual production (tonnes)
protease	protein	22.5
amylase	starch	18.0
pectinase	pectin in fruit	4.5
cellulase	cellulose in plants	13.5

5 Which bar chart in the diagram correctly represents the data in the table?

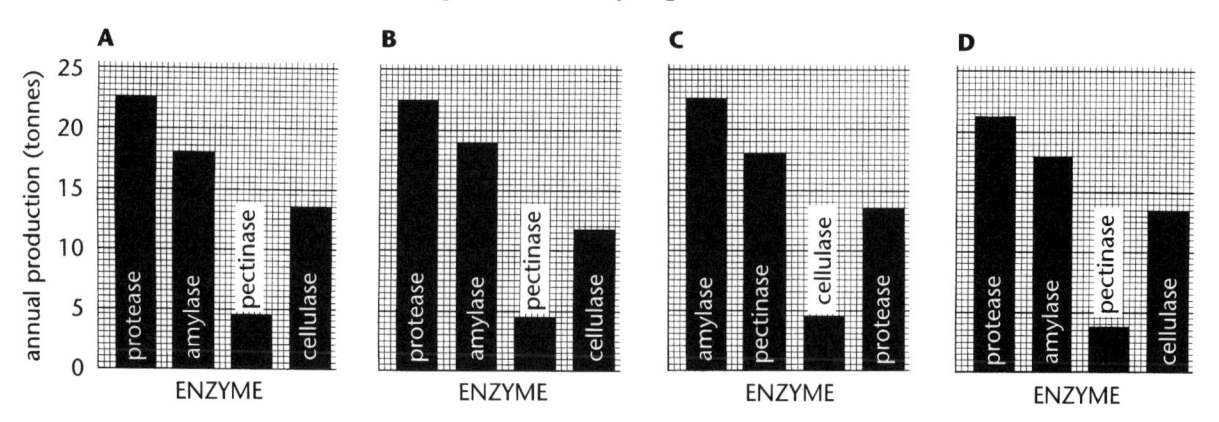

6 Which enzyme is used in dishwasher detergent to remove starchy food remains?

    A protease.   B amylase.   C pectinase.   D cellulase.

7 Which enzyme is used in detergent for removing blood stains rich in protein from butchers' aprons?

    A protease.   B amylase.   C pectinase.   D cellulase.

8 By how many times is the annual production of amylase greater than that of pectinase?

    A 3.0.   B 4.0.   C 13.5.   D 81.0.

9 What is the ratio of annual production of cellulase to that of pectinase?

    A 1:3.   B 1:4.   C 3:1.   D 4:1.

Unit 2 Biotechnological Industries

Multiple Choice Test 2 continued

Questions 10, 11 and 12 refer to the following information. Five test tubes like the one shown in the diagram were set up to test the effect of temperature on the action of an enzyme.

The enzyme causes the black chemical to be removed from the photographic film. The results are shown in the graph.

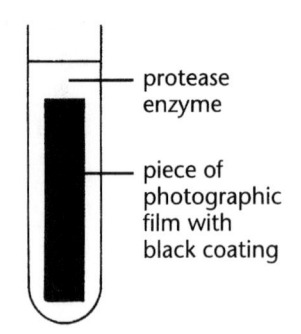

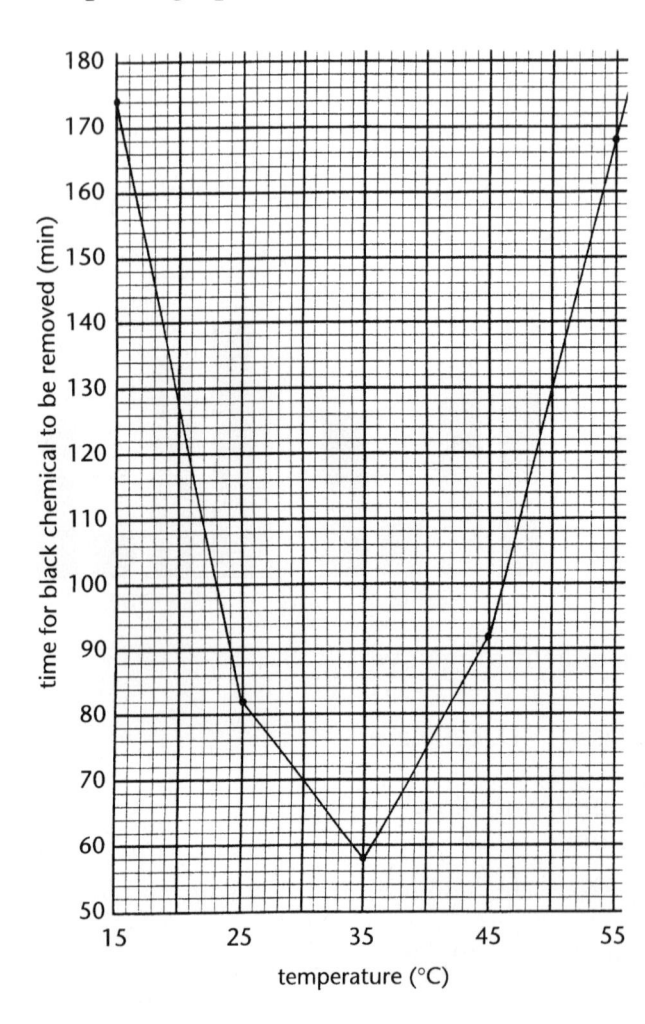

10 How much time (in minutes) was needed to remove the black chemical at 55°C?

A 164.   B 168.   C 169.   D 172.

11 From the graph, how long (in minutes) would it have taken to remove the black colour at 50°C?

A 105.   B 110.   C 120.   D 130.

Multiple Choice Test 2 continued

12 How much longer (in minutes) did it take to remove the black chemical at 25°C compared with 35°C?

   A   22.
   B   24.
   C   58.
   D   82.

Questions 13 and 14 refer to the accompanying chart.

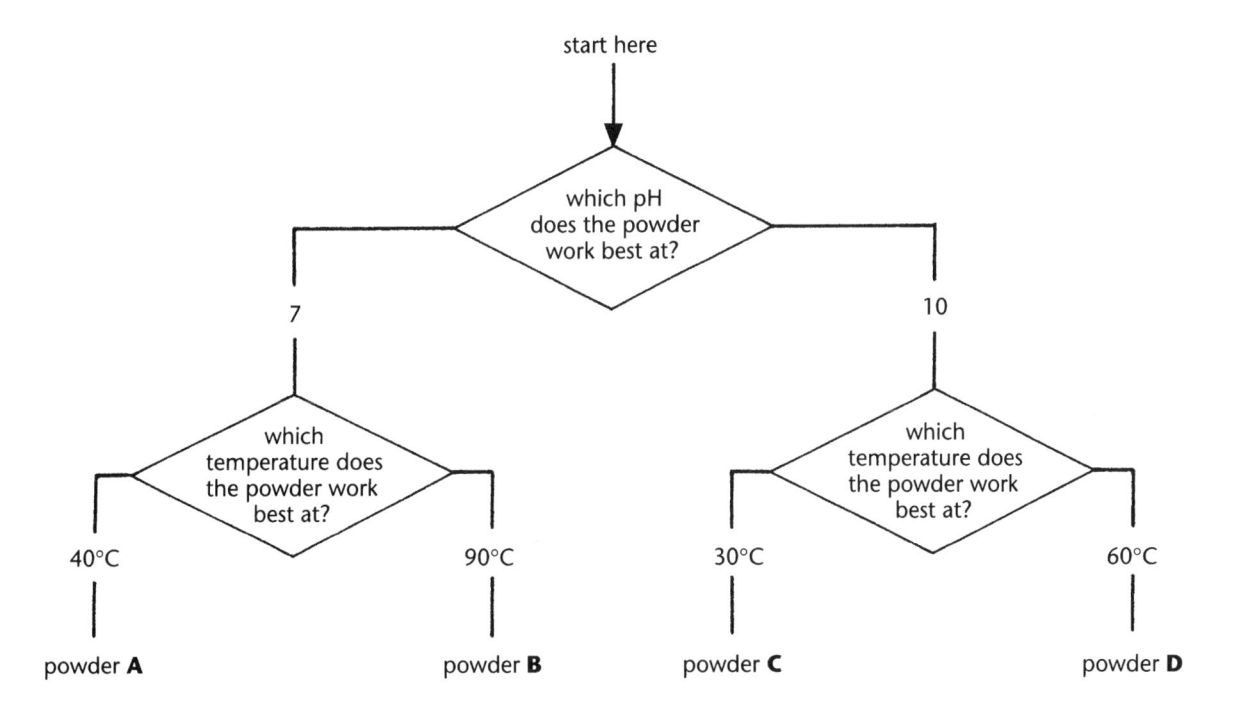

```
                    start here
                       │
                       ▼
                  which pH
                 does the powder
                 work best at?
            ┌─────────┴─────────┐
            7                   10
            │                   │
        which               which
    temperature does    temperature does
     the powder work     the powder work
       best at?            best at?
      ┌────┴────┐        ┌────┴────┐
    40°C      90°C     30°C      60°C
      │         │         │         │
   powder A  powder B  powder C  powder D
```

13 A certain brand of biological washing powder contains an enzyme that digests blood stains at 60°C and at pH 10. Identify its letter from the chart.

14 Which powder in the chart is the non-biological brand?

Unit 2 Biotechnological Industries

Multiple Choice Test 2 continued

Questions 15 and 16 refer to the six test tubes in the diagram set up to investigate the action of a non-biological and a biological detergent at 40°C and at 90°C.

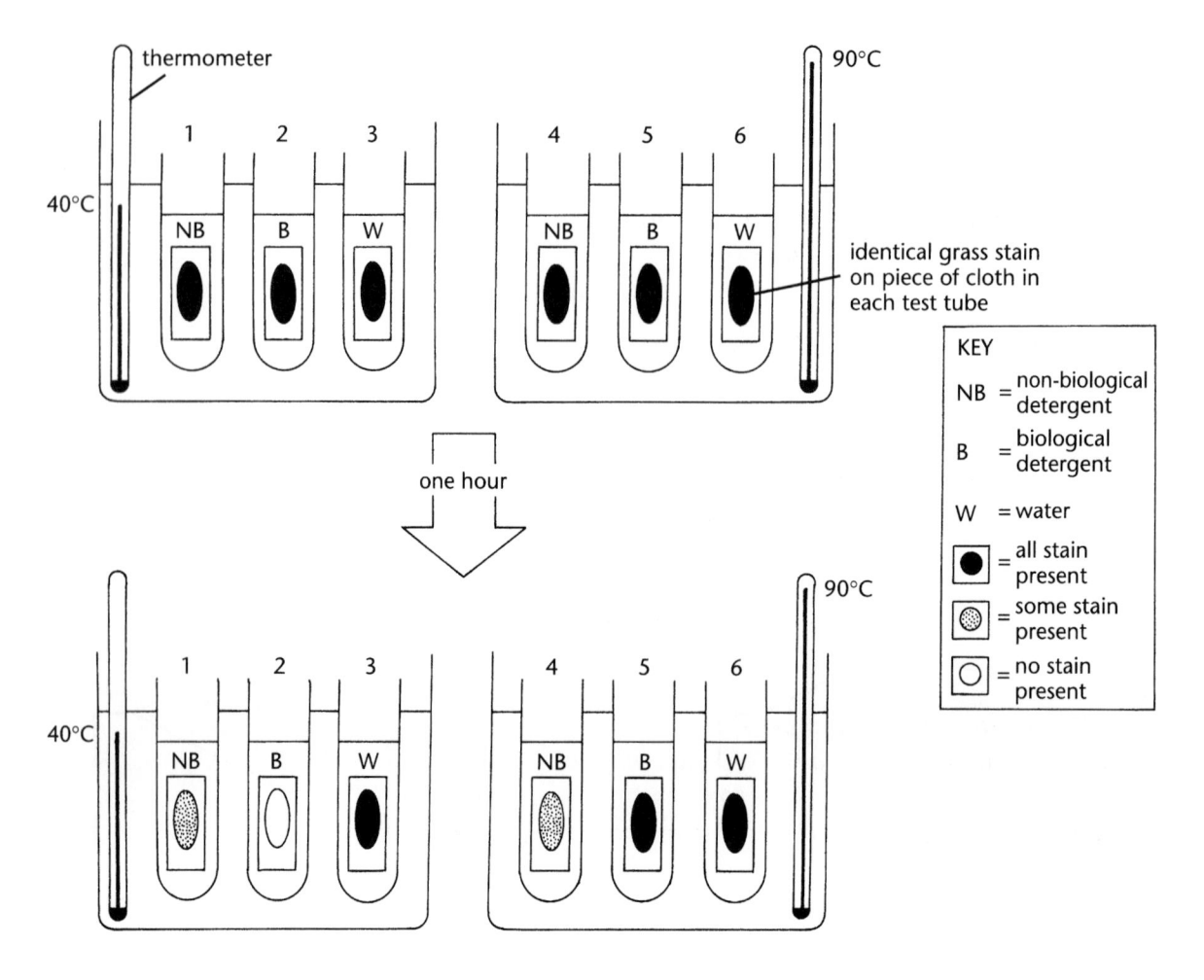

KEY

NB = non-biological detergent
B = biological detergent
W = water
● = all stain present
◉ = some stain present
○ = no stain present

15 Which line in the following table gives the combination of factors that removes the stain completely?

	type of detergent		temperature (°C)	
	non-biological	biological	40	90
A	✓		✓	
B		✓		✓
C		✓	✓	
D	✓			✓

Multiple Choice Test 2 continued

16 Why are test tubes 3 and 6 included in the experiment?
   A   to include suitable controls.
   B   to increase reliability.
   C   to make the results accurate.
   D   to make sure that the experiment is fair.

Questions 17 and 18 refer to the graph of the results from an experiment set up to test the effect of concentration on the action of a stain-removing enzyme.

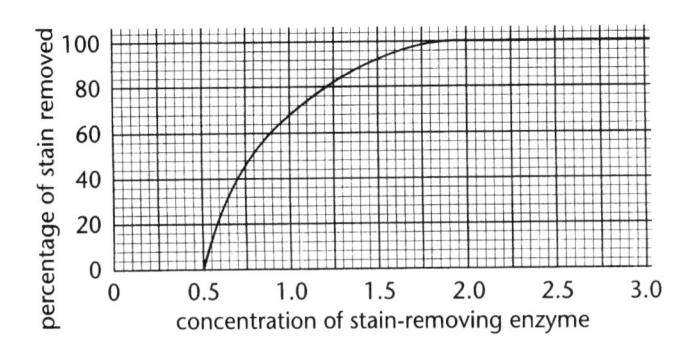

17 What percentage of stain was removed by an enzyme concentration of 1.0 per cent?
   A 62.   B 64.   C 68.   D 74.

18 What was the lowest concentration that removed all of the stain?
   A 0.5.   B 1.5.   C 2.0.   D 3.0.

19 Compared with a non-biological washing powder, use of a biological powder
   A   removes any chance of an allergic skin rash.
   B   uses more energy per load of washing.
   C   digests stains best at higher temperatures.
   D   causes less damage to delicate fabrics.

Unit 2 Biotechnological Industries

Multiple Choice Test 2 continued

Questions 20, 21 and 22 refer to the following table. It gives the results of a survey into a well known brand of biological detergent.

form of detergent	price of pack (£)	maximum number of washes	price per wash (£)
liquid	(see question 20)	20	0.15
powder	3.80	20	
sachets	2.50	10	
capsules	3.00	10	
tablets	2.20	10	

20 How much (in £) does the pack of liquid detergent referred to in the table cost?

A   3.00.

B   20.15.

C   30.00.

D   133.33.

21 Which form of detergent costs £0.22 per wash?

A   powder.

B   sachets.

C   capsules.

D   tablets.

22 Which form of detergent is the most expensive per wash?

A   powder.

B   sachets.

C   capsules.

D   tablets.

Chapter 7 Detergent Industries

Multiple Choice Test 2 continued

Questions 23 and 24 refer to the following information. Repeated sampling of the water from the river shown in the diagram was done at sample points 1–10. These were one kilometre apart. The results are summarised in the table that follows.

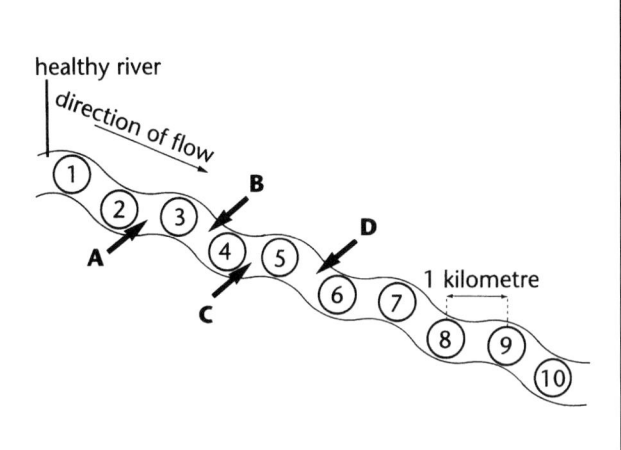

sample point	oxygen content of water (units)
1	90
2	90
3	90
4	5
5	25
6	40
7	65
8	80
9	90
10	90

23 At which lettered point was a large quantity of untreated detergent dumped into the river?

24 How many kilometres downstream from sample point 4 did the water travel before it was found to contain its original oxygen content?
  A 5.   B 6.   C 7.   D 9.

25 People can help to reduce the harmful impact of detergents on the environment by
  A changing from a biological to a non-biological brand.
  B adding extra fabric conditioner to every wash.
  C using powder instead of liquid detergent.
  D using the minimum during washing.

Unit 2
8 Pharmaceutical Industries

Matching Test 1

Match the words in list X with their descriptions in list Y.

List X

1) antibiotic
2) antifungal
3) athlete's foot
4) bacterium
5) fermenter
6) fungi
7) genetically engineered
8) purification
9) resistance
10) thrush

List Y

a) process by which the final product of fermentation is separated from micro-organisms and impurities
b) container in which fermentation is brought about by a micro-organism
c) words used to describe an organism that has had its genetic material altered to make it useful to mankind
d) simple plants, some of which can attack the human body and cause infections
e) type of fungal infection of the mouth and genitals
f) ability of a micro-organism to survive when it comes in contact with an antibiotic
g) word used to describe a chemical that prevents the growth of fungi
h) type of fungal infection of the skin
i) type of unicellular organism whose growth may be prevented by an antibiotic
j) chemical produced by one micro-organism (e.g. fungus) that prevents the growth of another micro-organism (e.g. bacterium)

Chapter 8 **Pharmaceutical Industries**

Multiple Choice Test 1

Choose the ONE correct answer to each of the following questions.

1. Antibiotics are made by
   A fungi and act on bacteria.
   B fungi and act on viruses.
   C bacteria and act on fungi.
   D bacteria and act on viruses.

2. Bacterial species Q is known to be resistant to penicillin (P) but sensitive to streptomycin (S). In an experiment, bacteria Q were spread evenly over a dish of nutrient agar and then a disc of P and a disc of S were added. Which of the diagrams shows the appearance of the dish after two days at a warm temperature?

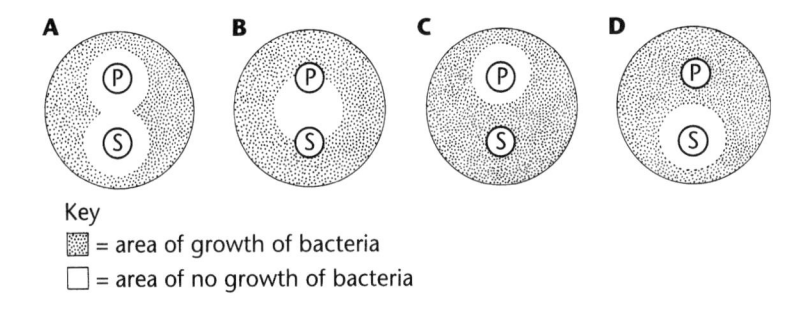

   Key
   ▓ = area of growth of bacteria
   □ = area of no growth of bacteria

3. A doctor has taken a throat swab from an infected patient and sent it to the local hospital. At the hospital a microbiologist follows the procedure shown in the diagram in order to find out which antibiotics(s) will work against the bacteria.

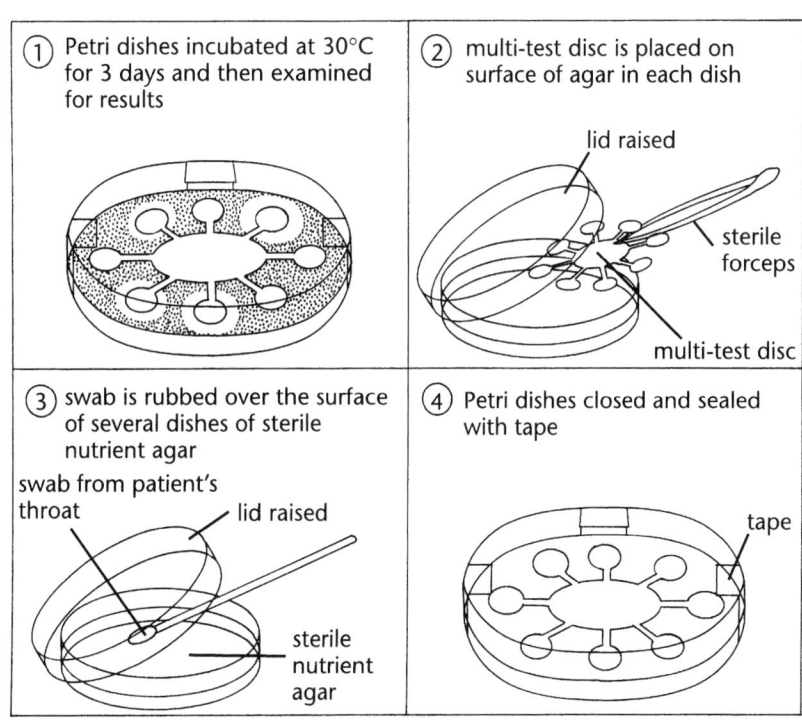

   ① Petri dishes incubated at 30°C for 3 days and then examined for results
   ② multi-test disc is placed on surface of agar in each dish
   ③ swab is rubbed over the surface of several dishes of sterile nutrient agar
   ④ Petri dishes closed and sealed with tape

   The correct order of the four steps is
   A 3, 2, 4, 1.
   B 3, 2, 1, 4.
   C 2, 3, 4, 1.
   D 2, 3, 1, 4.

Unit 2 Biotechnological Industries

Multiple Choice Test 1 continued

Questions 4, 5, 6 and 7 refer to the following table. It shows the results of testing four antibiotics on four bacterial species.

antibiotic	disease-causing bacterial species			
	1	2	3	4
J	+	−	−	+
K	+	+	−	−
L	+	+	−	+
M	−	−	+	−

Key
+ = antibiotic prevents growth of bacteria
− = antibiotic does not prevent growth of bacteria

4 Which antibiotic prevents the growth of only one species of disease-causing bacteria?
A J.
B K.
C L.
D M.

5 Which species of disease-causing bacterium is sensitive to three different antibiotics?
A 1.
B 2.
C 3.
D 4.

6 Which two species of disease-causing bacteria are each resistant to two different antibiotics?
A 1 and 3.
B 2 and 3.
C 2 and 4.
D 3 and 4.

7 Which antibiotic works over the widest range of bacterial species?
A J.   B K.   C L.   D M.

Multiple Choice Test 1 continued

Questions 8, 9, 10 and 11 refer to the information given in the following magazine article.

FUNGAL ATTACK!

At some point in their life, most people become infected by a fungus. This may be nappy rash, athlete's foot, sweat rash or ringworm, all of which attack the skin; or it could be thrush, a fungal disease of the mouth and genitals.

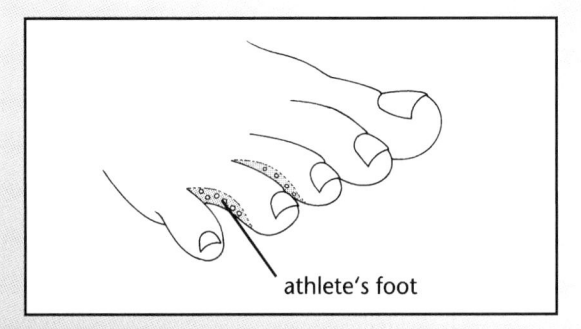

athlete's foot

One group of fungal infections are known as the tinea group. This includes athlete's foot (see diagram) and ringworm. These are easily spread by contact and give the sufferer an itchy, irritating rash. Ringworm is not a worm but its rash takes the form of itchy circular marks on the skin.

Another group of fungal infections are known as the candida group. This includes nappy rash, sweat rash and thrush. These are caused by types of yeast. When they infect the skin, it becomes itchy, swollen and sore.

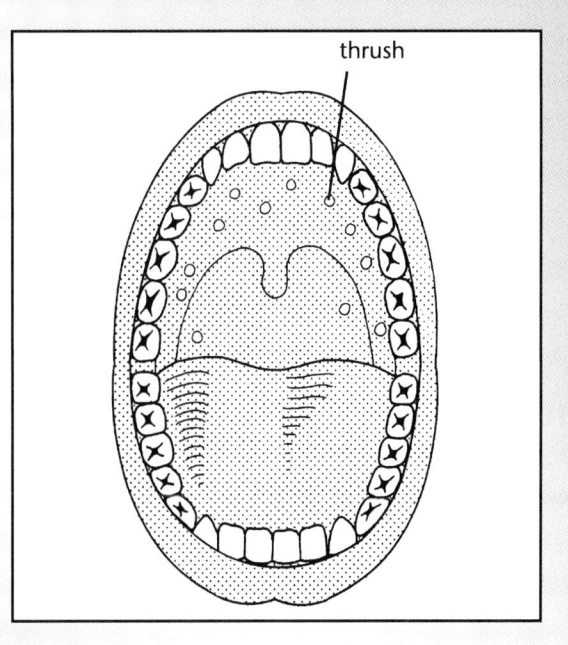

thrush

Fungal infections are normally successfully treated using antifungal chemicals such as clotrimazole.

8 Which of the following is not a fungal infection of the skin?
   A thrush.
   B ringworm.
   C nappy rash.
   D athlete's foot.

Unit 2 **Biotechnological Industries**

Multiple Choice Test 1 continued

9 The diagram summarises information given in the passage. The blank box should contain the entry

   A yeast.

   B ringworm.

   C sweat rash.

   D clotrimazole.

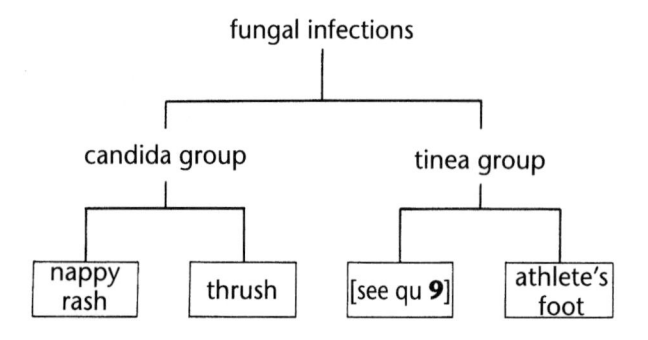

```
                    fungal infections
                   /                 \
           candida group          tinea group
           /        \              /        \
      nappy      thrush       [see qu 9]   athlete's
      rash                                   foot
```

10 Infections caused by the candida and tinea groups can be treated using chemicals called

   A antibiotics.

   B antifungals.

   C detergents.

   D disinfectants.

11 Which of the following is a symptom of athlete's foot?

   A A circular worm-shaped mark on the thigh.

   B A whitish spot on the lining of the mouth.

   C A persistent burning sensation in the armpit.

   D An itchy, irritating rash between the toes.

Chapter 8 **Pharmaceutical Industries**

Multiple Choice Test 1 continued

Questions 12 and 13 refer to the accompanying diagram. It shows an experiment set up to investigate the effect of concentration of SPOROCIDE (an antifungal powder) on red yeast cells.

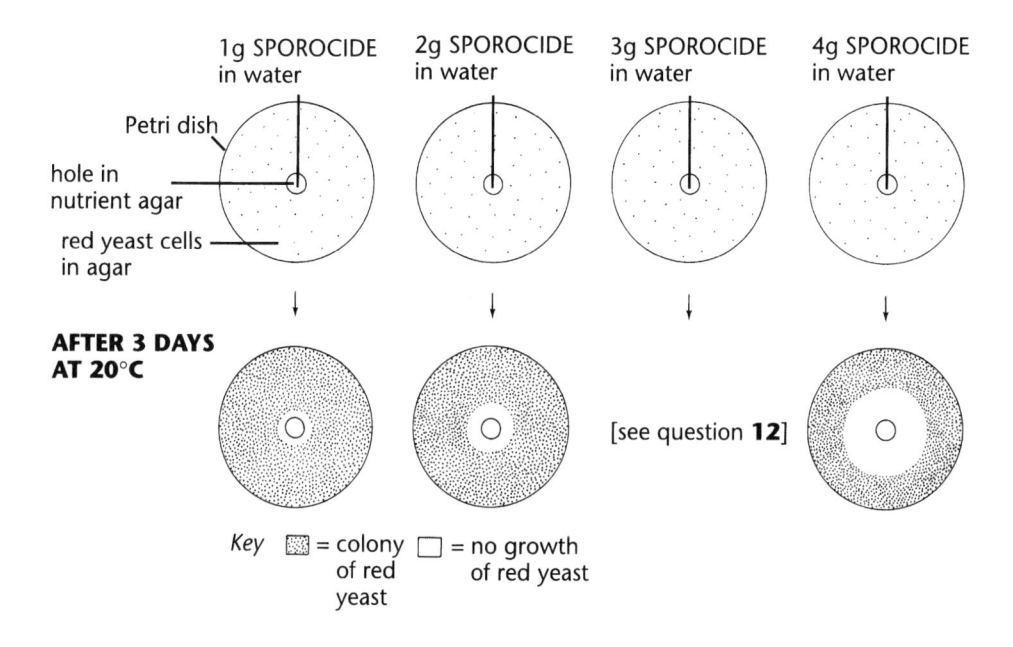

AT START

1g SPOROCIDE in water 2g SPOROCIDE in water 3g SPOROCIDE in water 4g SPOROCIDE in water

Petri dish
hole in nutrient agar
red yeast cells in agar

AFTER 3 DAYS AT 20°C

[see question 12]

Key: ▒ = colony of red yeast   ☐ = no growth of red yeast

12 Which of the Petri dishes in the accompanying diagram shows the missing result for 3 g of SPOROCIDE?

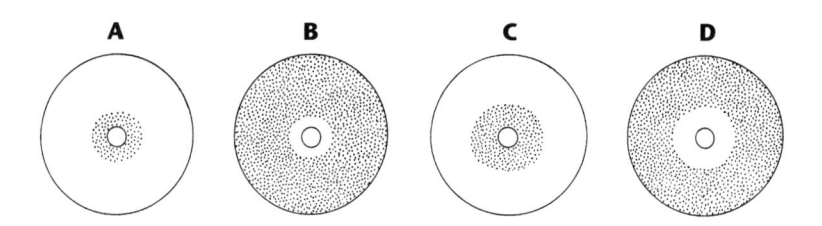

A   B   C   D

13 Which of the following was the factor that was varied from dish to dish in this experiment?
   A   concentration of antifungal powder.
   B   size of the red yeast colony.
   C   type of antifungal powder.
   D   type of red yeast cells.

135

Unit 2 Biotechnological Industries

Multiple Choice Test 1 continued

Questions 14, 15, 16 and 17 refer to the graph. It shows the results from an investigation into the effect of concentration of a new type of antifungal treatment on yeast cells.

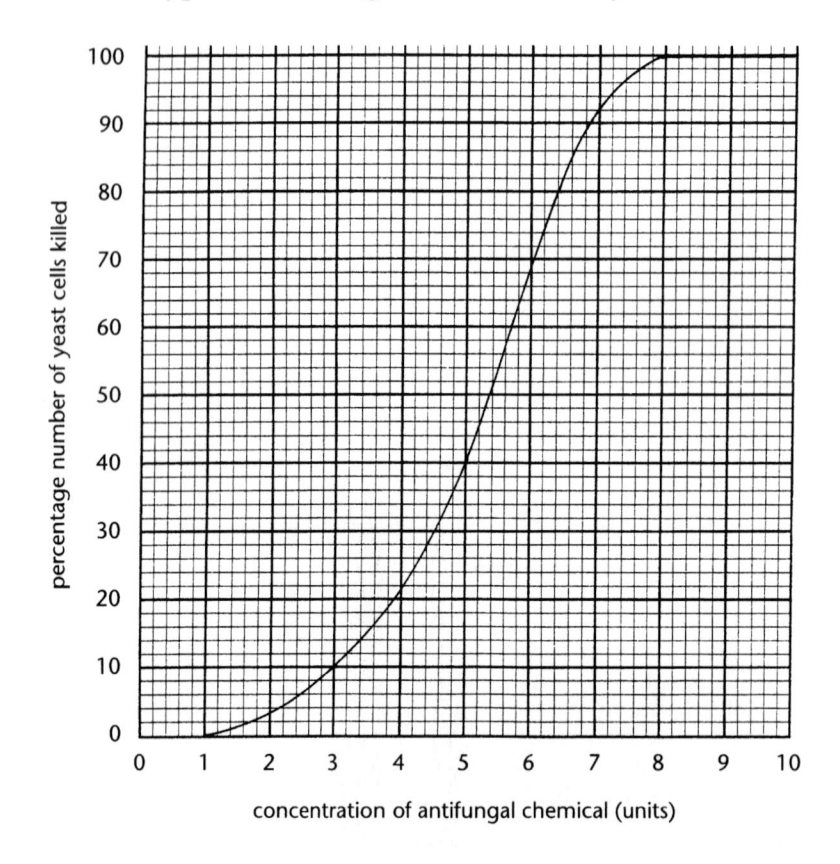

14 What percentage of yeast cells were killed by 7 units of the antifungal chemical?
   A 90.   B 91.   C 92.   D 94.

15 What percentage of yeast cells survived 5 units of antifungal chemical?
   A 5.   B 40.   C 50.   D 60.

16 What is the lowest concentration of antifungal chemical that will kill all the yeast cells?
   A 1.   B 8.   C 9.   D 10.

17 By how many times is a concentration of 5 units of antifungal chemical better at killing yeast cells than a concentration of 3 units?
   A 3.   B 4.   C 30.   D 40.

Chapter 8 **Pharmaceutical Industries**

Multiple Choice Test 1 continued

Questions 18, 19 and 20 refer to the diagram of three industrial fermenters. The numbers indicate the volumes of the fermenters in litres.

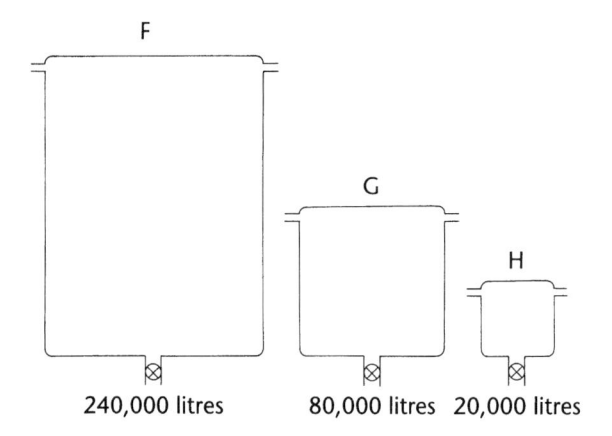

```
        F
                      G
                                 H
   240,000 litres  80,000 litres  20,000 litres
```

18 What is the ratio of the volume of fermenter F to that of G?

  A   2:1.
  B   3:1.
  C   4:1.
  D   5:1.

19 What is the ratio of the volume of fermenter G to that of H?

  A   2:1.
  B   3:1.
  C   4:1.
  D   5:1.

20 What is the ratio of the volume of fermenter F to that of G to that of H?

  A   8:3:1.
  B   8:4:1.
  C   12:3:1.
  D   12:4:1.

Unit 2 Biotechnological Industries

Multiple Choice Test 1 continued

21 The diagram shows a fermenter being used to grow a fungus that makes a useful antibiotic. The fungus only grows well in conditions of neutral pH.

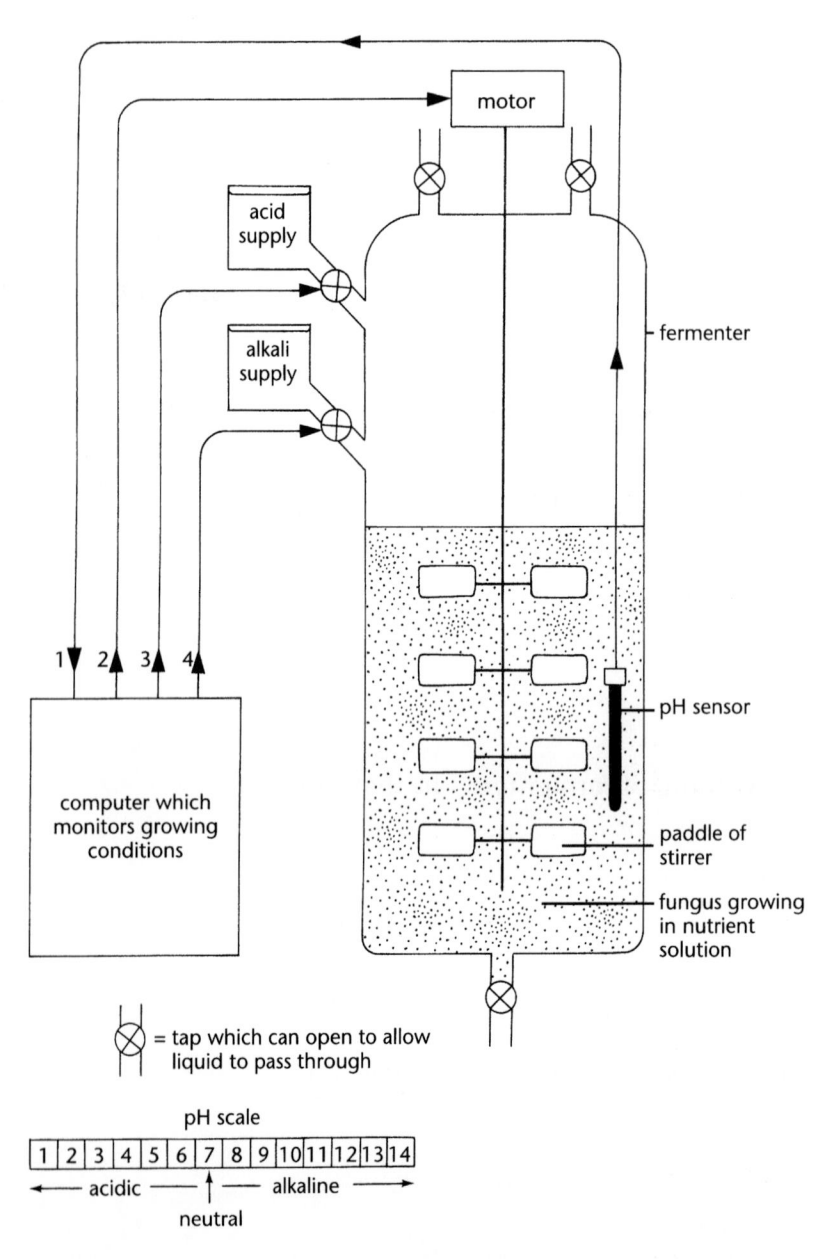

If the pH of the nutrient medium solution drops below 7, this problem is solved by information passing along route

A 1 and then 3. B 1 and then 4.
C 2 and then 3. D 2 and then 4.

Chapter 8 Pharmaceutical Industries

Multiple Choice Test 1 continued

22 The flow chart shows some of the steps carried out during the industrial production of an antibiotic. What should the missing step read?

A The fungus is altered by genetic engineering.

B The antibiotic is used to treat people who are ill.

C The fungus produces large quantities of the antibiotic.

D A second strain of the fungus containing the antibiotic is added.

> The fermenter is sterilised using heat treatment.
>
> ⇩
>
> One particular strain of fungus is grown in the fermenter.
>
> ⇩
>
> [see qu **22**]
>
> ⇩
>
> The antibiotic is purified and made ready for use.

23 The following table shows data which refer to Scottish cases of a type of chest infection caused by bacteria.

year	percentage of cases successfully treated by antibiotic erythromycin
1980	96
1982	90
1984	85
1986	74
1988	62
1990	48

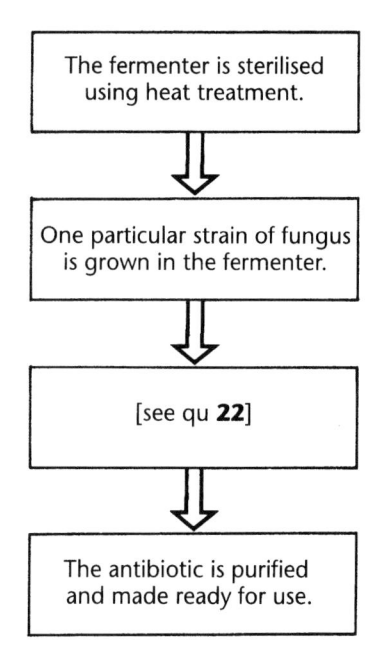

What is the most likely explanation for the trend shown in the table?

A People ate a poorer diet and were less healthy in 1990 than in 1980.

B Erythromycin used in 1980 was of a poorer quality than that used in 1990.

C More people were better able to resist the disease in 1990 than in 1980.

D Over-use of erythromycin has led to bacteria developing resistance to the antibiotic.

Unit 2 Biotechnological Industries

Multiple Choice Test 1 continued

Questions 24 and 25 refer to the following information. In an experiment it was found that an antibiotic slowed down the growth of a certain type of bacterium which was sensitive to the antibiotic. This type of bacterium was only able to double its number every two hours.

The antibiotic had no effect on a resistant strain of bacterium. It was able to increase its number every two hours by a factor of four times. The results are shown in the diagram.

time from start (h)	average number of bacterium types in a population sample
0	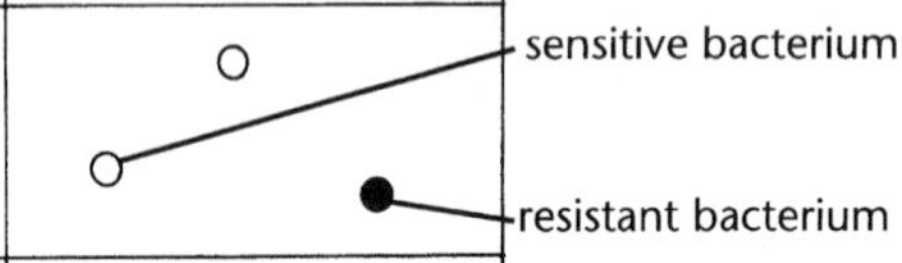 ○ — sensitive bacterium ● — resistant bacterium
2	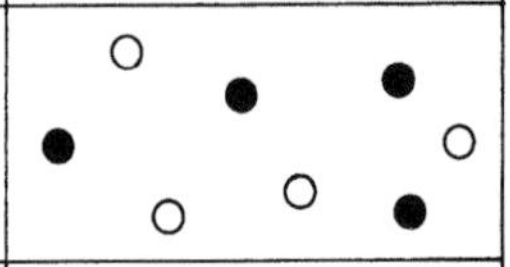 (mix of ○ and ●)
4	[see qu 25]

24 What is the ratio of sensitive to resistant bacteria at two hours from the start?

  A 1:1.   B 2:1.   C 4:1.   D 1:4.

25 Which of the diagrams should have been used to show the average number of bacteria in a population sample at four hours from the start?

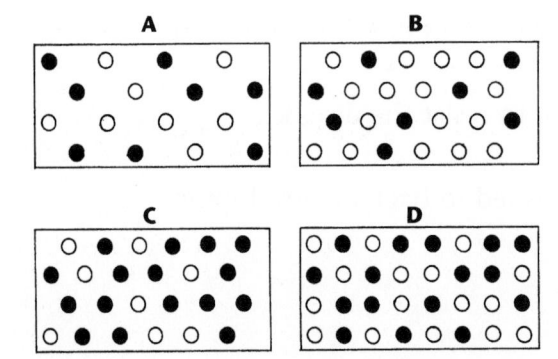

A

B

C

D

Chapter 8 Pharmaceutical Industries

Multiple Choice Test 2

Choose the ONE correct answer to each of the following questions.

1. In 1928, Scottish scientist, Alexander Fleming, set up several Petri dishes of the strain of bacterium that he was studying. Later when he examined the incubated dishes, he noticed that a fungus had got into one of them by mistake. The area around the fungal colony was clear of bacteria. This observation led to the discovery of penicillin. Which of the four accompanying diagrams represents Fleming's famous dish?

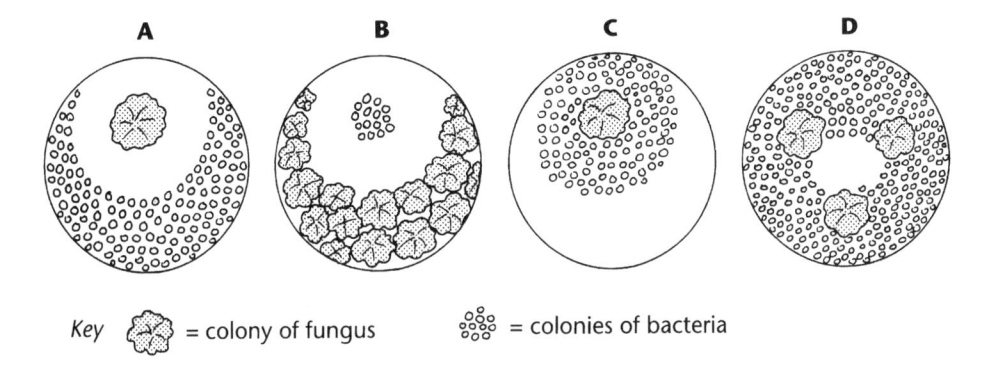

A   B   C   D

Key   = colony of fungus   = colonies of bacteria

2. A scientist wishes to set up an experiment to find out if two different species of bacteria (X and Y) are sensitive or resistant to the antibiotics penicillin (P) and streptomycin (S). Which of the set-ups shown in the diagram would be a fair test?

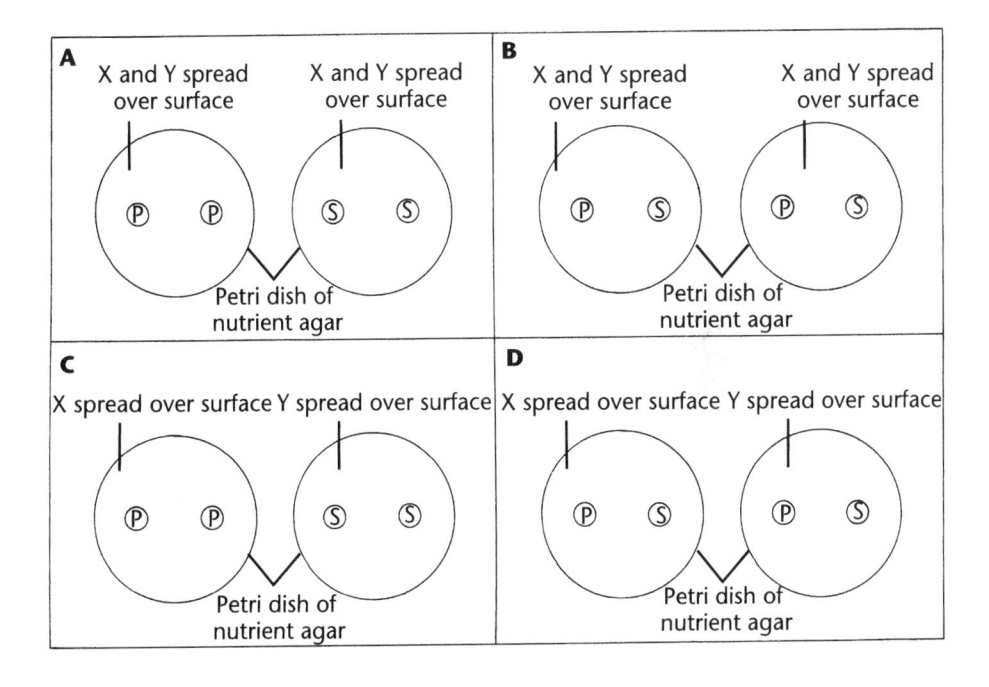

A
- X and Y spread over surface | X and Y spread over surface
- (P) (P) | (S) (S)
- Petri dish of nutrient agar

B
- X and Y spread over surface | X and Y spread over surface
- (P) (S) | (P) (S)
- Petri dish of nutrient agar

C
- X spread over surface | Y spread over surface
- (P) (P) | (S) (S)
- Petri dish of nutrient agar

D
- X spread over surface | Y spread over surface
- (P) (S) | (P) (S)
- Petri dish of nutrient agar

141

Unit 2 Biotechnological Industries

Multiple Choice Test 2 continued

Questions 3 and 4 refer to the flow chart. It shows the procedure carried out to select a suitable antibiotic to treat a patient's throat infection.

3 The step in the procedure that should have been given in box 3 in the chart is

   A Microbiologist rubs swab on to the surface of one Petri dish of sterile nutrient agar.

   B Microbiologist rubs swab on to surface of several Petri dishes of sterile nutrient agar.

   C Microbiologist rubs swab on to the surface of several Petri dishes of plain agar.

   D Microbiologist sterilises the swab in alcohol and then rubs it on to a Petri dish of sterile nutrient agar.

4 The step in the procedure that should have been given in box 5 in the chart is

   A Microbiologist adds a harmless strain of bacteria to each dish to give a control.

   B Microbiologist incubates the Petri dishes at different temperatures.

   C Microbiologist adds a second multidisc to some dishes to make the results more reliable.

   D Microbiologist incubates all the Petri dishes at 30°C for 3 days.

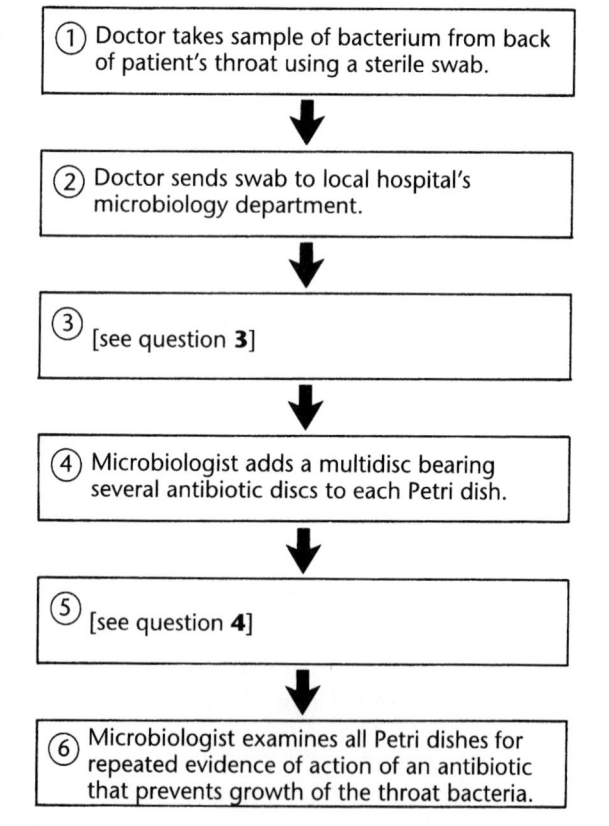

① Doctor takes sample of bacterium from back of patient's throat using a sterile swab.

② Doctor sends swab to local hospital's microbiology department.

③ [see question 3]

④ Microbiologist adds a multidisc bearing several antibiotic discs to each Petri dish.

⑤ [see question 4]

⑥ Microbiologist examines all Petri dishes for repeated evidence of action of an antibiotic that prevents growth of the throat bacteria.

Chapter 8 **Pharmaceutical Industries**

Multiple Choice Test 2 continued

Questions 5, 6, 7 and 8 refer to the following information. A multidisc bearing antibiotics 1 to 6 on its side arms was placed on a colony of bacterial species W growing on nutrient agar in a Petri dish. The procedure was repeated for bacterial species X, Y and Z and the four Petri dishes were incubated in warm conditions for two days. The accompanying diagram shows the results.

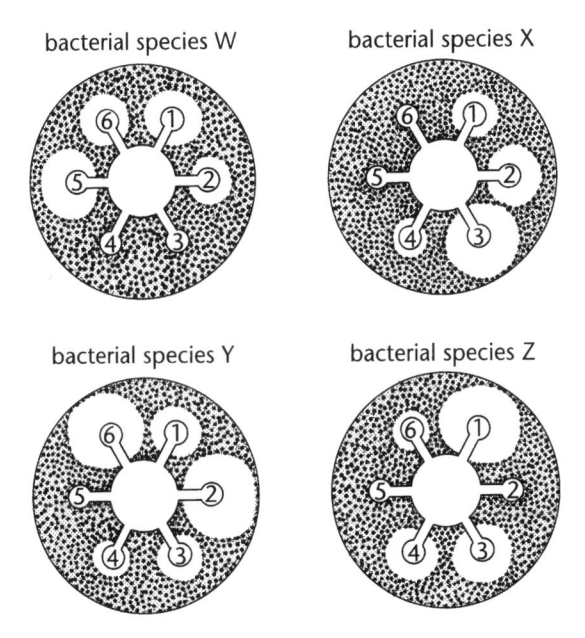

bacterial species W

bacterial species X

bacterial species Y

bacterial species Z

5   Which antibiotic worked best against bacterial species X?
    A 1.   B 2.   C 3.   D 4.

6   How many bacterial species were sensitive to antibiotic 1?
    A 1.   B 2.   C 3.   D 4.

7   How many bacterial species were resistant to antibiotic 2?
    A 0.   B 1.   C 2.   D 3.

8   Which bacterial species were sensitive to antibiotic 3?
    A   W only.   B   X, Y and Z only.
    C   W, Y and Z only.   D   W, X, Y and Z.

9   Antifungal chemicals are used to treat both
    A   athlete's foot and thrush.   B   thrush and bronchitis.
    C   bronchitis and AIDS.   D   AIDS and athlete's foot.

Unit 2 **Biotechnological Industries**

Multiple Choice Test 2 continued

Questions 10 and 11 refer to the accompanying diagram. It shows four steps that are followed when setting up an investigation to find out how effective an antifungal cream is at preventing growth of yeast.

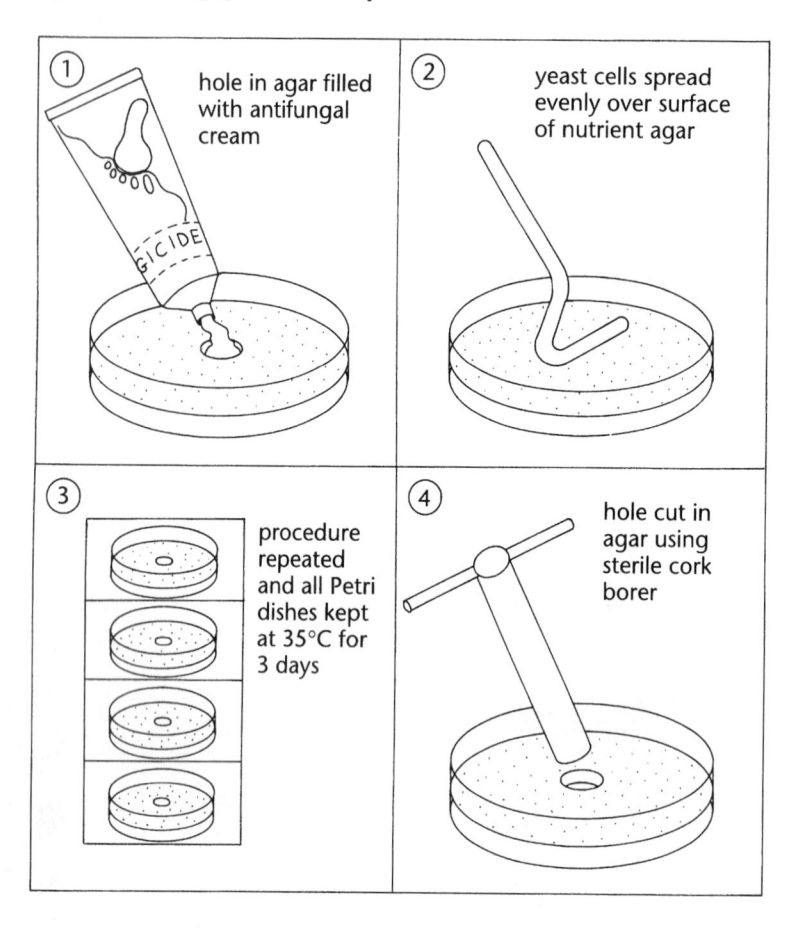

① hole in agar filled with antifungal cream

② yeast cells spread evenly over surface of nutrient agar

③ procedure repeated and all Petri dishes kept at 35°C for 3 days

④ hole cut in agar using sterile cork borer

10 What is the correct order of the four steps?
  A 2, 4, 1, 3.   B 2, 4, 3, 1.   C 4, 1, 2, 3.   D 4, 2, 3, 1.

11 Which Petri dish shown in the accompanying diagram shows the best control for this experiment?

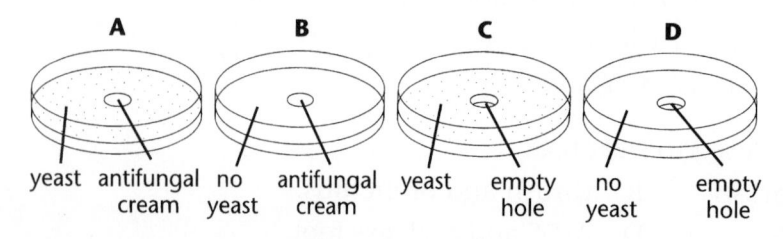

A yeast antifungal cream
B no yeast antifungal cream
C yeast empty hole
D no yeast empty hole

Chapter 8 Pharmaceutical Industries

Multiple Choice Test 2 continued

12 The accompanying diagram shows the results from an experiment to investigate how well antifungal creams X and Y work on two types of yeast cell.

What conclusion can be correctly drawn from these results?

A X works better against baker's yeast.
B X works better against brewer's yeast.
C Y works better against baker's yeast.
D X and Y work equally well against both yeasts.

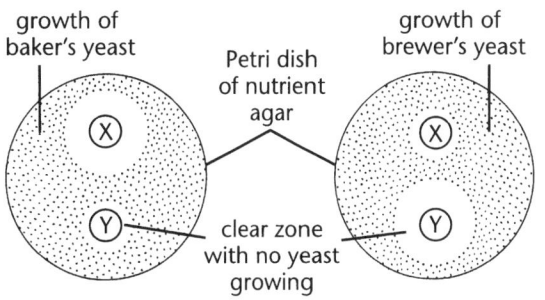

Questions 13, 14 and 15 refer to the accompanying bar chart. It shows the results from an experiment to test the effect of four antifungal treatments (P, Q, R and S) on two types of yeast (Y_1 and Y_2).

13 Which antifungal treatment worked equally well on both types of yeast cell?

A P.
B Q.
C R.
D S.

14 What percentage of Y_1 cells survived treatment S?

A 60.
B 80.
C 85.
D 90.

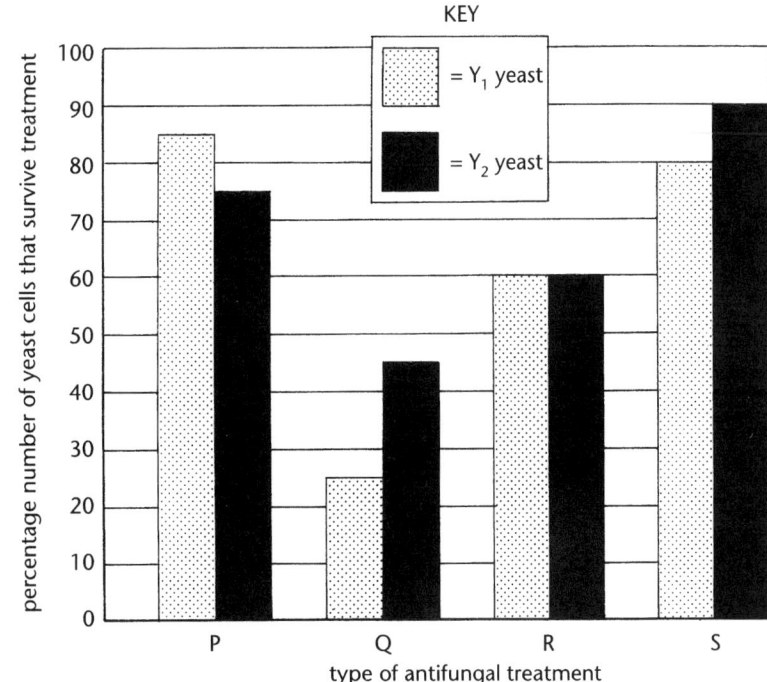

15 What percentage of Y_2 yeast cells were killed by antifungal treatment Q?

A 25.   B 45.   C 55.   D 75.

Unit 2 Biotechnological Industries

Multiple Choice Test 2 continued

16 Which of the accompanying diagrams shows a simple fermenter correctly set up and ready for use?

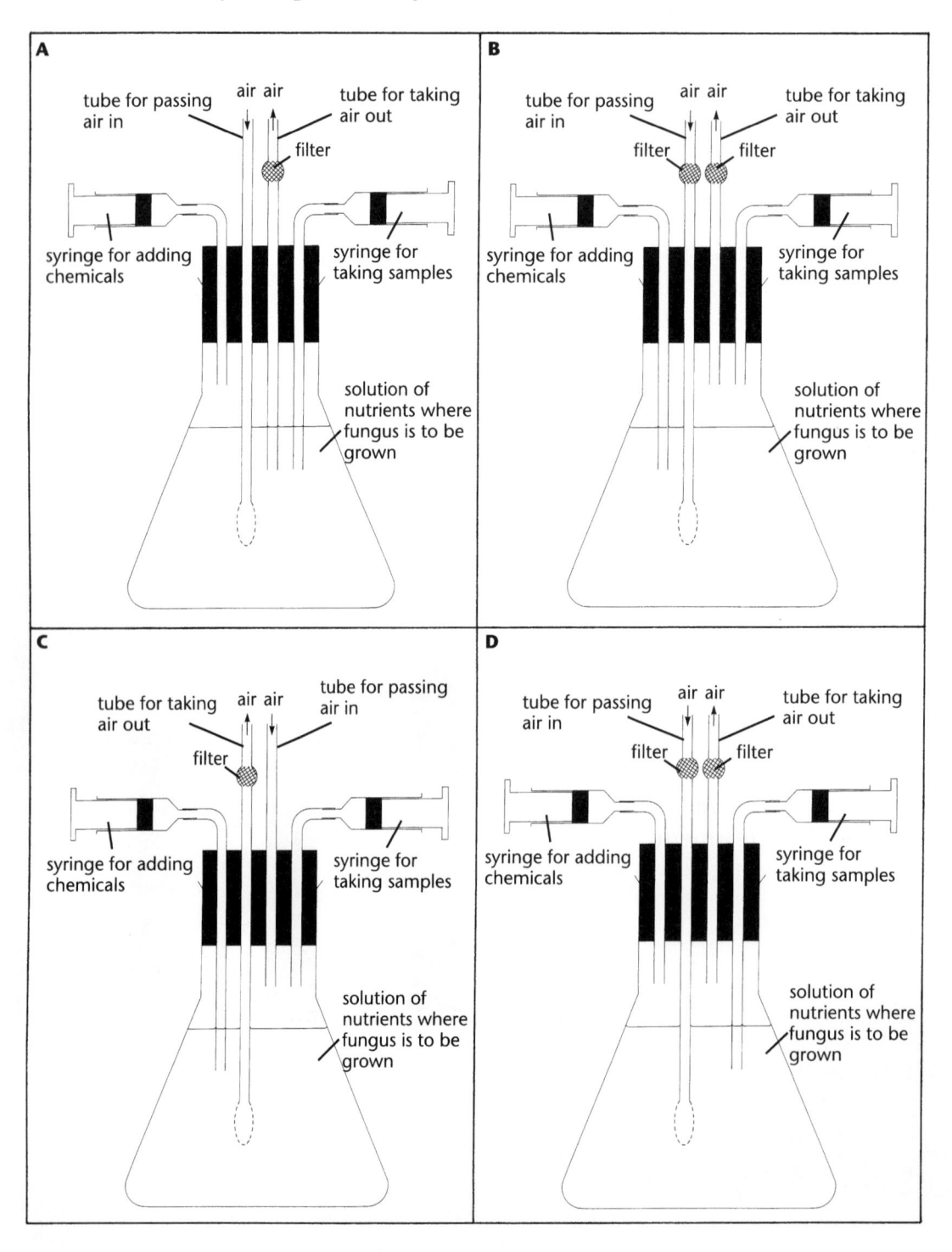

A
- tube for passing air in
- air air
- tube for taking air out
- filter
- syringe for adding chemicals
- syringe for taking samples
- solution of nutrients where fungus is to be grown

B
- tube for passing air in
- air air
- tube for taking air out
- filter filter
- syringe for adding chemicals
- syringe for taking samples
- solution of nutrients where fungus is to be grown

C
- tube for taking air out
- air air
- tube for passing air in
- filter
- syringe for adding chemicals
- syringe for taking samples
- solution of nutrients where fungus is to be grown

D
- tube for passing air in
- air air
- tube for taking air out
- filter filter
- syringe for adding chemicals
- syringe for taking samples
- solution of nutrients where fungus is to be grown

Chapter 8 Pharmaceutical Industries

Multiple Choice Test 2 continued

Questions 17 and 18 refer to the accompanying diagram. It shows a fermenter used to grow a fungus and make large quantities of an antibiotic.

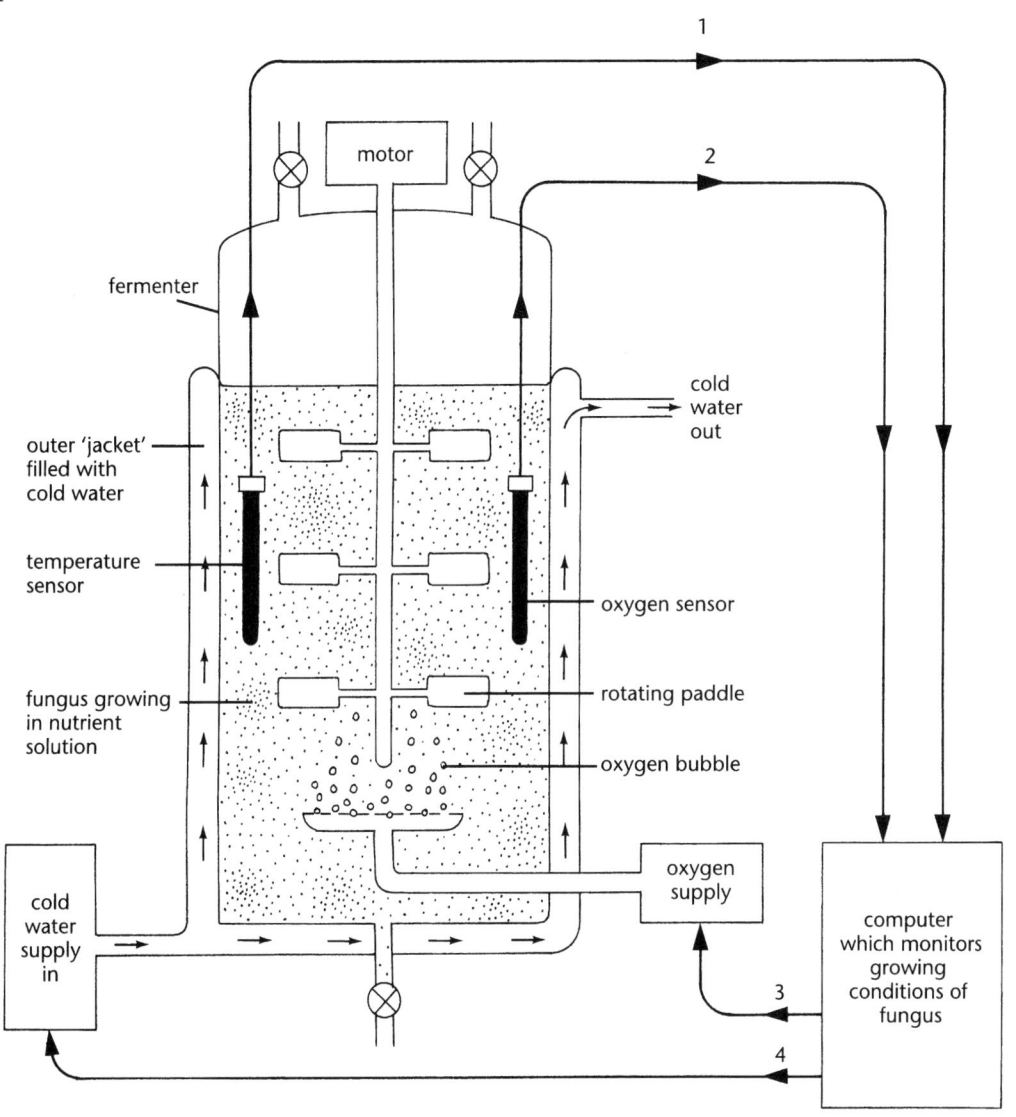

17 If the oxygen level in the fermenter drops, this problem is solved by information passing along route

    A 1 and then 3.   B 1 and then 4.   C 2 and then 3.   D 2 and then 4.

18 If the growing conditions become too warm, this problem is solved by information passing along route

    A 1 and then 3.   B 1 and then 4.   C 2 and then 3.   D 2 and then 4.

Unit 2 Biotechnological Industries

Multiple Choice Test 2 continued

Questions 19 and 20 refer to the accompanying graph. It shows the results of culturing a fungus to produce the antibiotic penicillin.

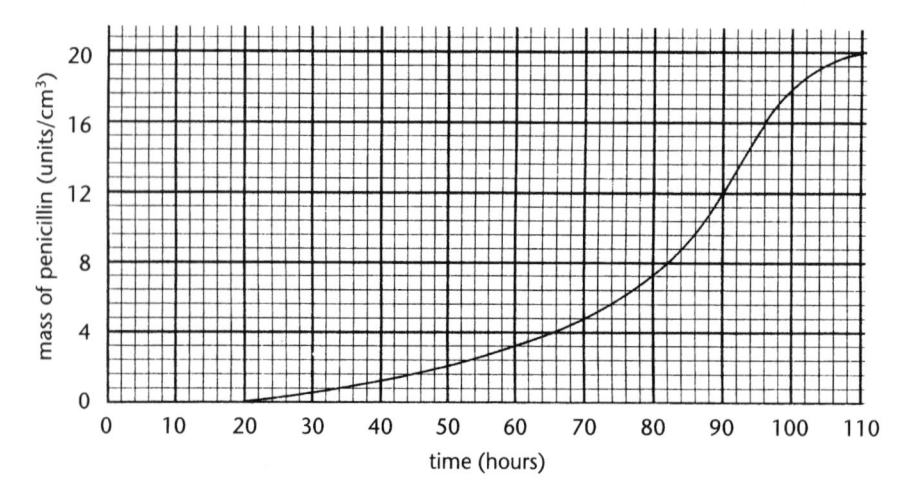

19 The mass of penicillin showed the greatest gain between hours
   A 20 and 40.   B 40 and 60.   C 60 and 80.   D 80 and 100.

20 The final mass of penicillin was 20 units/cm^3. What percentage of this final mass was present at 90 hours?
   A 8.   B 12.   C 60.   D 240.

21 In the diagram the person's sore throat is treated using antibiotic Q. The diagram also shows four close-ups of the throat after treatment. Which one is the most likely result?

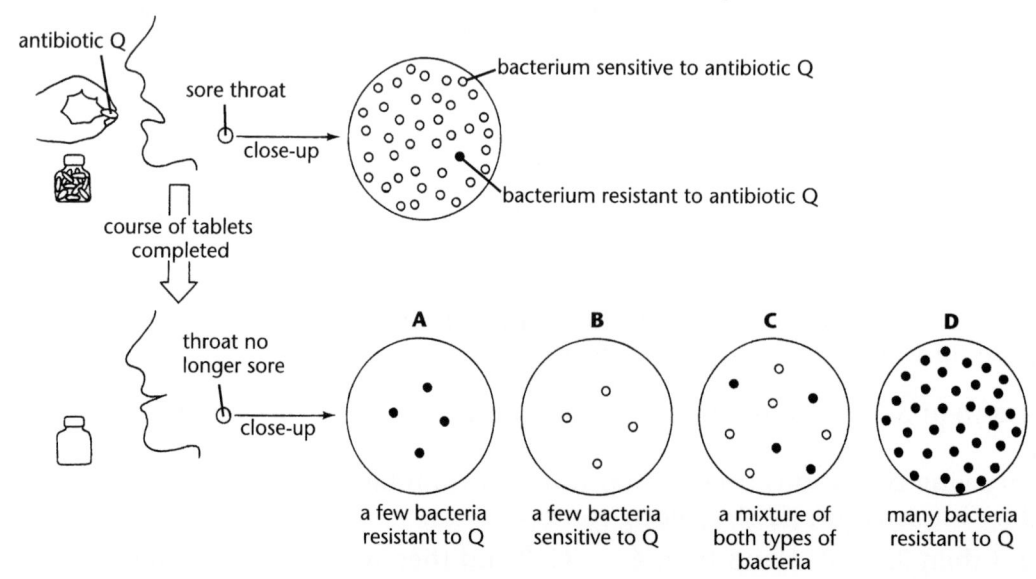

A a few bacteria resistant to Q
B a few bacteria sensitive to Q
C a mixture of both types of bacteria
D many bacteria resistant to Q

Chapter 8 Pharmaceutical Industries

Multiple Choice Test 2 continued

Questions 22 and 23 refer to the accompanying four graphs.

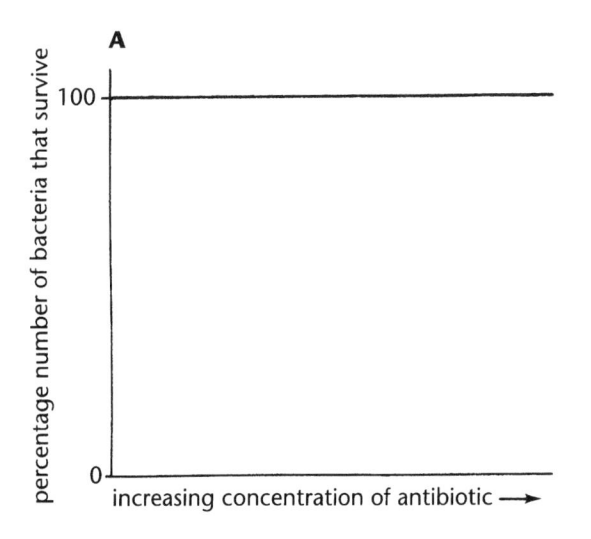

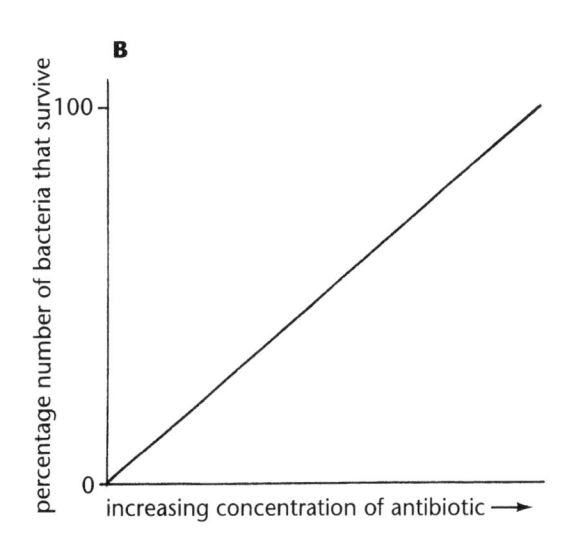

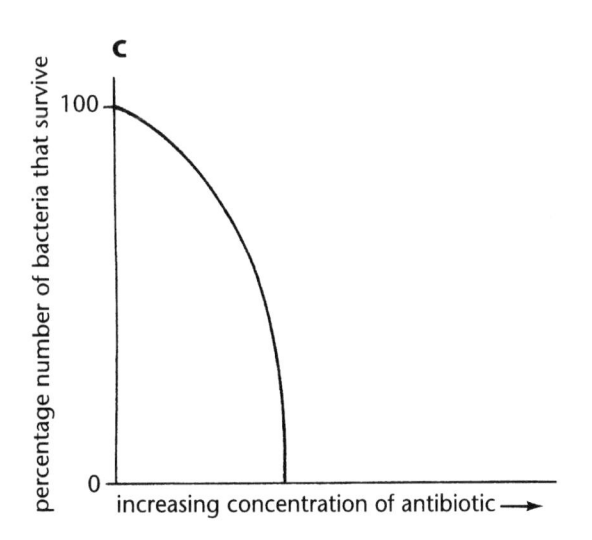

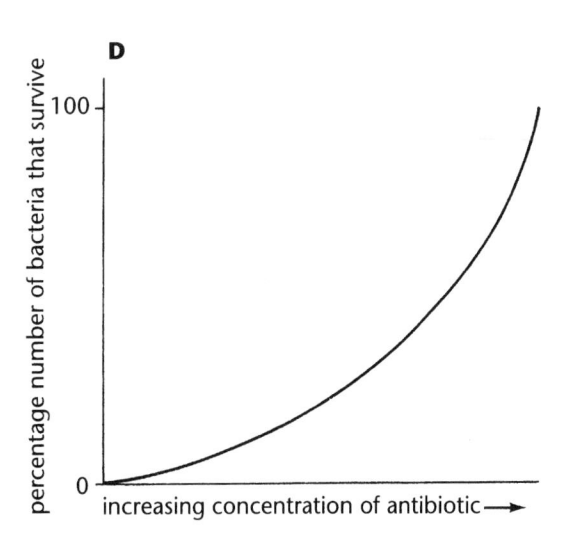

A
percentage number of bacteria that survive (y-axis, 0 to 100)
increasing concentration of antibiotic (x-axis)
horizontal line at 100

B
percentage number of bacteria that survive (y-axis, 0 to 100)
increasing concentration of antibiotic (x-axis)
linear line from 0 to 100

C
percentage number of bacteria that survive (y-axis, 0 to 100)
increasing concentration of antibiotic (x-axis)
curve starting at 100, decreasing to 0

D
percentage number of bacteria that survive (y-axis, 0 to 100)
increasing concentration of antibiotic (x-axis)
curve starting at 0, increasing to 100

22 Which graph shows the effect of increasing concentration of an antibiotic on bacteria that are sensitive to it?

23 Which graph shows the effect of increasing concentration of an antibiotic on bacteria that are resistant to it?

Unit 2 Biotechnological Industries

Multiple Choice Test 2 continued

Questions 24 and 25 refer to the following information. In an experiment it was found that the use of an antibiotic slowed down the growth rate of a certain type of bacterium that was sensitive to the antibiotic. This type of bacterium was only able to double its number once every two hours.

The antibiotic had no effect on a resistant strain of bacterium. It was able to increase its number every two hours by a factor of four times. The accompanying table shows the results.

time (h)	average number of bacteria in a population sample	
	sensitive strain	resistant strain
0	4	1
2	8	4
4	16	16
6	?	?
8	64	256
10	128	1024

24 The two entries missing from the table at 6 hours are

	sensitive strain	resistant strain
A	24	64
B	32	64
C	24	128
D	32	128

25 What overall trend is shown by the results in the table?
  A Both types of bacteria are increasing in number at the same rate.
  B Sensitive bacteria are increasing in number more quickly than the resistant strain.
  C Resistant bacteria are increasing in number more slowly that the sensitive strain.
  D Resistant bacteria are increasing in number more quickly than the sensitive strain.

Unit 3
Growing Plants

Unit 3

9 Growing Plants from Seeds

Matching Test 1

Match the words in list X with their descriptions in list Y.

List X	List Y
1) albustix	a) structure inside a seed that develops into an independent plant with green leaves
2) clinistix	b) tissue inside a seed containing starch or sugar to feed the embryo plant
3) embryo plant	c) tough protective layer surrounding a seed
4) food store	d) red-brown liquid used to test for starch; blue-black indicates a positive result
5) germination	e) strip of material used to test for glucose sugar; purple indicates a positive result
6) iodine solution	f) strip of material used to test for protein; green indicates a positive result
7) seed coat	g) development of the embryo plant into an independent plant with green leaves

Chapter 9 **Growing Plants from Seeds**

Matching Test 2

Match the words in list X with their descriptions in list Y.

List X

1) chitted
2) dormancy
3) pelleted
4) photosynthesis
5) pregerminated
6) propagator
7) silver sand

List Y

a) shallow box with heating element and cover used to give germinating seeds ideal growing conditions

b) word describing a seed that has had its hard seed coat broken open to allow water in and speed up germination

c) word describing a seed that has been made to start the process of germination before being planted

d) word describing a seed that has been coated with several layers of clay

e) grains of rock that are mixed with tiny seeds during sowing to space them out

f) state of inhibited growth that prevents some types of seeds from germinating during winter

g) process by which green plants convert light energy to chemical energy stored in food

Unit 3 Growing Plants

Multiple Choice Test 1

Choose the ONE correct answer to each of the following questions.

1. Which line in the following table refers correctly to the germinating pea seed shown in the diagram?

	1	2	3
A	food store	seed coat	embryo plant
B	embryo plant	food store	seed coat
C	embryo plant	seed coat	food store
D	seed coat	embryo plant	food store

Questions 2, 3 and 4 refer to the following table. It shows the results from an experiment set up to measure the water content of stored ('dry') peas seeds and fresh pea seeds.

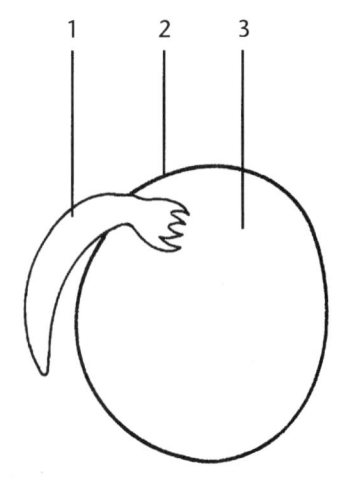

	stored ('dry') peas seeds	fresh pea seeds
mass of 100 seeds before drying (g)	30	40
mass of 100 dried seeds (g)	24	16
mass of water lost by 100 seeds (g)	[see question 2]	24
% water content	20	[see question 3]

2. What mass of water (in g) was lost by 100 stored ('dry') pea seeds?

    A 5.   B 6.   C 20.   D 54.

3. What was the percentage water content of fresh pea seeds?

    A 40.   B 60.   C 67.   D 80.

4. As many as 100 pea seeds were used each time to make sure that the results were

    A fair.   B correct.   C reliable.   D accurate.

Chapter 9 Growing Plants from Seeds

Multiple Choice Test 1 continued

5 Which line in the following table is correct?

	chemical reagent	food being tested for	colour that indicates a positive result
A	albustix	protein	green
B	clinistix	protein	purple
C	albustix	sugar	purple
D	clinistix	sugar	green

Questions 6, 7, 8 and 9 refer to the accompanying diagram. It shows an experiment set up to investigate the conditions needed by seeds to germinate.

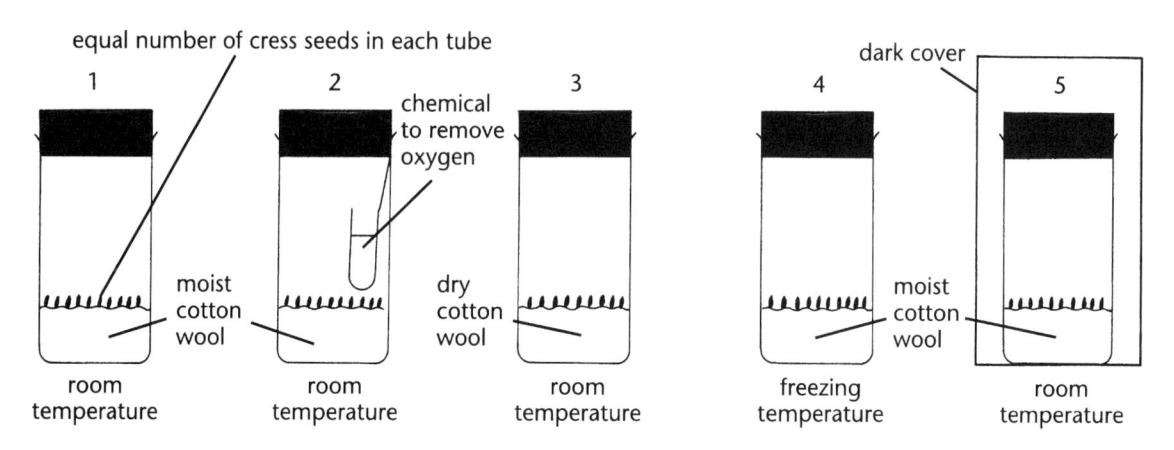

6 It is correct to say that cress seeds would germinate in
  A tube 1 only.   B tube 5 only.   C tubes 1 and 5.   D all of the tubes.

7 After a few days, which tube should be compared with tube 1 to find out if cress seeds need water to germinate?
  A 2.   B 3.   C 4.   D 5.

8 To find out if cress seeds need room temperature to germinate, a comparison should be made of the results for tubes
  A 1 and 4.   B 2 and 4.   C 3 and 4.   D 4 and 5.

9 A comparison of tubes 1 and 5 after four days would allow you to find out if one of the following factors is needed by cress seeds to germinate. Which one?
  A water.   B oxygen.   C warmth.   D light.

155

Unit 3 **Growing Plants**

Multiple Choice Test 1 continued

Questions 10 and 11 refer to the diagram. It shows an experiment set up to investigate the germination of mung bean seeds under different conditions.

10 To investigate the effect of depth of planting on germination, you should compare the results from pots
 A 1, 4 and 7.
 B 1, 5 and 9.
 C 2, 5 and 8.
 D 3, 6 and 9.

11 To investigate the effect of number of seeds on germination, you should compare the results from pots
 A 1, 2 and 3.
 B 1, 5 and 9.
 C 4, 5 and 6.
 D 7, 8 and 9.

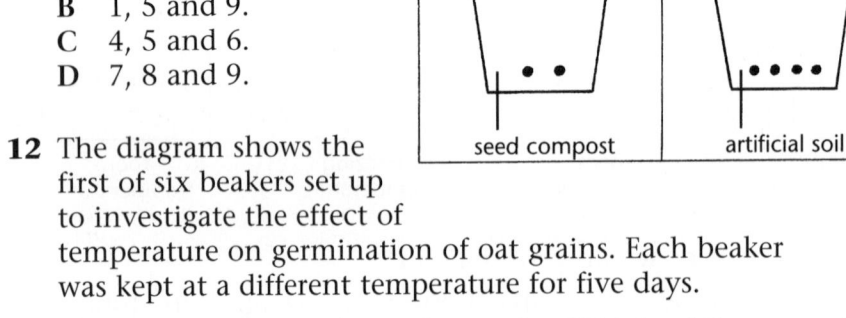

12 The diagram shows the first of six beakers set up to investigate the effect of temperature on germination of oat grains. Each beaker was kept at a different temperature for five days.

The following table shows the results. Which of the graphs in the second of the accompanying diagrams on the next page, correctly represents these results?

temperature (°C)	germination (%)
0	0
5	4
20	60
25	80
30	10
40	0

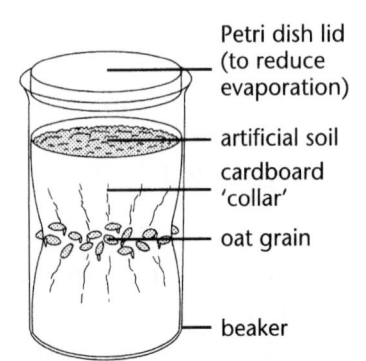

Multiple Choice Test 1 continued

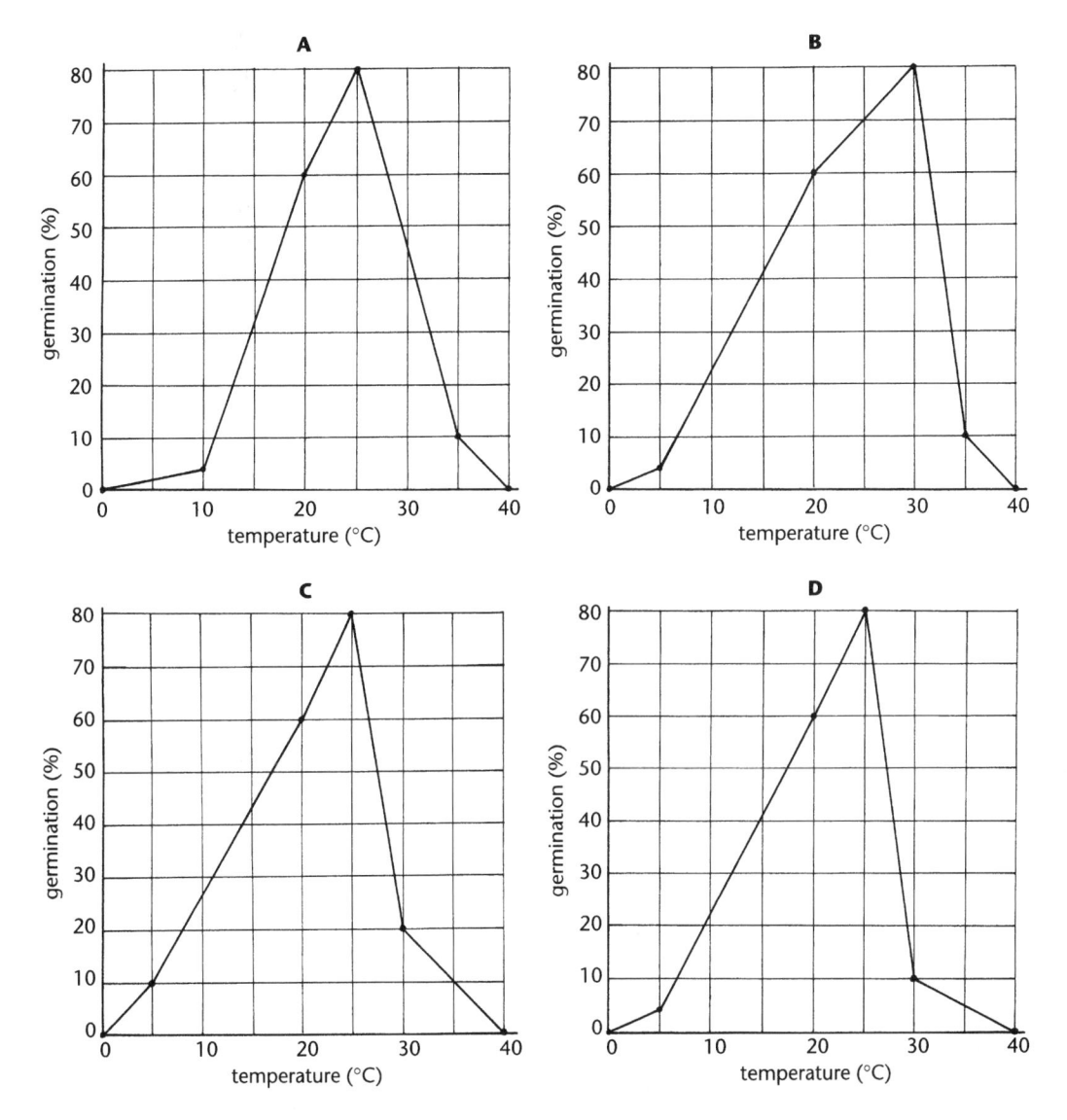

13 Why is a period of dormancy in seeds during the winter an advantage?

    A It enables the embryo plant to develop green leaves ready for germination.

    B It allows the seed time to build up a starchy food store from the parent plant.

    C It makes the seed coat become a tough barrier for protecting the embryo.

    D It delays germination until favourable growing conditions arrive in spring.

Unit 3 **Growing Plants**

Multiple Choice Test 1 continued

Questions 14 and 15 refer to the accompanying graph. It shows the results from an experiment set up to measure changes in dry mass of mung bean seedlings over a period of 35 days.

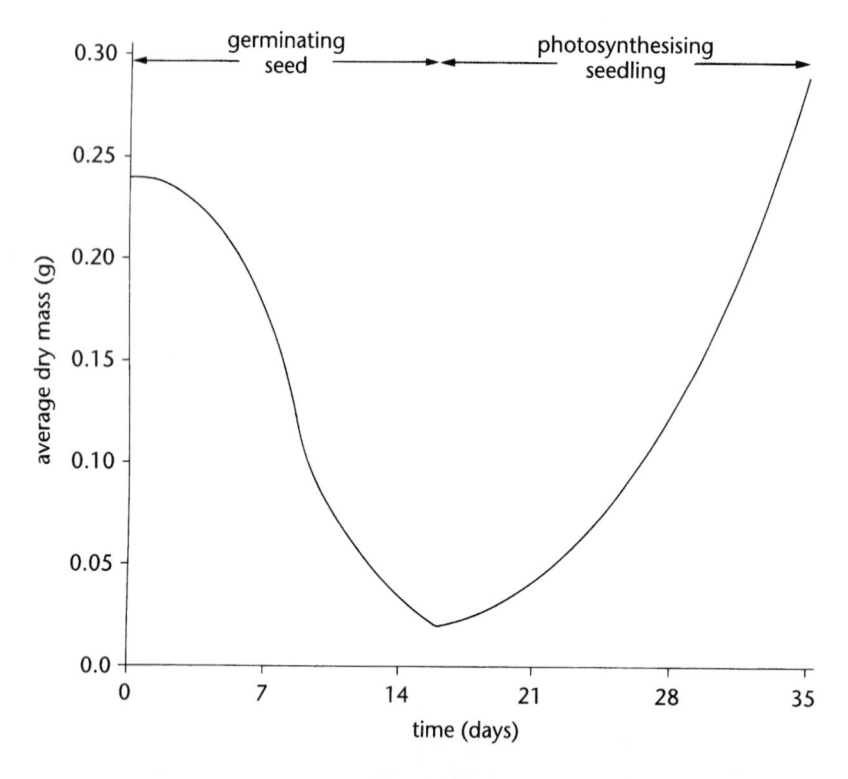

14 Which line in the following table represents a conclusion that can be correctly drawn from the graph?

| | average dry mass ||
	germinating seeds	photosynthesising seedlings
A	↑	↓
B	↓	↓
C	↑	↑
D	↓	↑

Key
↑ = increase   ↓ = decrease

15 On which day did a seedling's green leaves begin to photosynthesise and gain mass?

A 0.   B 16.   C 24.   D 35.

Chapter 9 **Growing Plants from Seeds**

Multiple Choice Test 1 continued

Questions 16 and 17 refer to the accompanying diagram. It shows some of the steps carried out to test a leaf for the presence of starch.

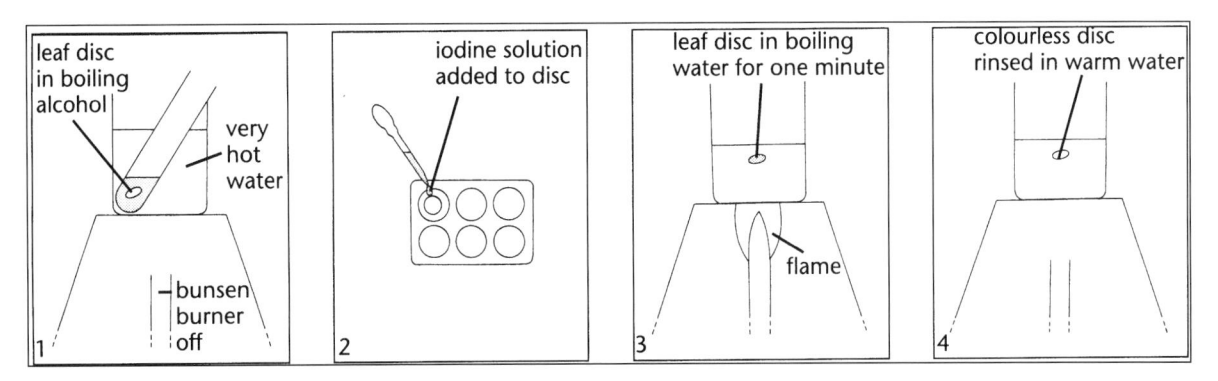

16 The correct sequence of the steps is
- A 3, 1, 4, 2.
- C 3, 1, 2, 4.
- B 4, 1, 3, 2.
- D 4, 3, 1, 2.

17 The reason for carrying out step 3 is to
- A kill the leaf cells.
- B soften the leaf discs.
- C remove the chlorophyll from the leaf cells.
- D extract oxygen bubbles from the leaf discs.

18 A leaf on a destarched ivy plant was treated as shown in the accompanying diagram.

Which part of the second diagram shows the appearance of the leaf after testing it for starch?

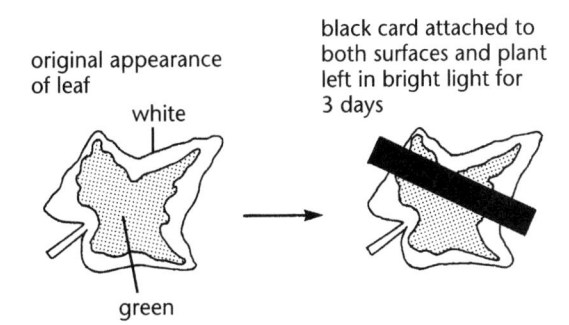

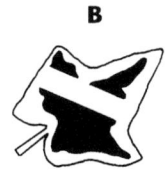

Key ■ = blue-black
□ = non blue-black

159

Unit 3 Growing Plants

Multiple Choice Test 1 continued

Questions 19, 20, 21 and 22 refer to the accompanying diagram on page 187. It shows a branched key of 8 types of garden plant classified according to the requirements of their seeds.

19 Which plant needs dark for its seeds to germinate and prefers well-drained soil for its seedlings to develop?

    A Coleus.   B Busy Lizzie.   C California Bluebell.   D Violet.

20 Which plant needs its seeds to be chilled before sowing and prefers well-drained soil for its seedlings to develop?

    A Monkshood.   B Blue Poppy.   C Geranium.   D Black-eyed Susan.

21 It is correct to say that before sowing Geranium seeds, they should be

    A chilled and chitted.   B chilled but not chitted.
    C chitted but not chilled.   D neither chitted nor chilled.

22 Three types of plant that do not prefer well-drained soil for their seedlings are

    A Coleus, California Bluebell and Monkshood.
    B Violet, Blue Poppy and Black-eyed Susan.
    C California Bluebell, Monkshood and Geranium.
    D Busy Lizzie, Violet and Blue Poppy.

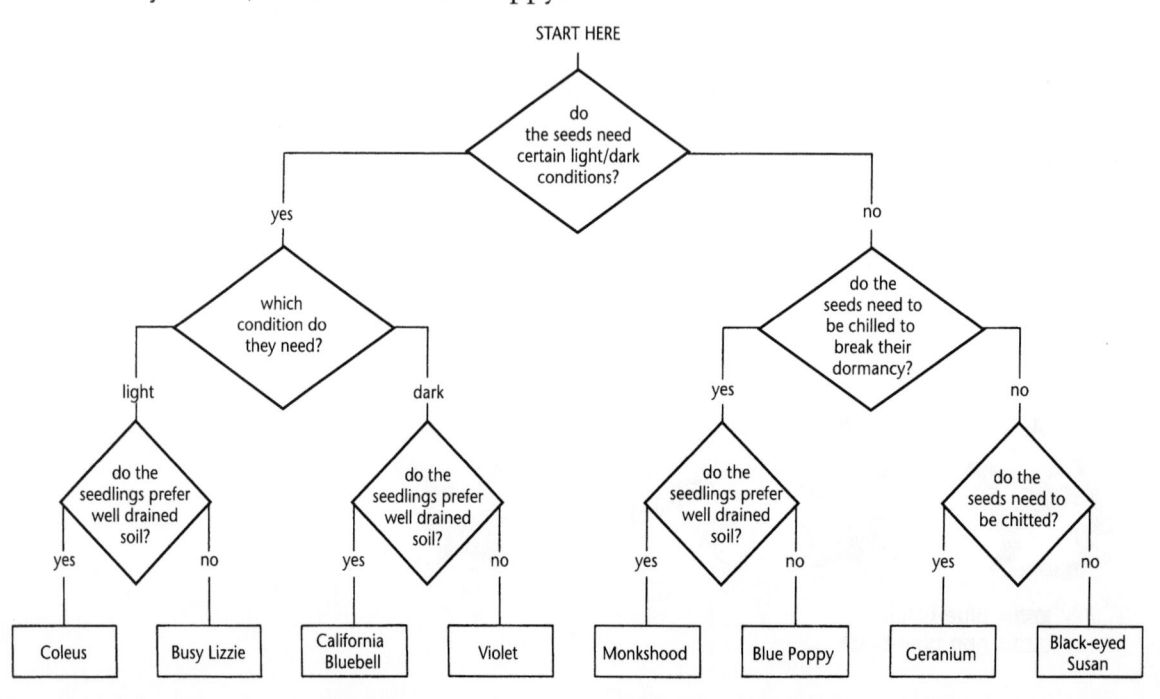

START HERE

do the seeds need certain light/dark conditions?

- yes → which condition do they need?
  - light → do the seedlings prefer well drained soil?
    - yes → Coleus
    - no → Busy Lizzie
  - dark → do the seedlings prefer well drained soil?
    - yes → California Bluebell
    - no → Violet
- no → do the seeds need to be chilled to break their dormancy?
  - yes → do the seedlings prefer well drained soil?
    - yes → Monkshood
    - no → Blue Poppy
  - no → do the seeds need to be chitted?
    - yes → Geranium
    - no → Black-eyed Susan

Multiple Choice Test 1 continued

Questions 23, 24 and 25 refer to the following possible answers.

    1   Sowing the seeds individually by hand.
    2   Applying a coating of clay to the seeds before sowing.
    3   Mixing the seeds with silver sand before sowing.
    4   Nicking the seed coats with a sharp knife.

23 Which procedure is used to speed up the entry of water through a tough seed coat before the seed is sown?
    A   1.
    B   2.
    C   3.
    D   4.

24 Which procedure produces pelleted seeds?
    A   1.
    B   2.
    C   3.
    D   4.

25 Which two procedures are both useful when dealing with tiny seeds that tend to stick together and need to be spaced out during sowing?
    A   1 and 2.
    B   1 and 3.
    C   2 and 3.
    D   3 and 4.

Unit 3 Growing Plants

Multiple Choice Test 2

Choose the ONE correct answer to each of the following questions.

Questions 1, 2 and 3 refer to the accompanying diagram of a Horse chestnut seed.

1. Which structure protects the seed from damage?
   A 1.   B 2.   C 3.   D 4.

2. Which structure would turn blue-black if iodine solution was added to it?
   A 1.   B 2.   C 3.   D 4.

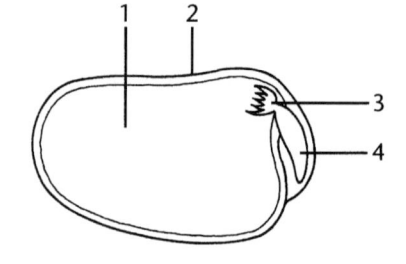

3. Which structures are both parts of the embryo plant?
   A 1 and 2.   B 1 and 4.   C 2 and 3.   D 3 and 4.

4. The first of the accompanying diagrams shows two broad bean seeds three days after germination. Part X was removed from seed 2 but not from seed 1.

   Which part of the second diagram shows the two seedlings after two further weeks of growth?

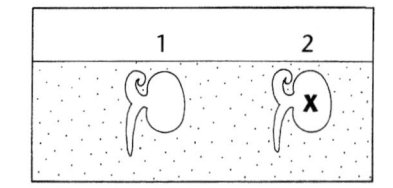

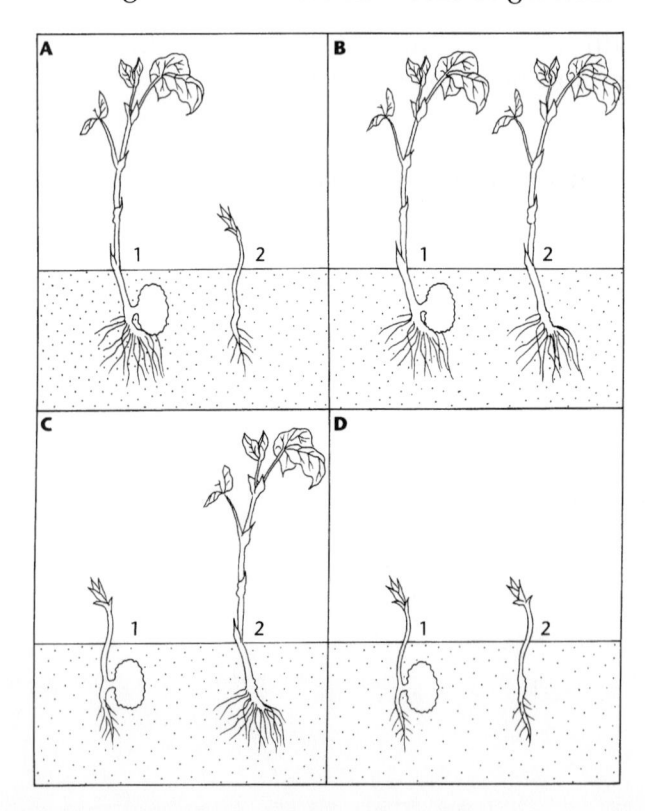

Chapter 9 **Growing Plants from Seeds**

Multiple Choice Test 2 continued

Questions 5, 6 and 7 refer to the following table. It shows the results from an experiment where food tests were carried out on seeds from eight different plants.

plant	chemical reagent used for food test		
	clinistix	albustix	iodine solution
barley	−	−	+
bean	−	+	+
cabbage	+	−	−
cauliflower	+	−	−
mustard	+	+	−
oat	−	−	+
pea	−	+	+
radish	+	+	−

5   Which seed contains sugar but not starch or protein?

   A   barley.

   B   bean.

   C   cabbage.

   D   mustard.

6   Which pair of plants have protein and starch in their seeds but not sugar?

   A   bean and pea.

   B   mustard and radish.

   C   barley and oat.

   D   cabbage and cauliflower.

7   Which of the following conditions is correct?

   A   Seeds of plants always contain starch in their food store.

   B   Protein always forms part of a seed's food store.

   C   If a seed contains sugar then it also contains starch.

   D   The type of food stored in a seed varies from plant to plant.

Unit 3 Growing Plants

Multiple Choice Test 2 continued

Questions 8 and 9 refer to the diagram of six test tubes which were set up and left at room temperature in an attempt to investigate the conditions needed by cress seeds to germinate.

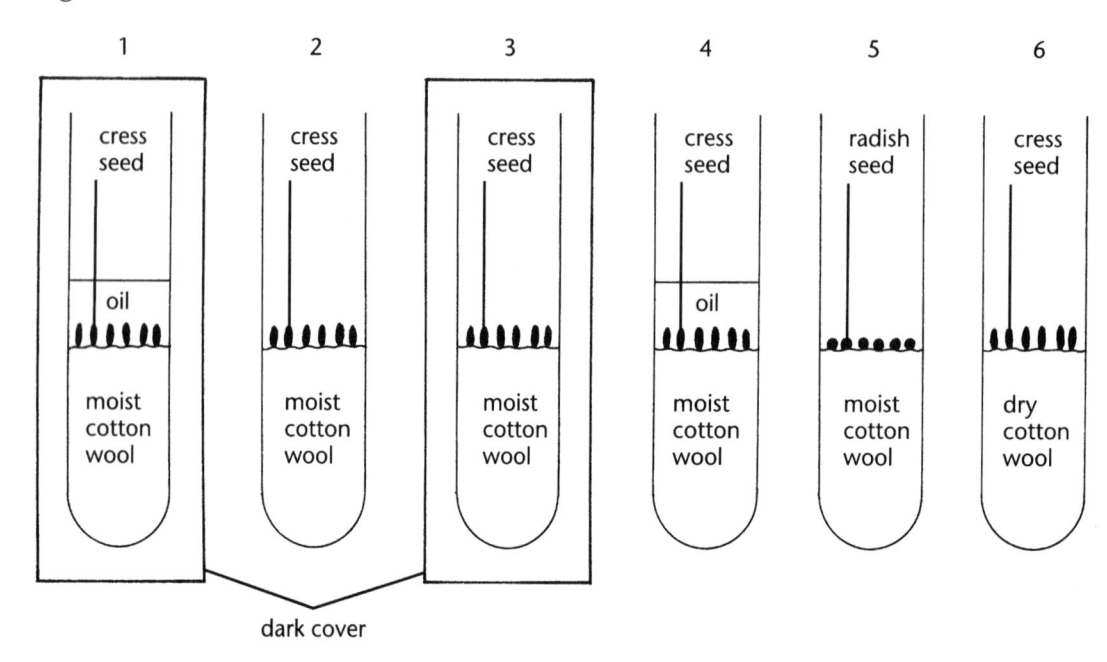

8 Which two test tubes should not have been included in this experiment?

A 1 and 2.
B 1 and 5.
C 3 and 4.
D 5 and 6.

9 Which of the test tubes shown in the diagram should have been included in the original experiment?

A 7.
B 8.
C 9.
D 10.

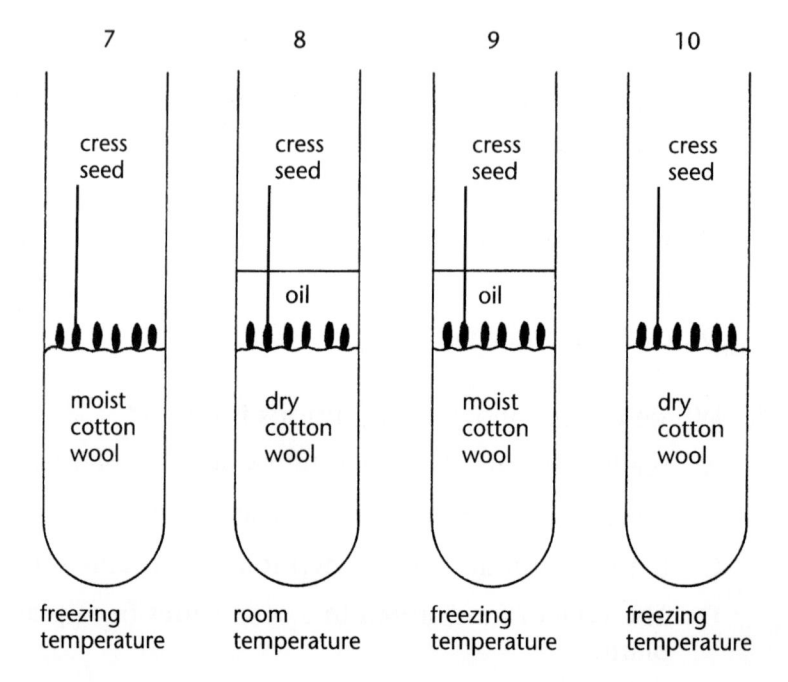

Multiple Choice Test 2 continued

10 The first of the diagrams (which is incomplete) shows a method of investigating the effect of competition on germinating cress seeds.

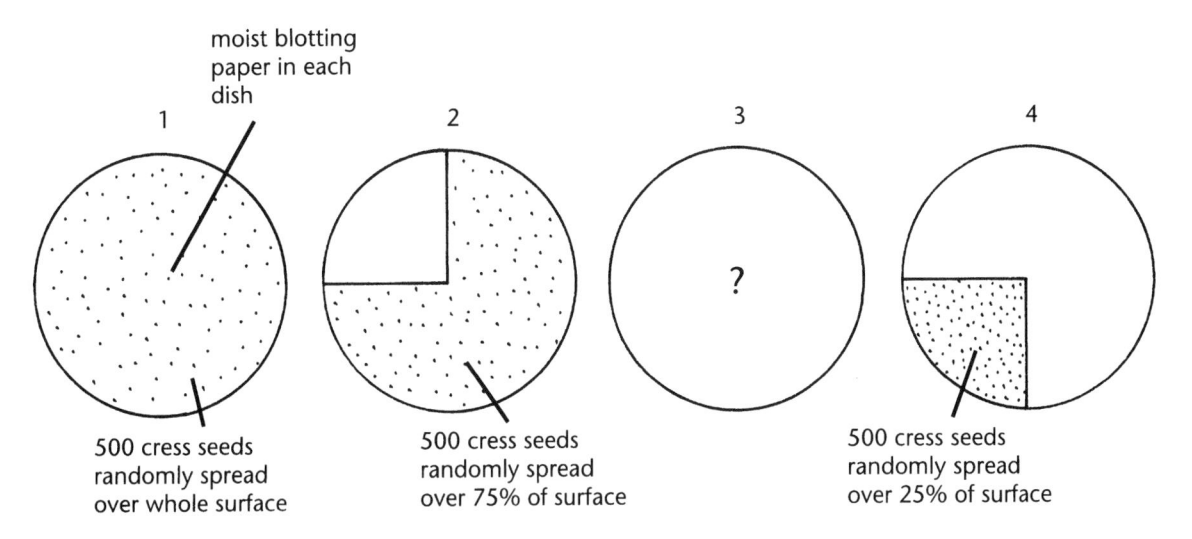

Dish 1: moist blotting paper in each dish — 500 cress seeds randomly spread over whole surface

Dish 2: 500 cress seeds randomly spread over 75% of surface

Dish 3: ?

Dish 4: 500 cress seeds randomly spread over 25% of surface

Which part of the second diagram shows the correct set-up for Petri dish 3?

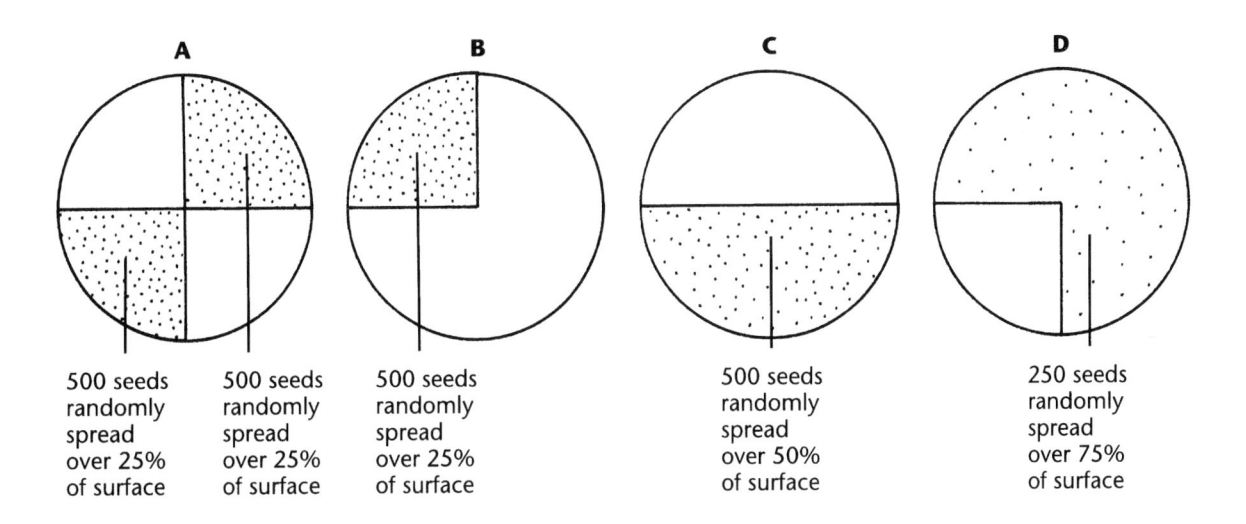

A 500 seeds randomly spread over 25% of surface | 500 seeds randomly spread over 25% of surface

B 500 seeds randomly spread over 25% of surface

C 500 seeds randomly spread over 50% of surface

D 250 seeds randomly spread over 75% of surface

Unit 3 Growing Plants

Multiple Choice Test 2 continued

Questions 11 and 12 refer to the following table. It shows the results from an experiment set up to investigate the effect of temperature on germination of cress seeds.

temperature (°C)	number of seeds germinating out of 25	percentage germination
5	0	0
10	3	12
15	25	100
20	25	100
25	17	[see question 11]
30	5	20
35	1	4

11 What was the percentage germination at 25°C?

   A   17.
   B   42.
   C   68.
   D   85.

12 What would be the most likely result for number of seeds germinating out of 25 at 50°C?

   A   0.
   B   3.
   C   5.
   D   8.

Questions 13 and 14 refer to the accompanying graph. It shows the effect of 90 days of low temperature chilling on the percentage germination of dormant seeds of Mountain ash tree.

13 What percentage of Mountain ash seeds germinated after they had been chilled at 7°C?

   A 50.   B 60.   C 70.   D 80.

14 The highest percentage of seeds have their dormancy broken when they have been chilled at temperature

   A   0–2°C.
   B   3–5°C.
   C   6–8°C.
   D   9–10°C.

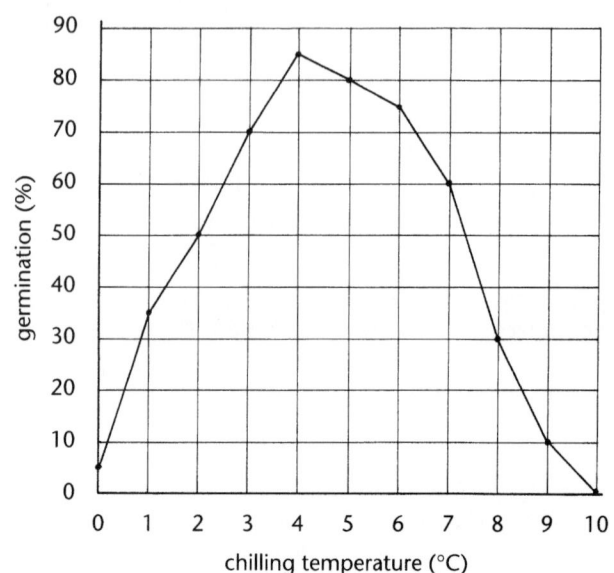

Chapter 9 Growing Plants from Seeds

Multiple Choice Test 2 continued

Questions 15, 16, 17, 18 and 19 refer to the accompanying diagram. It shows an experiment to measure changes in dry mass of germinating seeds and young seedlings in light and dark.

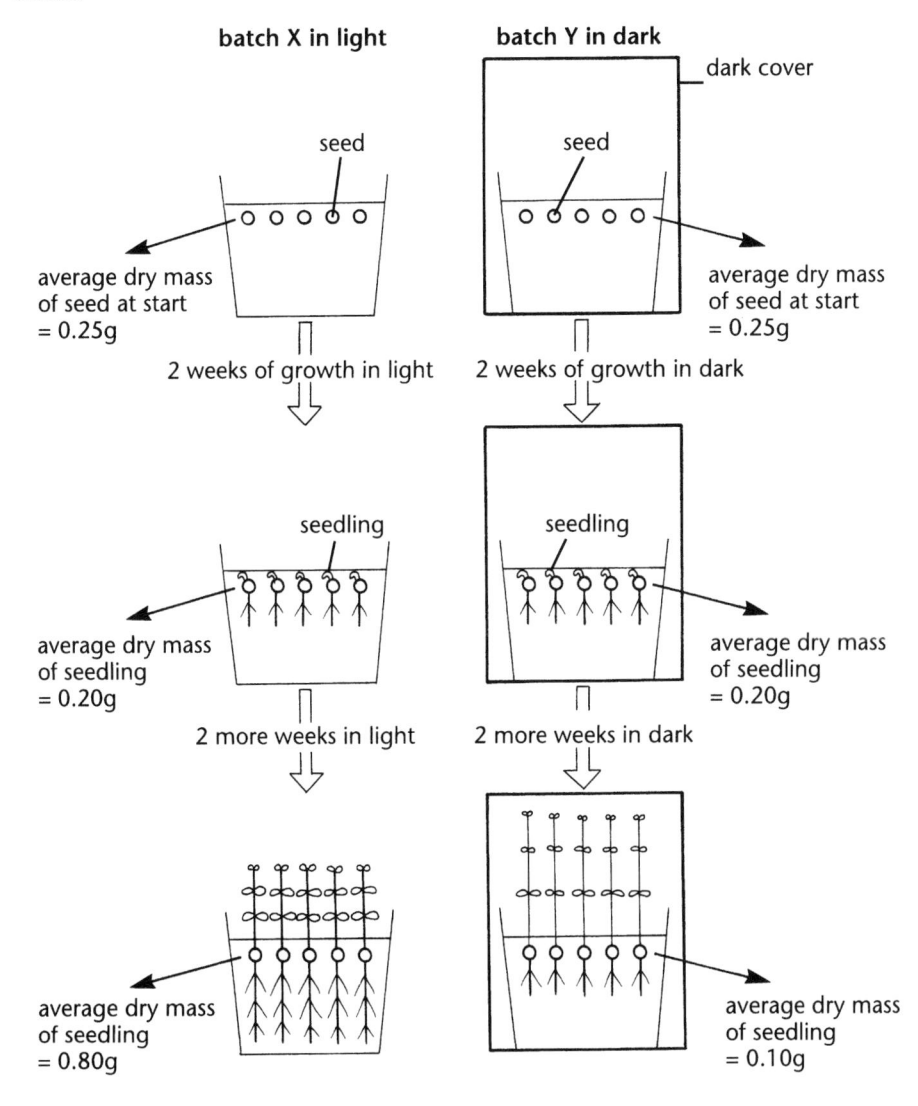

batch X in light

seed

average dry mass of seed at start = 0.25g

⇩ 2 weeks of growth in light

seedling

average dry mass of seedling = 0.20g

⇩ 2 more weeks in light

average dry mass of seedling = 0.80g

batch Y in dark

dark cover

seed

average dry mass of seed at start = 0.25g

⇩ 2 weeks of growth in dark

seedling

average dry mass of seedling = 0.20g

⇩ 2 more weeks in dark

average dry mass of seedling = 0.10g

15 What is the average loss in dry mass (in g) by a germinating seedling during the first two weeks of growth?

  A 0.05.
  B 0.20.
  C 0.25.
  D 0.50.

Unit 3 **Growing Plants**

Multiple Choice Test 2 *continued*

16 The loss in dry mass during the first two weeks is due to stored food being used up for
   A dormancy.   B respiration.
   C pregermination.   D photosynthesis.

17 What is the average percentage loss in dry mass by a seedling growing in the dark over the four-week period?
   A 20.   B 50.   C 60.   D 80.

18 What is the average percentage gain in dry mass by a seedling growing in light during the second two-week period?
   A 25.   B 33.   C 300.   D 400.

19 The gain in dry mass during the second two-week period by seedlings in batch X is due to the process of
   A dormancy.   B respiration.
   C pregermination.   D photosynthesis.

20 The diagram below shows the procedure for sowing seeds. The steps are in a mixed-up order.

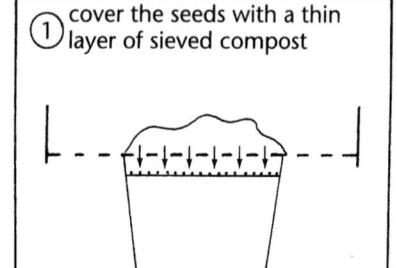

① cover the seeds with a thin layer of sieved compost

② cover the pot with a plastic sheet and put in seed propagator

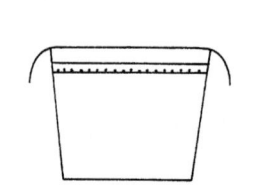

③ fill pot with moist seed compost and use a presser to firm compost to about 1 cm below the rim

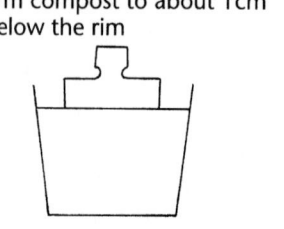

④ using a piece of folded paper, scatter the seeds thinly over the compost

⑤ water the seeds with a fine rose attached to the watering can

Multiple Choice Test 2 *continued*

The correct sequence is
A 1, 3, 5, 2, 4. B 3, 4, 1, 5, 2. C 1, 3, 4, 5, 2. D 3, 5, 4, 2, 1.

21 Some seeds germinate more successfully if they have had their seed coat chitted. This can be done by nicking large seeds with a knife or rubbing small seeds with abrasive paper. Why is chitting useful?

A It keeps out harmful pests and parasites.
B It allows the embryo to develop green leaves.
C It speeds up the storage of starchy food.
D It lets the seed absorb water more easily.

Questions 22, 23, 24 and 25 refer to the following magazine article.

YOUR QUESTIONS ABOUT PELLETED SEEDS ANSWERED

What is a pelleted seed?
It is a seed that has been coated with several layers of material such as chalk or clay as shown in the diagram.

How are these layers applied?
They are added by rotating the seeds in a tumbling machine.

Why are seeds pelleted?
The process makes irregularly-shaped seeds round and smooth. Therefore they do not tend to stick together and can be easily planted. Planting is often done using a machine called a drill that spaces the seeds out evenly.

What chemicals can be added to the layers in a pellet?
The inside layer of a pellet may contain fungicide to control fungal spores on the surface of the seed that might cause disease. A pellet sometimes contains pesticide in its outer layer to kill pests in the soil but leave the seed unaffected. Sometimes the pellet contains nutrients to encourage growth of the young seedling.

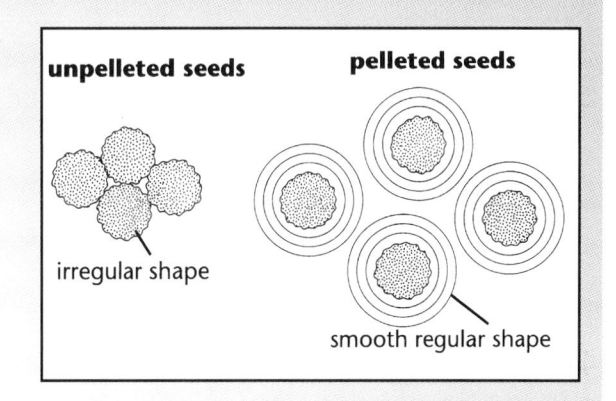

Which types of seed are pelleted?
It is commonly done to small seeds such as carrot, onion, tomato, lettuce and sugar beet but not to larger, more easily handled seeds such as bean, pea, sweet pea and Aster.

Unit 3 Growing Plants

Multiple Choice Test 2 continued

22 A pelleted seed is one that has been coated with a substance such as
   A clay.
   B carbon.
   C plastic.
   D polythene.

23 Because pelleted seeds have a round shape they
   A grow into dense colonies of seedlings that compete well with weeds.
   B compete with one another during germination and eliminate the weakest strain.
   C stick closely together during sowing giving a dense clump of seedlings.
   D do not stick together and can be handled more easily during planting.

24 Which of the following chemicals would not be added to the layers in a pellet?
   A fungicide.
   B nutrients.
   C pesticide.
   D iodine.

25 Which of the following types of seed is often pelleted before sowing?
   A pea.
   B bean.
   C carrot.
   D sweet pea.

Unit 3 · 10 Vegetative Propagation

Matching Test 1 — Match the words in list X with their descriptions in list Y.

List X

1) bulb
2) corm
3) offset
4) plantlet
5) runner
6) vegetative propagation

List Y

a) method of producing genetically identical offspring from one parent

b) young plant formed by vegetative propagation at the edge of a leaf of the parent plant

c) stem that spreads out from a plant and has a new plantlet at its end

d) young plant formed by vegetative propagation at the base of the parent plant

e) plant propagation structure with its food store in swollen underground leaf bases

f) plant propagation structure with its food store in a swollen underground stem

171

Unit 3 **Growing Plants**

Matching Test 2

Match the words in list X with their descriptions in list Y.

List X	List Y
1) crock	a) small pair of shears with sprung handles for pruning plants
2) dibber	b) chemical used in low concentrations to encourage root production by cuttings
3) layering	c) shallow box with heating element and cover used to give cuttings ideal growing conditions
4) node	d) tool for making a hole in soil to take the stem of a new cutting
5) propagator	e) piece of broken clay pot used to cover a drainage hole of a plant pot and stop soil escaping
6) rooting powder	f) removal and planting of side shoots from a parent plant
7) secateurs	g) method of propagation by which a shoot is made to root while still attached to the parent plant
8) taking cuttings	h) part of a stem from which leaves or side branches grow

Chapter 10 **Vegetative Propagation**

Multiple Choice Test 1

Choose the ONE correct answer to each of the following questions.

Questions 1, 2 and 3 refer to the diagram of a branched key.

1. Into which box should the words 'using a storage organ' have been put?

2. Which box should contain the words 'side branch of Ivy'?

3. Which box should say 'artificial'?

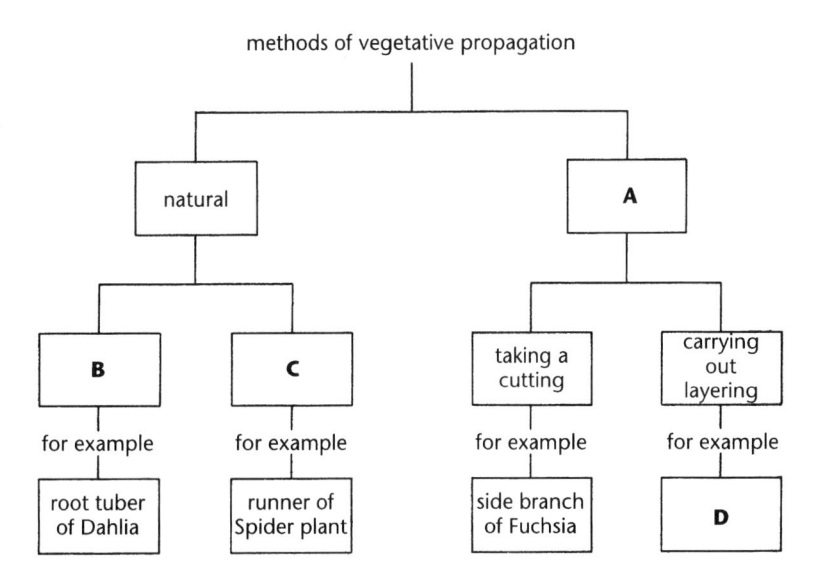

Questions 4 and 5 refer to the set of four diagrams that follow.

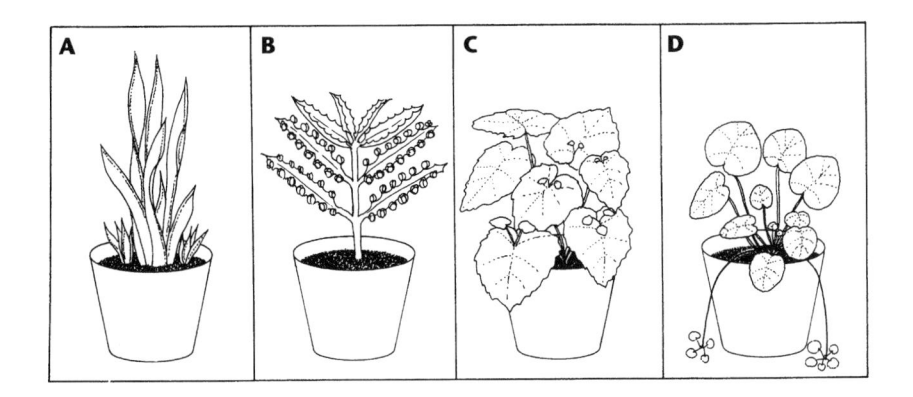

4. Which shows a parent plant producing plantlets as offsets?

5. Which shows a parent plant producing plantlets in the centres of its leaves?

Unit 3 Growing Plants

Multiple Choice Test 1 continued

6 When Crocus corms are planted in a garden, they should be given a layer of soil above them of about twice their height. They should also be placed about two corm widths apart. The first of the diagrams shows what is meant by height and width of a corm.

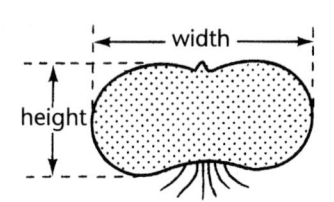

Which part of the second diagram shows Crocus corms correctly planted in a garden?

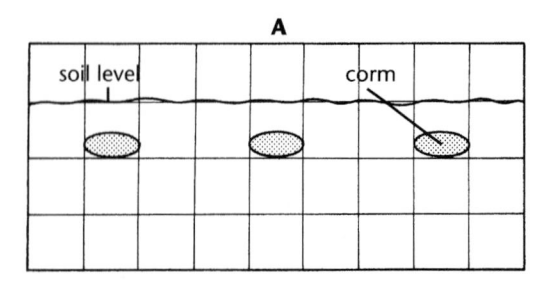

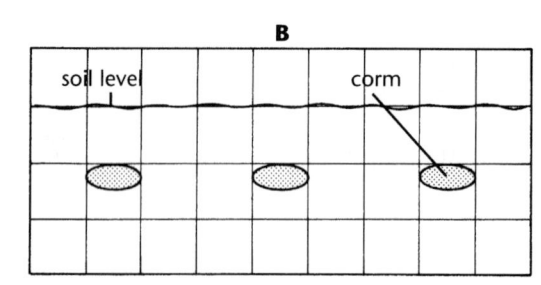

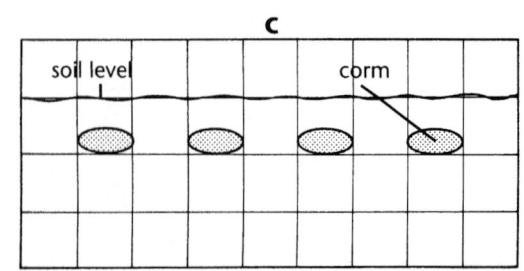

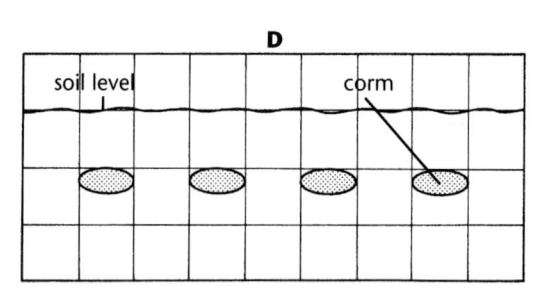

7 The food store in a bulb allows it to
   A store starch in its tubers.
   B withstand extreme summer temperatures.
   C grow early in spring before many other plants.
   D make its flowers in autumn before winter sets in.

8 The accompanying diagram shows four steps carried out when growing bulbs indoors in a bowl. The steps are given in a mixed-up order. The correct sequence is

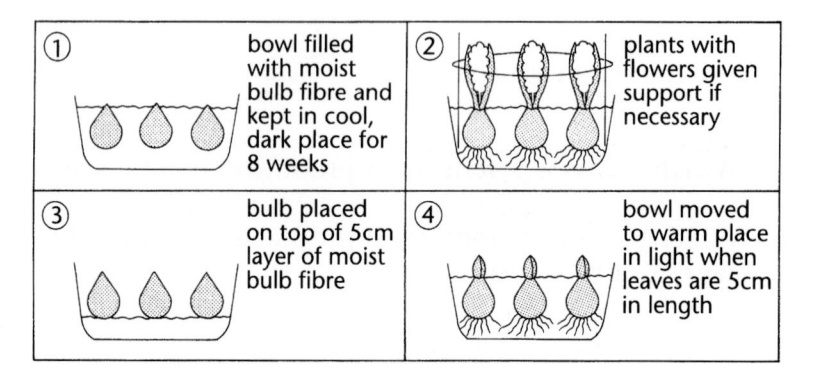

① bowl filled with moist bulb fibre and kept in cool, dark place for 8 weeks
② plants with flowers given support if necessary
③ bulb placed on top of 5cm layer of moist bulb fibre
④ bowl moved to warm place in light when leaves are 5cm in length

   A 3, 1, 4, 2.
   B 3, 1, 2, 4.
   C 1, 3, 4, 2.
   D 1, 3, 2, 4.

Chapter 10 **Vegetative Propagation**

Multiple Choice Test 1 *continued*

Questions 9 and 10 refer to the following table. It shows the percentage content of three classes of food present in onion bulbs and potato tubers.

food type present in storage organ	percentage content of food	
	onion bulb	potato tuber
protein	0.7	2.1
sugar	5.2	0.5
starch	0.0	19.0

9 Which of the bar charts correctly compares the sugar content of the two types of storage organ?

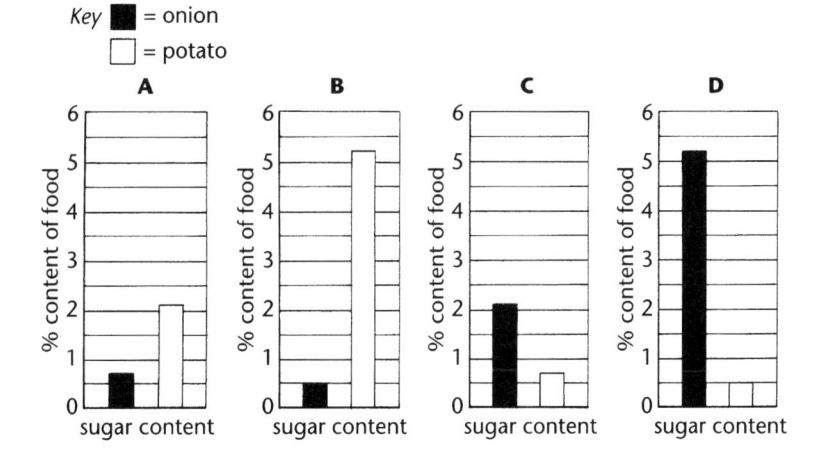

Key ■ = onion
☐ = potato

10 By how many times is the protein content of a potato tuber greater than that of an onion bulb?

A 0.3.
B 1.4.
C 3.0.
D 3.3.

11 The diagram shows a Potato plant forming new tubers.

Which route would be taken by most of the food at this time?

A 1 ⟶ 4 ⟶ 2 ⟶ 3.
B 6 ⟶ 5 ⟶ 2 ⟶ 3.
C 1 ⟶ 4 ⟶ 5 ⟶ 6.
D 6 ⟶ 5 ⟶ 4 ⟶ 1.

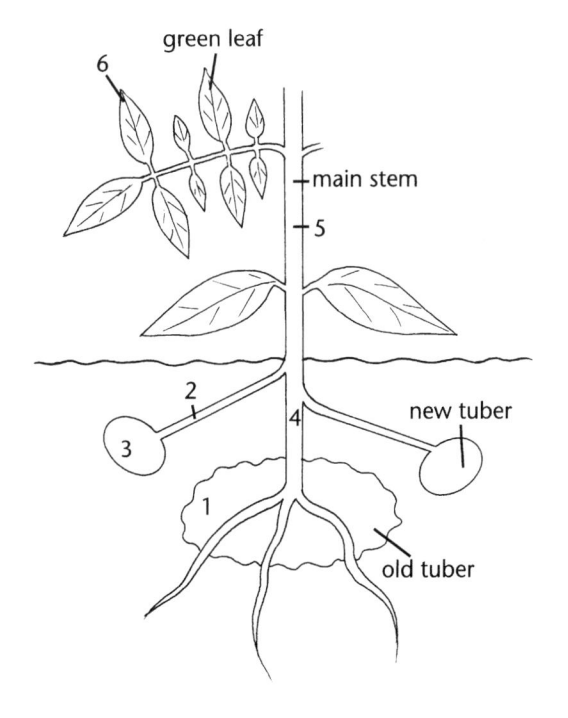

Unit 3 Growing Plants

Multiple Choice Test 1 continued

12 The diagram shows four steps carried out when propagating by offsets. The steps are in a mixed-up order. The correct sequence is

   A   1, 4, 2, 3.
   B   4, 2, 3, 1.
   C   2, 3, 1, 4.
   D   4, 2, 1, 3.

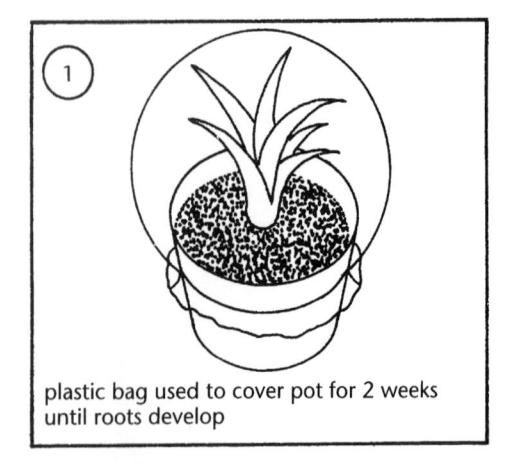

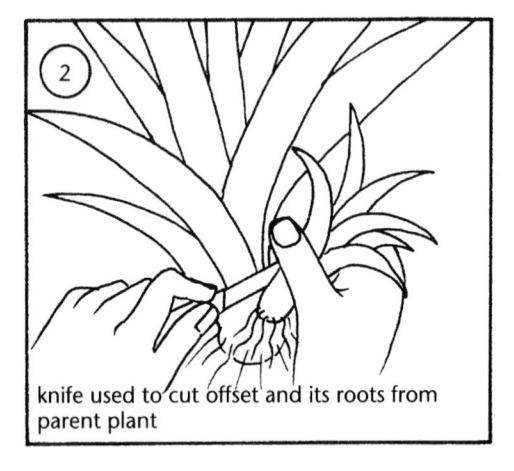

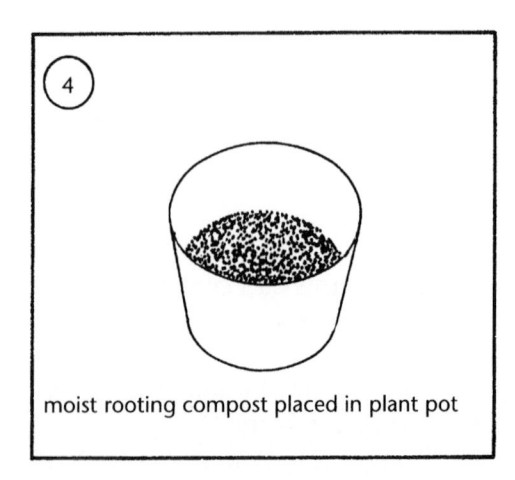

1 — plastic bag used to cover pot for 2 weeks until roots develop

2 — knife used to cut offset and its roots from parent plant

3 — offset pressed lightly into soil and more rooting compost added

4 — moist rooting compost placed in plant pot

Chapter 10 **Vegetative Propagation**

Multiple Choice Test 1 continued

13 The young Strawberry plant in the accompanying diagram is kept attached to the parent plant for a few weeks.

This procedure is carried out to make sure that the young plant will
- A continue to get water until it has developed roots.
- B develop a branched rooting system on its runner.
- C continue to send sugar made by photosynthesis to the parent.
- D develop new stem runners bearing further plantlets.

14 Which letter on the plant in the diagram points to a node?

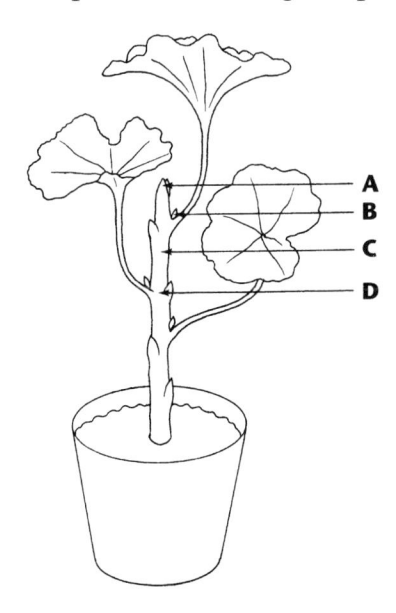

15 Which line in the following table gives methods which all help to prevent cuttings from losing too much water?

	put in mist propagator	cut off top bud	surround with plastic bag	leave uncovered in sunny room	remove lower leaves
A	✔	✘	✔	✘	✔
B	✔	✔	✘	✘	✔
C	✘	✘	✔	✔	✔
D	✔	✔	✔	✔	✘

Unit 3 Growing Plants

Multiple Choice Test 1 continued

16 The following table shows a set of results. They come from an investigation into the effect of a type of rooting powder on the rooting success of cuttings from four species of plant.

plant species	stem type	successful rooting without powder (%)	successful rooting with powder (%)
W	softwood	32	0
X	hardwood	41	76
Y	softwood	60	60
Z	hardwood	35	72

From the information in the table, it can be concluded that this type of rooting powder

A prevents rooting in species W and X.

B encourages rooting in species Y and Z.

C prevents rooting in both softwood species.

D encourages rooting in both hardwood species.

17 The diagram shows a side branch of an Ivy plant about to be propagated by layering. Which letter indicates the place where the plant should be cut and rooting powder added?

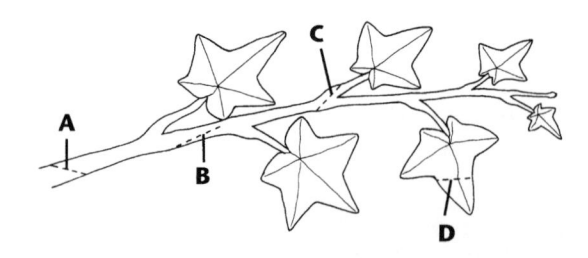

Chapter 10 Vegetative Propagation

Multiple Choice Test 1 continued

Questions 18, 19 and 20 refer to the accompanying diagram. It shows six different experiments set up to investigate the best conditions for layering Carnation plants.

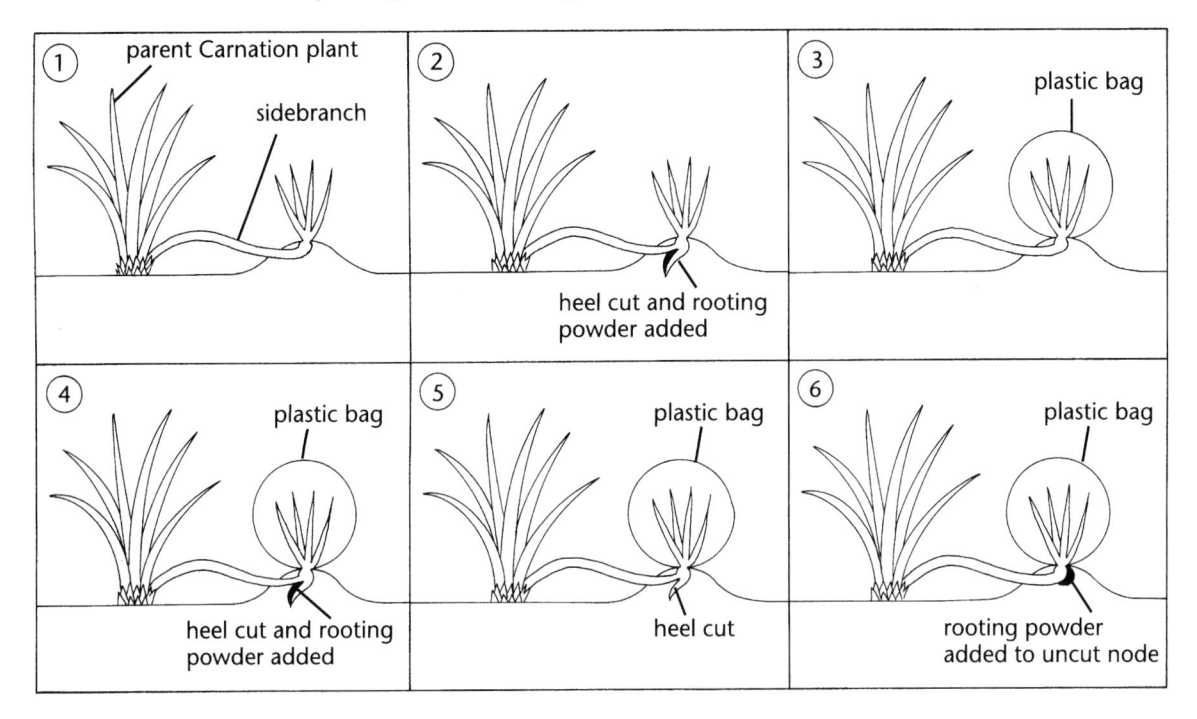

1 parent Carnation plant, sidebranch

2 heel cut and rooting powder added

3 plastic bag

4 plastic bag, heel cut and rooting powder added

5 plastic bag, heel cut

6 plastic bag, rooting powder added to uncut node

18 To investigate the effect of a plastic bag on the layered plant, set-up 1 should be compared with
   A 3.   B 4.   C 5.   D 6.

19 Which of the following set-ups should be compared in order to investigate the effect of rooting powder on layering?
   A 1 and 2.
   B 3 and 4.
   C 4 and 5.
   D 5 and 6.

20 Which of the following set-ups should be compared in order to investigate the effect on layering of cutting the stem to form a heel?
   A 1 and 2.
   B 2 and 4.
   C 3 and 5.
   D 3 and 6.

Unit 3 Growing Plants

Multiple Choice Test 1 continued

21 A hundred different species of plants were investigated to find out which methods could be used to propagate them. The following table shows the results.

number of plant species	method of propagation	code letter
25	runners	R
5	layering	L
50	taking cuttings	C
20	plantlets	P

Which pie chart correctly represents this information?

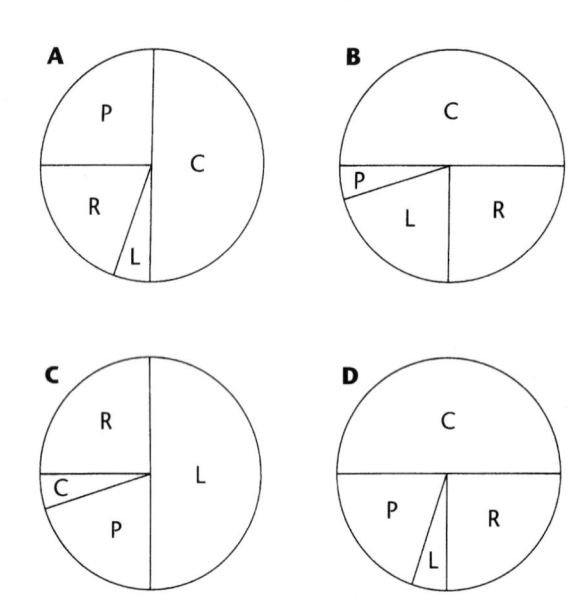

Multiple Choice Test 1 *continued*

Questions 22, 23, 24 and 25 refer to the following magazine article.

MIST PROPAGATION UNIT

Stem cuttings that are planted in soil and left to grow in a sunny room need to be watered frequently. Sometimes they are over-watered or under-watered. In addition the temperature in the room may become too high during the day and too low at night to promote root growth. These problems can be overcome using a mist propagator unit (see accompanying diagram)

When the temperature drops below the pre-set level ideal for rooting, the soil thermostat detects this change and switches on the soil-warming cable. The system heats up until the required temperature is reached. The thermostat cuts out again and the soil-warming cable switches off until it is needed.

When the air in the unit becomes drier than it should be, this is detected by the mist control sensor. It sends a message to the mist control box which turns on the water supply. A fine mist is now released into the air by the misting head. When the atmosphere is moist enough to prevent dehydration of plants and encourage rooting, the mist control sensor cuts out and the water supply switches off until it is needed again

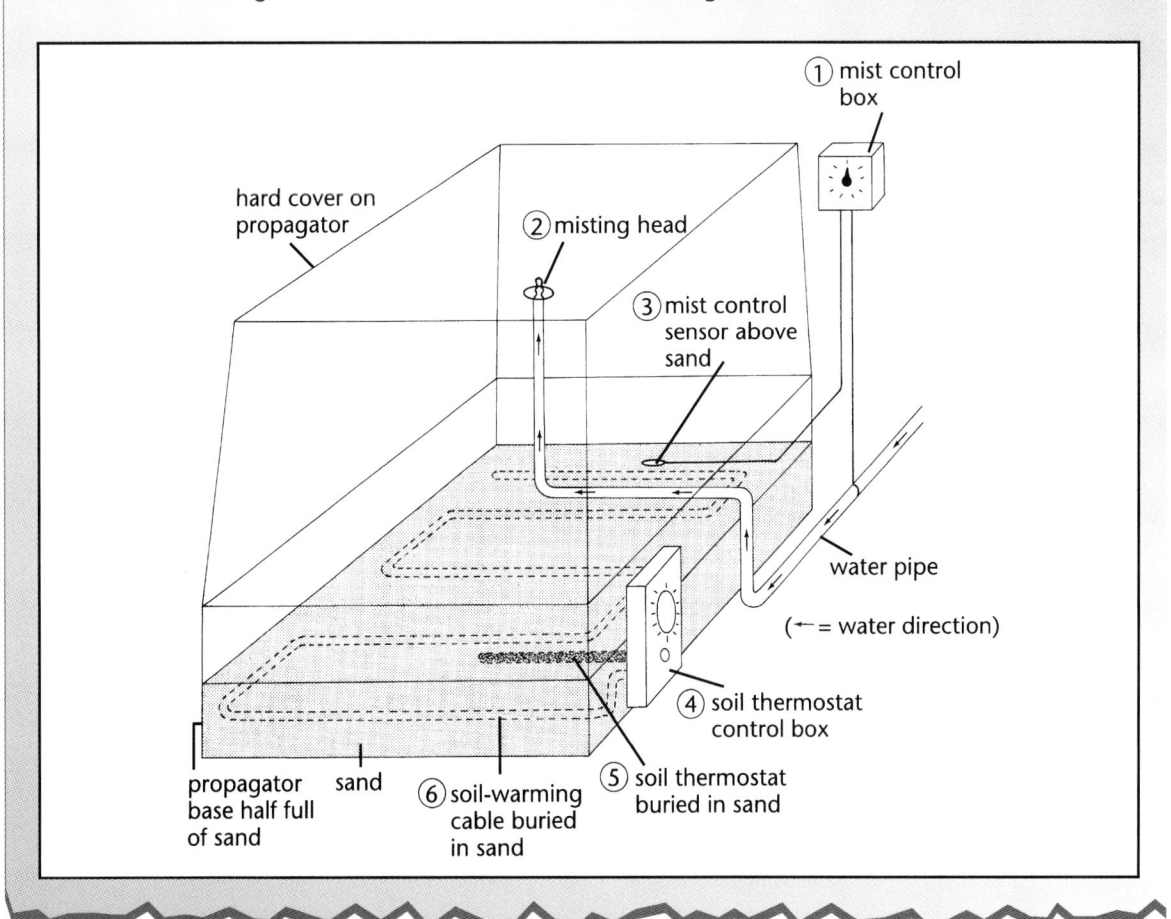

① mist control box
② misting head
③ mist control sensor above sand
④ soil thermostat control box
⑤ soil thermostat buried in sand
⑥ soil-warming cable buried in sand

hard cover on propagator

water pipe

(← = water direction)

propagator base half full of sand

sand

Unit 3 **Growing Plants**

Multiple Choice Test 1 continued

22 Which numbered structure in the diagram first detects that the air is too dry and triggers the system of mist release?

   A 1.
   B 2.
   C 3.
   D 4.

23 Which structure in the diagram releases mist into the air when required?

   A 1.
   B 2.
   C 3.
   D 4.

24 Which structure first detects that the conditions have become too cold?

   A 3.
   B 4.
   C 5.
   D 6.

25 Which structure, on being switched on, supplies the system with heat?

   A 3.
   B 4.
   C 5.
   D 6.

Chapter 10 **Vegetative Propagation**

Multiple Choice Test 2

Choose the ONE correct answer to each of the following questions.

Questions 1, 2 and 3 refer to the accompanying diagram. It shows a branched key of several types of plant propagation structure.

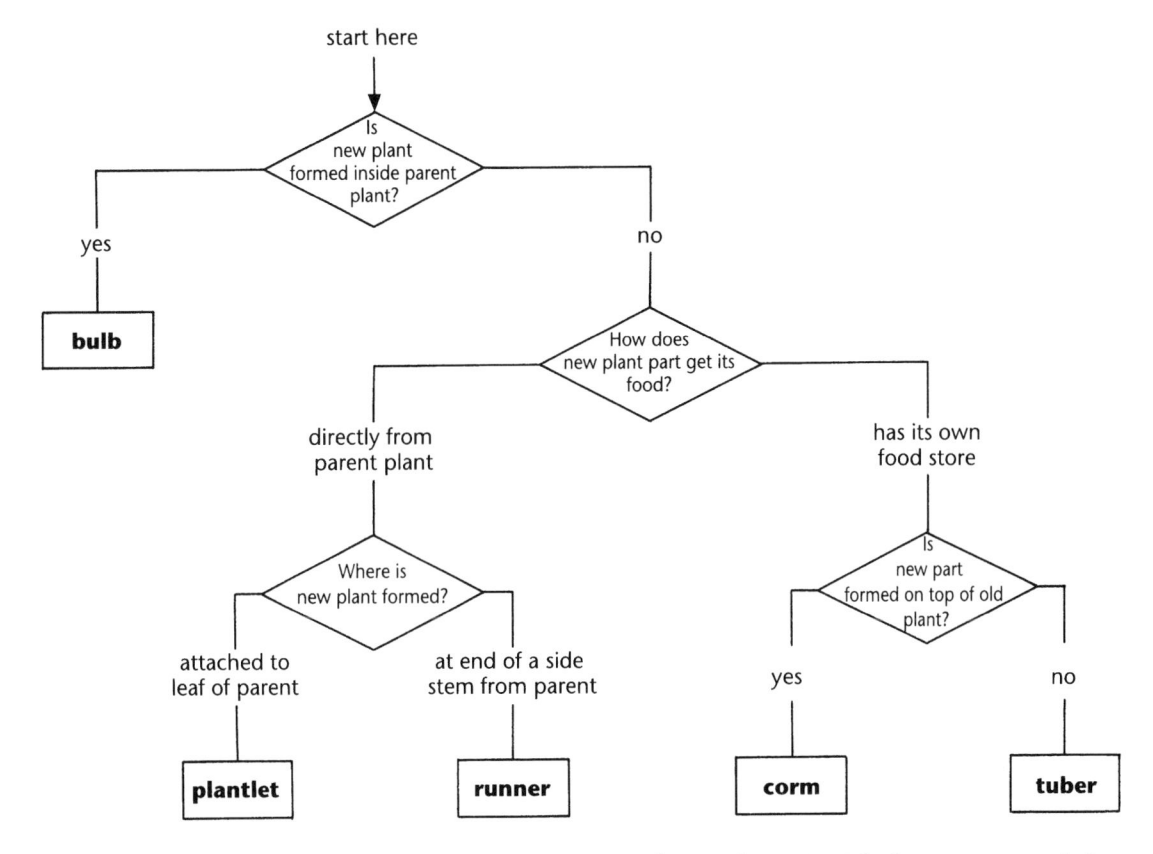

```
                        start here
                            ↓
                    Is new plant
                 formed inside parent
                        plant?
         yes ←                    → no
         bulb              How does
                       new plant part get its
                              food?
             directly from              has its own
             parent plant                food store
                  ↓                          ↓
            Where is                    Is new part
         new plant formed?           formed on top of old
                                           plant?
   attached to      at end of a side    yes         no
   leaf of parent   stem from parent
       ↓                 ↓               ↓           ↓
    plantlet           runner           corm       tuber
```

1 Which of the following plant structures is formed not inside but on top of the parent plant and has its own food store?

    A bulb.   B runner.   C corm.   D tuber.

2 Which line in the following table refers to a plantlet?

	Attached to a leaf of the parent plant?	Formed inside the parent plant?	Gets its food from the parent plant?	Has its own food store?
A	no	yes	no	yes
B	no	yes	yes	no
C	yes	no	no	yes
D	yes	no	yes	no

183

Unit 3 Growing Plants

Multiple Choice Test 2 continued

3 Each propagation structure made by a plant called the Lesser Celandine has its own food store and is formed outside the parent but not on top of it. What name is given to this type of propagation structure?

A bulb.   B runner.   C corm.   D tuber.

4 To produce large numbers of a desirable type of plant for sale, garden centres often use vegetative propagation. Which line in the table summarises their reasons for choosing this method?

	speed of process compared with growing from seed	state of new plants produced
A	faster	varied
B	slower	varied
C	faster	identical
D	slower	identical

Questions 5 and 6 refer to the following table and bar chart.

bulb	average height of bulb (cm)	recommended depth of planting in a garden (cm)
snowdrop	2	4
hyacinth	5	12
tulip	3	8
daffodil	7	14

5 Which bar in the chart represents the depth of planting recommended for snowdrop bulbs?

6 Which bar represents the depth of planting recommended for hyacinth bulbs?

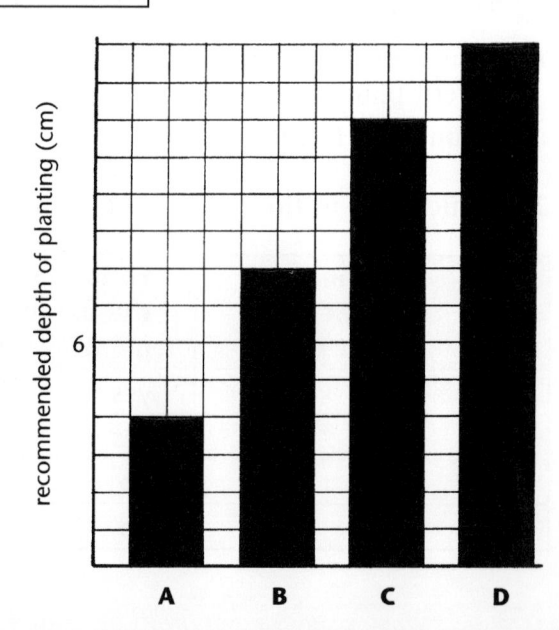

Chapter 10 **Vegetative Propagation**

Multiple Choice Test 2 continued

7   The diagram shows a daffodil bulb cut longitudinally down its centre. Which lettered structure will develop into a daughter bulb?

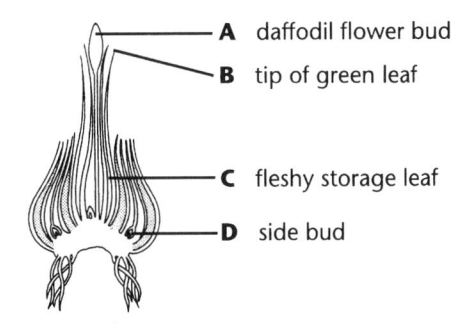

- **A** daffodil flower bud
- **B** tip of green leaf
- **C** fleshy storage leaf
- **D** side bud

8   Which line in the following table is correct?

	chemical reagent	food being tested for	colour that indicates positive result
A	iodine solution	sugar	purple
B	iodine solution	starch	blue-black
C	clinistix	starch	purple
D	clinistix	sugar	blue-black

9   The following table gives the results of carrying out two food tests on twenty bulbs from two different plants.

type of bulb	chemical used for food test	
	iodine solution	clinistix
daffodil	+	−
onion	−	+

What conclusion can be drawn from these results?

- **A** An onion bulb contains starch but not sugar.
- **B** An onion bulb contains sugar but not starch.
- **C** A daffodil bulb contains starch but not protein.
- **D** A daffodil bulb contains protein but not starch.

Unit 3 Growing Plants

Multiple Choice Test 2 continued

Questions 10, 11, 12 and 13 refer to the accompanying diagram. It shows the life cycle of a type of potato plant.

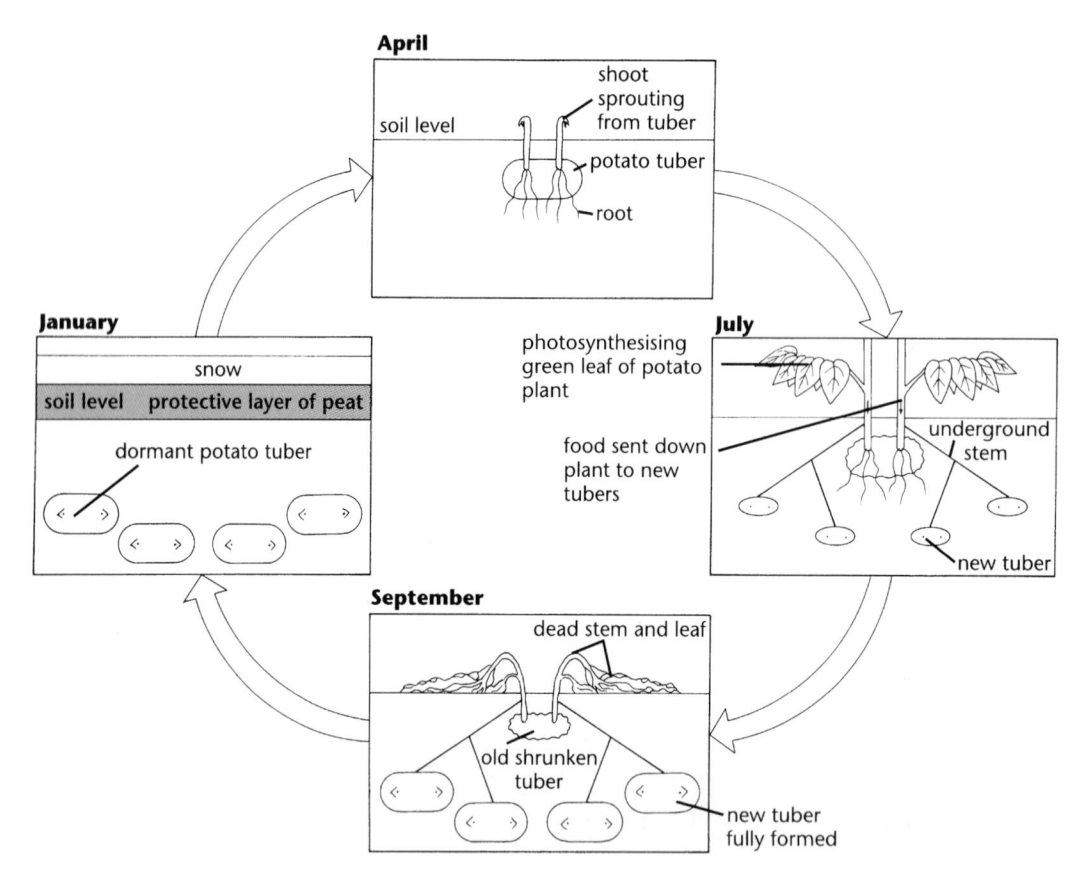

10 When would be the best time to plant tubers to grow a crop of new potatoes?

A March.   B June.   C August.   D December.

11 New tubers are formed at the end of underground

A stems.   B roots.   C leaves.   D corms.

12 During which period of time does the greatest increase in size of new potato tubers take place?

A January to March.   C July to September.

B April to June.   D October to December.

13 New tubers get their food from the plant's

A roots.   B old tuber.   C green leaves.   D other new tubers.

Chapter 10 **Vegetative Propagation**

Multiple Choice Test 2 continued

14 Which of the plants shown in the diagram could not be propagated by division of offsets?

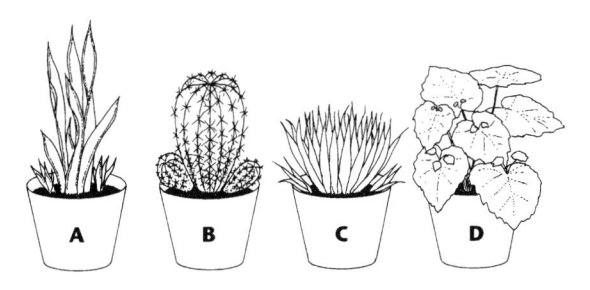

Questions 15 and 16 refer to the accompanying diagram. It shows the procedure carried out when taking a stem cutting. The five steps are in a mixed-up order.

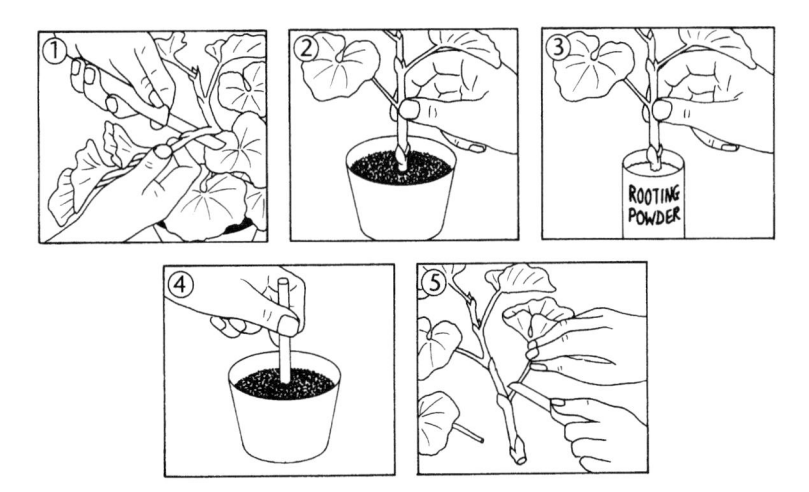

15 What is the correct sequence of the five steps?

    A 1, 5, 2, 3, 4.   C 3, 4, 2, 5, 1.

    B 2, 5, 1, 3, 2.   D 4, 1, 5, 3, 2.

16 Step 5 is carried out so that during the plant's time in the propagator

    A water loss from the cutting is reduced.

    B growth of roots from exposed nodes is promoted.

    C leaf cuttings can be planted in the same pot.

    D side buds are encouraged to grow into shoots.

Unit 3 **Growing Plants**

Multiple Choice Test 2 continued

Questions 17 and 18 refer to the experiment shown in the accompanying diagram. It was set up to investigate the effect of different concentrations of rooting powder on the rooting success of cuttings.

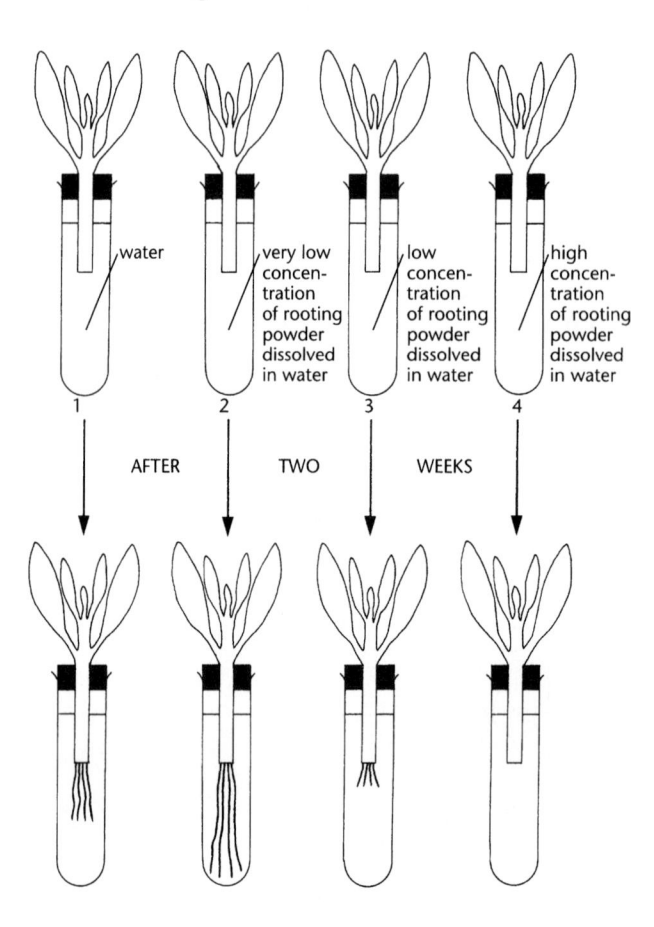

17 From the results, it can be concluded that in this type of plant
  A the highest concentration of rooting powder produces the longest roots.
  B a very low concentration of rooting powder is the most effective at encouraging root formation.
  C water is better for promoting root production than any concentration of rooting powder.
  D a low concentration of rooting powder promotes the formation of the biggest number of roots.

18 Which tube is the control in this experiment?
  A 1.   B 2.   C 3.   D 4.

Multiple Choice Test 2 continued

19 What is the reason for putting the cuttings into the propagator shown in the diagram?

   A to supply extra light to promote photosynthesis.
   B to supply heat to encourage growth of roots.
   C to keep the temperature constant to increase water loss.
   D to remove light to decrease water loss.

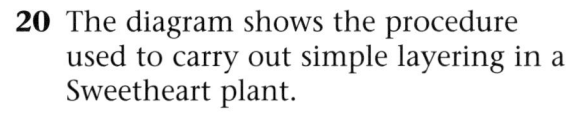

20 The diagram shows the procedure used to carry out simple layering in a Sweetheart plant.

   What does the gardener do at stage X?

   A She pegs down the side shoot so that the node touches the compost.
   B She cuts the side shoot at the node to separate it from the parent plant.
   C She dips the cut end of the side shoot in hormone rooting powder.
   D She uses a U-shaped piece of wire to support the parent plant.

21 One advantage of layering as a method of propagation is that it makes sure that the young plant gets

   A nutrients from the parent plant.
   B started in the same pot as the parent plant.
   C water without the help of the parent plant.
   D sugar from the parent plant's fruit.

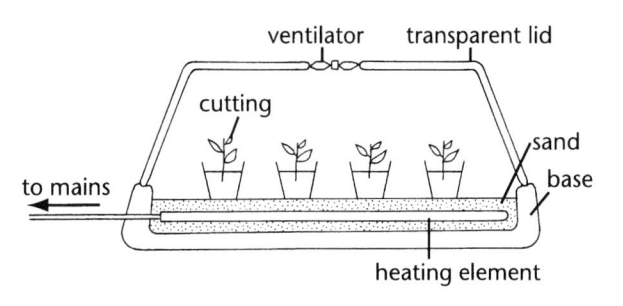

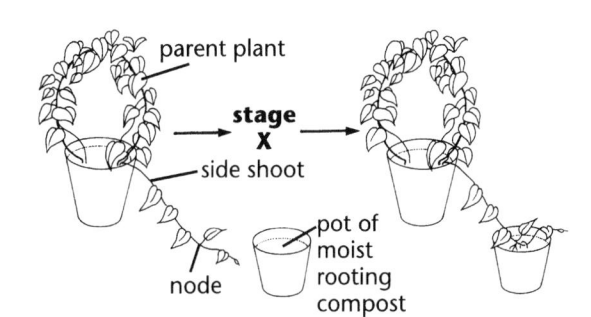

Unit 3 Growing Plants

Multiple Choice Test 2 continued

Questions 22, 23, 24 and 25 refer to the following magazine article.

CLONING PLANTS

In a plant-cloning laboratory, all staff must wear sterile clothing. Gone are the muddy pots of soil found in greenhouses and potting sheds. In their place are countless rows of spotless culture tubes. Here thousands of plants of the one type are produced by micro-propagation.

First a plant with useful features such as a sweet-tasting fruit is chosen. Then it is tissue-cultured by cutting buds from this parent plant into tiny pieces and growing them in sterile nutrient agar jelly in culture tubes (see diagram).

Each piece of tissue is kept in ideal conditions of light and temperature until it develops into a miniature plant. Once it has been checked for disease, it is supplied in a batch to a commercial grower.

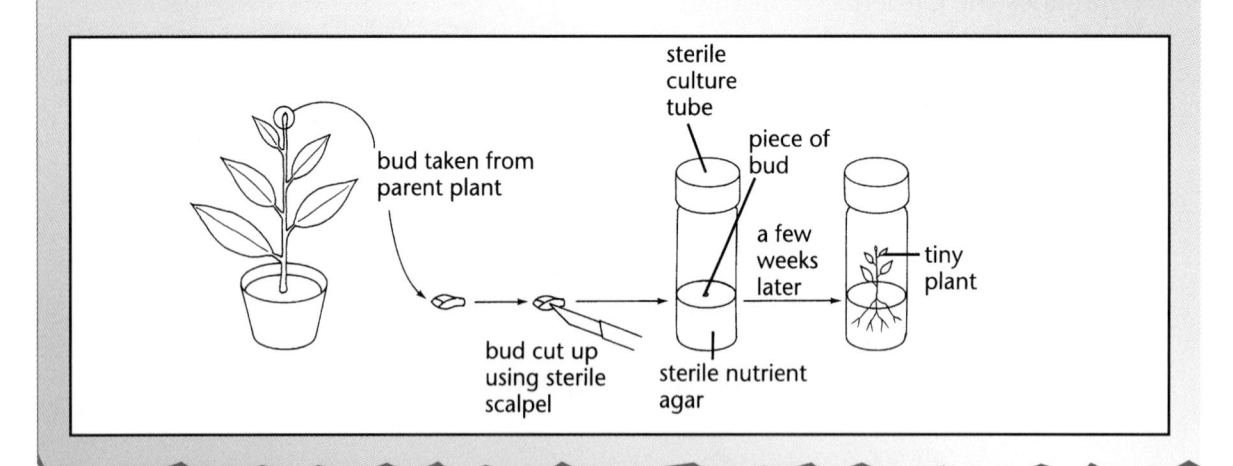

22 Which of the following states the main theme of the passage?
  A Investigating new diseases of fruit.
  B Micro-propagation by tissue-culturing.
  C Producing new varieties of useful plant.
  D Natural methods of vegetative propagation.

23 Which of the following is least likely to carry micro-organisms that could spread disease among plants?
  A muddy pot.   B greenhouse.   C sterile agar.   D potting shed.

Chapter 10 Vegetative Propagation

Multiple Choice Test 2 continued

Questions 24 and 25 refer to the flow diagram. It summarises the information given in the article above as a set of instructions.

24 Which instruction should box X contain?

A Transplant young plants into pots of compost.

B Cut bud tissue from parent plant into tiny pieces.

C Check all young plants thoroughly for disease.

D Put young plants into a mist propagation unit.

25 Which instruction should box Y contain?

A Cut bud tissue from parent plant into tiny pieces.

B Increase supply of young plants by layering.

C Take offsets of new young plants using sterile scalpel.

D Check all young plants thoroughly for disease.

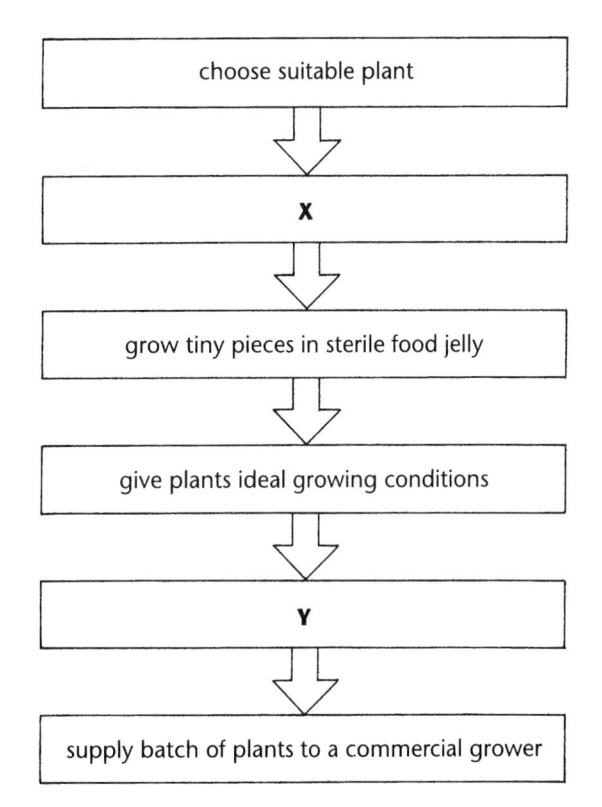

```
┌─────────────────────────────────┐
│      choose suitable plant      │
└─────────────────────────────────┘
                ⇩
┌─────────────────────────────────┐
│                X                │
└─────────────────────────────────┘
                ⇩
┌─────────────────────────────────┐
│ grow tiny pieces in sterile food jelly │
└─────────────────────────────────┘
                ⇩
┌─────────────────────────────────┐
│  give plants ideal growing conditions  │
└─────────────────────────────────┘
                ⇩
┌─────────────────────────────────┐
│                Y                │
└─────────────────────────────────┘
                ⇩
┌─────────────────────────────────┐
│ supply batch of plants to a commercial grower │
└─────────────────────────────────┘
```

Unit 3 · 11 Plant Production

Matching Test 1

Match the words in list X with their descriptions in list Y.

List X

1) coconut fibre
2) drainage
3) loam
4) loam-based compost
5) loamless compost
6) nutrients
7) peat
8) perlite
9) retention
10) sand and grit

List Y

a) fertile soil containing sand, clay and decaying organic material
b) small hard particles of stone that improve soil drainage
c) mineral substances required for plant growth that are absorbed by roots
d) dead plant material from boggy moorland that improves soil's water-holding capacity
e) mass of small globules of volcanic rock used in some loamless composts
f) process by which water flows down, through and out of a soil
g) growing medium for plants that lacks loam
h) growing medium for plants that is rich in garden soil
i) substitute for peat in some loamless composts
j) process by which soil holds on to water and does not let it drain away

Chapter 11 **Plant Production**

Matching Test 1

Match the words in list X with their descriptions in list Y.

List X

1) automatic irrigation
2) capillary matting
3) fertiliser
4) K
5) N
6) P
7) trace elements
8) ventilation
9) water retentive gel
10) watering

List Y

a) process by which an enclosed system is supplied with fresh air
b) symbol for the element nitrogen needed by plants especially for leaf growth
c) general name for process by which the soil around a plant is moistened
d) unattended system of pipeline and nozzles for supplying water to many plant pots
e) chemical that absorbs several hundreds of times its own weight of water
f) material that draws up water and supplies it to soil in plant pots
g) symbol for the element potassium needed by plants especially for growth of flowers and fruit
h) mixture of chemical substances added to soil or water to improve plant growth
i) symbol for element phosphorus needed by plant especially for growth of roots
j) chemicals such as iron and copper needed by plants in tiny quantities for healthy growth

Unit 3 Growing Plants

Matching Test 1

Match the words in list X with their descriptions in list Y.

List X	List Y
1) aphid	a) removal of old flowers to encourage plants to make more flowers
2) cloche	b) transfer of seedlings from a crowded site to a container or bed with more space
3) dead-heading	c) type of fungus that attacks plants kept in air that is too damp
4) floating fleece	d) framework covered with glass or polythene used to protect young plants
5) fungicide	e) general name for a chemical that kills pests on plants
6) grey mould	f) chemical used to kill fungal pests on plants
7) insecticide	g) transfer of a potted plant into a larger container
8) pricking out	h) layer of light-weight insulating material used to protect young plants from extremes of temperature
9) pesticide	i) small insect (e.g. greenfly and blackfly) that feeds by sucking juices from plants
10) potting on	j) chemical used to kill insect pests on a plant

Chapter 11 **Plant Production**

Multiple Choice Test 1

Choose the ONE correct answer to each of the following questions.

1. The following table gives differences between two types of compost. Which line in the table is correct?

		loam-based compost	loamless compost
A	Does it contain soil?	no	yes
B	Does it contain fertiliser?	yes	no
C	Does it need to be sterilised?	yes	no
D	Is peat its main component?	yes	no

Questions 2 and 3 refer to the following information and accompanying diagram of possible answers. The ratio of peat to sharp sand in a rooting compost is 1:1 and in a potting compost is 3:1.

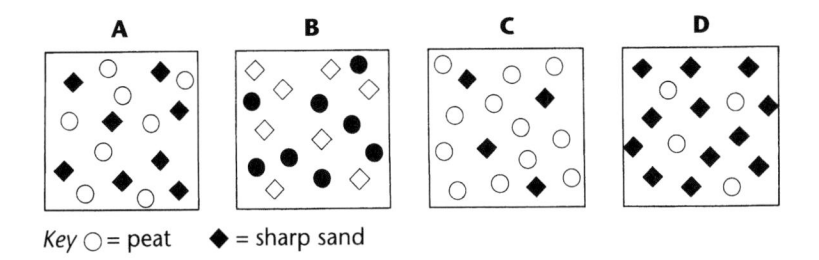

Key ○ = peat   ◆ = sharp sand

2. Which diagram best represents the rooting compost?

3. Which diagram best represents the potting compost?

Unit 3 Growing Plants

Multiple Choice Test 1 continued

Questions 4, 5, 6 and 7 refer to the accompanying diagram. It shows the results of an experiment where 50 ml of water was added to each of four compost types. Any water that passed through the compost was collected in a measuring cylinder.

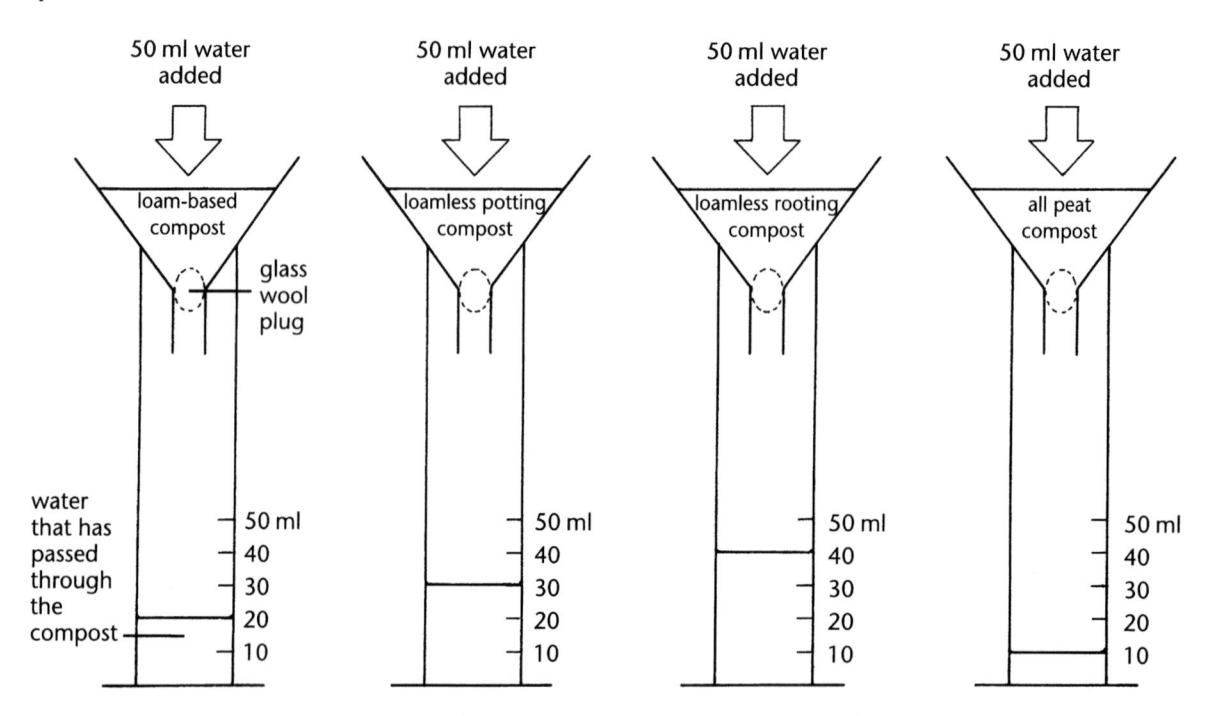

4 Which compost allows most water to drain through it?
  A loam-based.   B loamless potting.
  C loamless rooting.   D all peat.

5 Which compost has the greatest water-holding capacity?
  A loam-based.   B loamless potting.
  C loamless rooting.   D all peat.

6 What volume of water (in ml) was retained by loamless potting compost?
  A 10.   B 20.   C 30.   D 40.

7 What percentage volume of water drained through loam-based compost?
  A 20.   B 30.   C 40.   D 60.

Chapter 11 **Plant Production**

Multiple Choice Test 1 continued

Questions 8 and 9 refer to the following table.

brand of fertiliser	percentage of element present in fertiliser		
	N (nitrogen)	P (phosphorus)	K (potassium)
A	4	4	7
B	7	7	7
C	40	10	0
D	0	30	15

8   Which brand is the general purpose fertiliser?

9   Which brand would be useful to promote growth of tomato plants and, in particular, boost fruit growth?

Questions 10 and 11 refer to the diagram. It shows an experiment set up to investigate the importance of three mineral elements on the growth of a type of cereal plant.

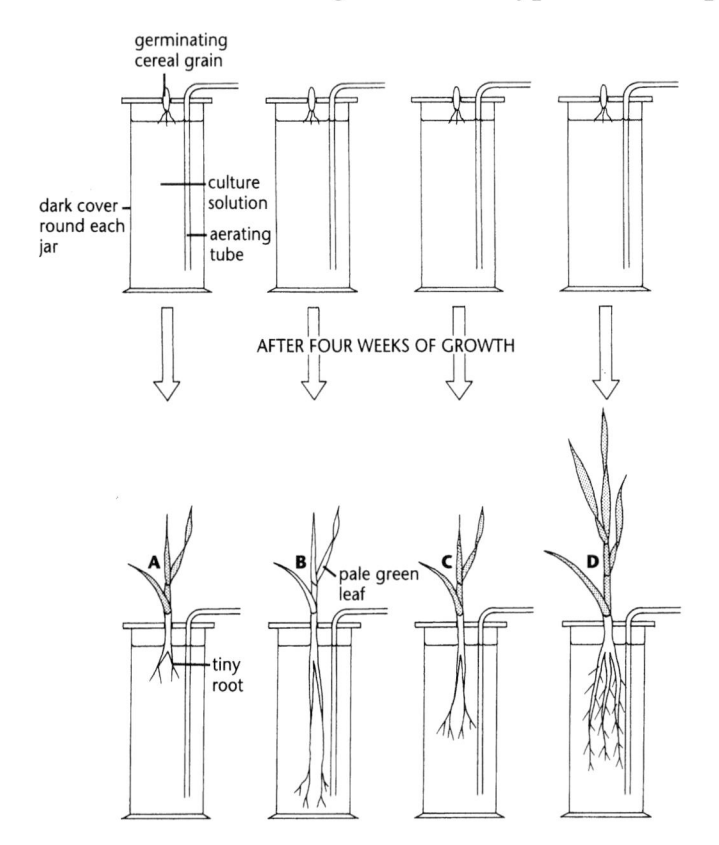

Unit 3 **Growing Plants**

Multiple Choice Test 1 continued

10 Which plant was given a culture solution containing all the chemical nutrients needed for healthy growth?

11 Which plant was grown in a culture solution that contained no phosphorus?

12 The accompanying diagram shows a system designed to water a house plant while the owner is away on holiday.

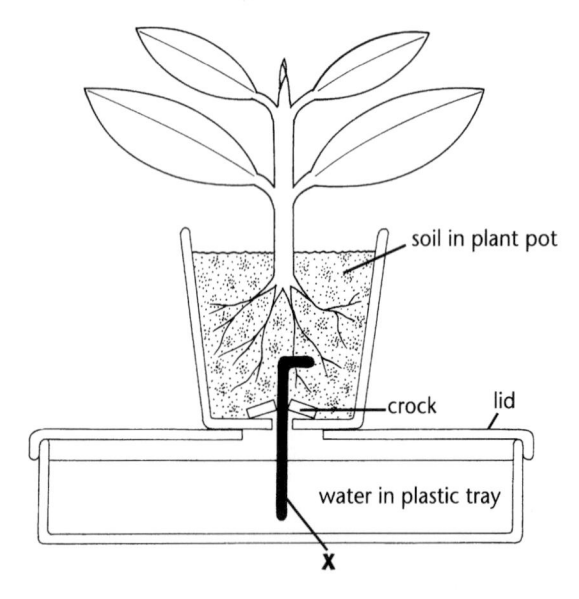

For the best results, material X should be made of
A   water retentive gel.   B   capillary matting.
C   filter paper.   D   plastic pipe.

13 The diagram shows a maximum and minimum thermometer that has been set up for 24 hours.

Which line in the following table is correct?

	temperature (°C)	
	minimum during last 24 hours	maximum during last 24 hours
A	−5	40
B	5	30
C	15	15
D	5	40

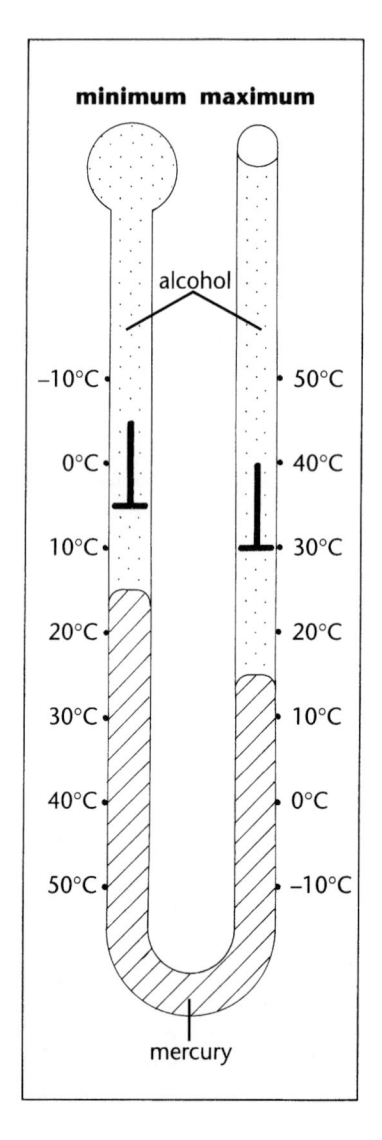

Chapter 11 **Plant Production**

Multiple Choice Test 1 continued

Questions 14 and 15 refer to the following table. It shows the results from an experiment set up to investigate the effect of different night temperatures on the growth of tomato plants.

day temperature (°C)	night temperature (°C)	average increase in height (mm/day)
26	13	24
26	17	29
26	19	26
26	26	21

14 Averages were calculated so that the results would be
 A reliable.   B accurate.   C fair.   D correct.

15 From these results it can be concluded that tomato plants grow better when the
 A day temperature is lower than the night temperature.
 B night temperature is lower than the day temperature.
 C day and night temperatures are kept equal.
 D temperature varies from day to day and night to night.

Questions 16, 17, 18 and 19 refer to the branched key to some common house plants on the following page.

16 Which plant likes medium light (not bright sunshine), has attractive leaves and does not grow well at 10–15°C?
 A Aspidistra.
 B Rubber Plant.
 C African Violet.
 D Aluminium Plant.

17 Which plant develops attractive leaves, likes bright sunlight and needs plenty of water?
 A Coleus.   B Geranium.
 C Busy Lizzie.   D Piggyback Plant.

Unit 3 Growing Plants

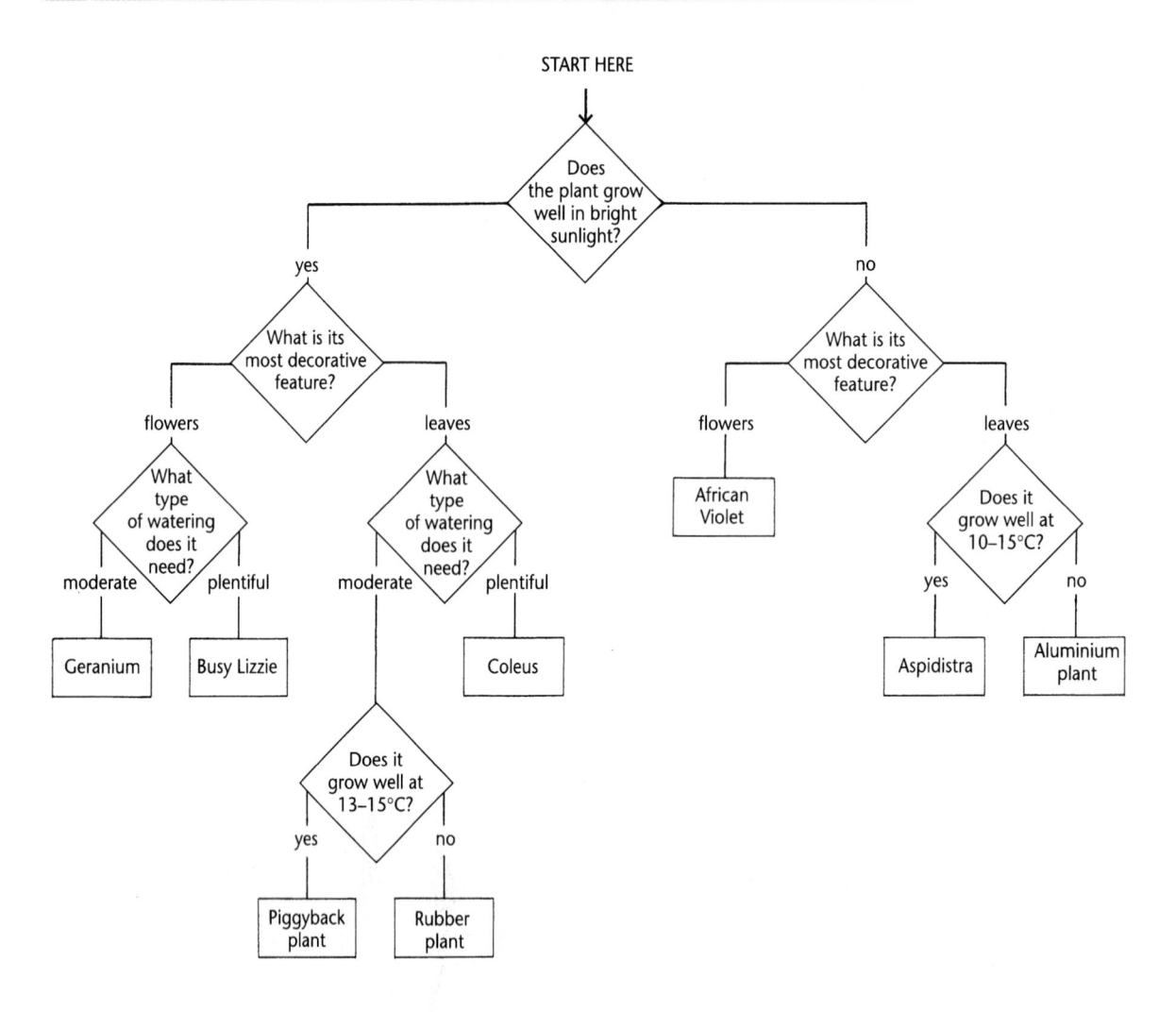

Multiple Choice Test 1 continued

```
                    START HERE
                        ↓
                 ┌─────────────┐
                 │ Does the    │
                 │ plant grow  │
                 │ well in bright
                 │ sunlight?   │
                 └─────────────┘
              yes ╱           ╲ no
```

18 Which line in the table indicates the best growing conditions for a Geranium plant?

	shady	bright	moderate watering	plentiful watering
A	✔	✘	✔	✘
B	✘	✔	✘	✔
C	✔	✘	✘	✔
D	✘	✔	✔	✘

19 Two plants that will grow well at 14°C are

    A Piggyback and Aspidistra.

    B Piggyback and Aluminium Plant.

    C Rubber Plant and Aspidistra.

    D Rubber Plant and Aluminium Plant.

Chapter 11 **Plant Production**

Multiple Choice Test 1 continued

20 Which part of the accompanying diagram shows the process of 'dead-heading' being carried out?

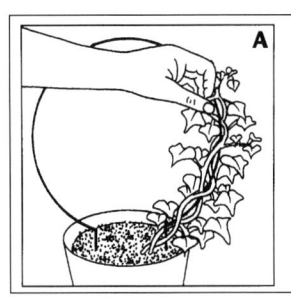

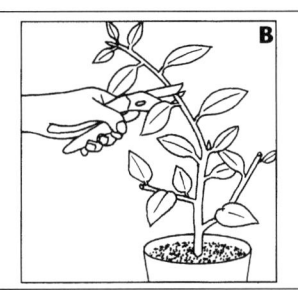

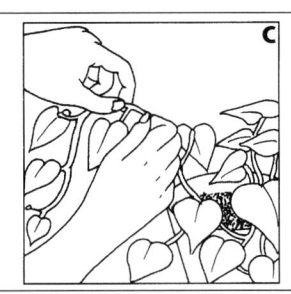

21 The following boxes give five steps carried out during 'pricking out' of seedlings. They are given in the wrong order.

| 1 Dig up a clump of seedlings and gently separate one from the others at the roots. |

| 2 Fill every hole with a seedling and water the tray. |

| 3 Add seed compost to a tray, then level and firm it. |

| 4 Lower the seedling into a hole and press soil around it. |

| 5 Make many evenly spread-out holes in the compost. |

What is the correct sequence of the five steps?

    A 3, 1, 5, 4, 2.   C 1, 3, 5, 2, 4.
    B 3, 5, 1, 4, 2.   D 1, 3, 5, 4, 2.

22 Disease spreads most easily from plant to plant in a greenhouse when the air is

    A overheated and humid.   C underheated and humid.
    B overheated and dry.   D underheated and dry.

Unit 3 Growing Plants

Multiple Choice Test 1 continued

23 The diagram shows a diseased leaf. What is the name of this condition?

   A whitefly.
   B greenfly.
   C grey mould.
   D green mould.

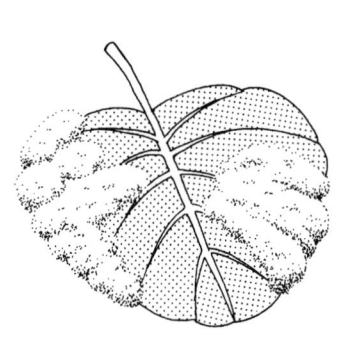

Questions 24 and 25 refer to the following table. It shows the results of an investigation into the effects of a new pesticide chemical.

pest	% of plants affected when pesticide is NOT used	% of plants affected when pesticide is used
aphid	28	9
white fly	16	5
red spider mite	8	7
caterpillar	9	1

24 The percentage number of plants saved from attack by aphids following use of the pesticide was

   A 9.
   B 11.
   C 19.
   D 37.

25 On which pest did the chemical have hardly any effect?

   A aphid.
   B whitefly.
   C caterpillar.
   D red spider mite.

Chapter 11 **Plant Production**

Multiple Choice Test 2

Choose the ONE correct answer to each of the following questions.

Questions 1, 2 and 3 refer to the following table. It gives the ingredients of four different brands of compost.

brand of compost	compost ingredient					
	sand	peat	perlite	fertiliser	loam	coconut fibre
W	✗	✓	✓	✓	✗	✗
X	✓	✗	✗	✓	✗	✓
Y	✗	✓	✓	✓	✗	✗
Z	✓	✓	✗	✓	✓	✗

Key
✓ = present   ✗ = absent

1. Which brand of compost would be described as environmentally friendly since it contains a peat substitute?
   A W.   B X.   C Y.   D Z.

2. How many of these brands of compost are loamless?
   A 1.   B 2.   C 3.   D 4.

3. Which ingredient is present in all of these brands of compost?
   A sand.
   B peat.
   C perlite.
   D fertiliser.

4. A pupil was asked to make up 12 litres of a potting compost using peat and perlite in a 3:1 ratio. Which of the following gives the correct volumes of the ingredients in litres?

	peat	perlite
A	3	1
B	3	9
C	9	3
D	18	6

Unit 3 Growing Plants

Multiple Choice Test 2 continued

Questions 5, 6, 7 and 8 refer to the information in the following table.

plant type	time when fertiliser should be used			
	fertiliser W	fertiliser X	fertiliser Y	fertiliser Z
bean	–	at all times	–	–
cucumber	at all times	–	–	–
leek	up to the end of June	from July on	–	–
lettuce	at all times	–	–	–
onion	up to the end of June	from July on	–	–
pea	–	at all times	–	–
potato	–	–	at all times	–
tomato	–	–	up to the end of August	from September on

5   The number of types of plant that can be given fertiliser W at all times is

   A 1.   B 2.   C 3.   D 4.

6   At which time of the year should use of fertiliser X on leek plants be started?

   A   June.
   B   July.
   C   August.
   D   September.

7   Which fertiliser should be used for tomato plants in July?
   A W.   B X.   C Y.   D Z.

8   On which **two** types of plant can fertiliser X be used during June?

   A   onion and pea.
   B   bean and leek.
   C   leek and onion.
   D   bean and pea.

Chapter 11 **Plant Production**

Multiple Choice Test 2 continued

Questions 9 and 10 refer to the accompanying diagram. It shows a packet of fertiliser.

9   The proportions of elements N, P and K are shown on the packet. Which of the following pie charts represents this information?

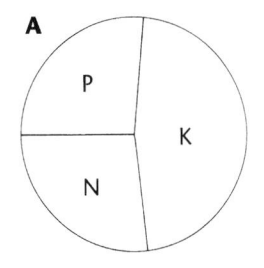

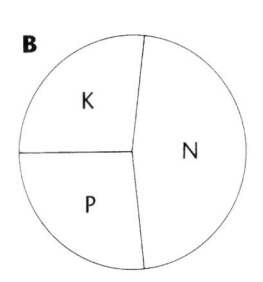

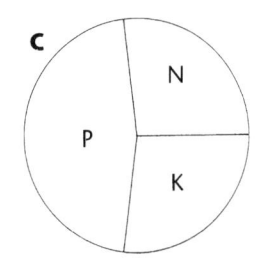

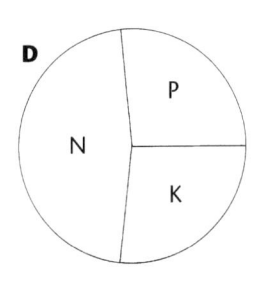

A

B

C

D

Kantfale
FERTILISER

N:P:K = 4:4:7

10 The information N : P : K = 4 : 4 : 7 also means that this packet contains 4 per cent N, 4 per cent P and 7 per cent K. If the packet's contents weigh 500 g, then the mass of P present (in grams) is
    A   20.
    B   35.
    C   71.
    D   125.

11 The mineral element that is especially important for promoting growth of flowers and fruit is
    A   N.
    B   P.
    C   K.
    D   S.

205

Unit 3 Growing Plants

Multiple Choice Test 2 continued

12 The diagram below shows an automatic watering system. However it will not begin to work until the

  A volume of container W is reduced.
  B length of absorbent material X is extended.
  C number of plant pots at Y is increased.
  D space at Z is eliminated by removing the two stones.

13 To cut down on the number of times that a hanging basket needs to be watered, the owner often adds one of the following to the soil when setting it up. Which one?

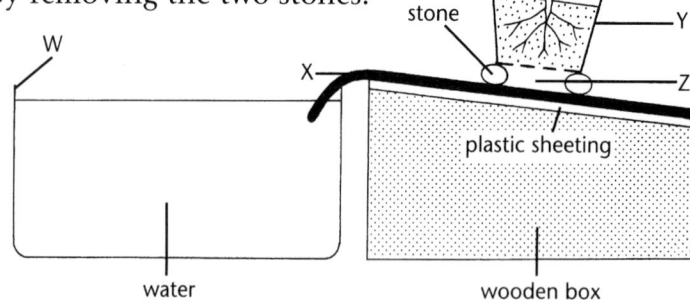

  A trickle tubing.
  B extra sharp sand.   C polythene sheeting.   D water retentive gel.

14 The following table gives data collected using a maximum and minimum thermometer.

day	maximum temperature (°C)	minimum temperature (°C)
1	30	10
2	25	5
3	35	15
4	20	5

Which of the following bar graphs correctly represents this data?

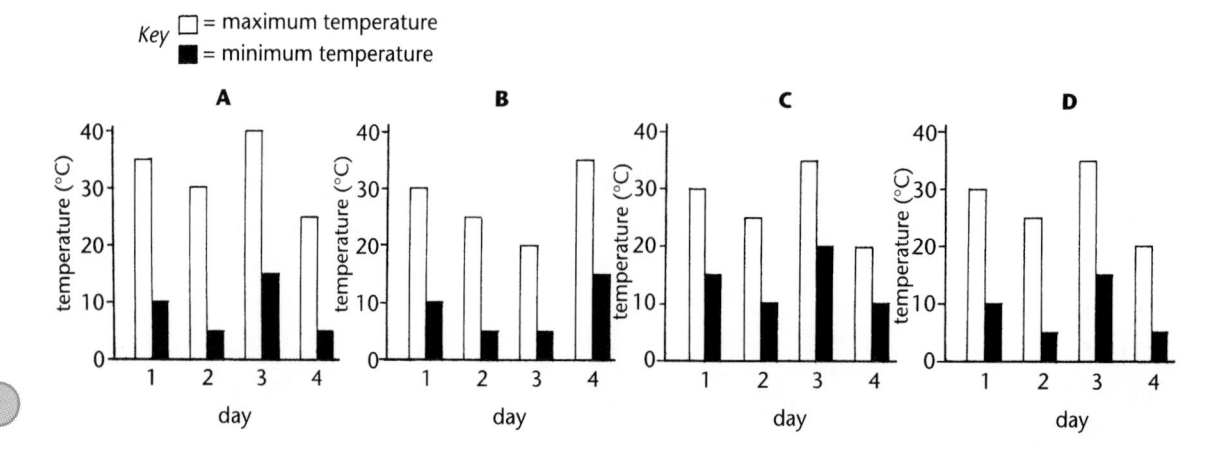

Chapter 11 **Plant Production**

Multiple Choice Test 2 continued

Questions 15, 16 and 17 refer to the accompanying diagram. Each of its boxes shows a plant, its ideal temperature range, its watering needs and its preferred conditions of light.

15 Which plant grows best when given moderate watering, bright light but not direct sunlight and a temperature range of 16–21°C?

   A   Mexican Hat Plant.
   B   Aloe.
   C   Easter Cactus.
   D   Money Tree.

16 How many of the plants in the diagram would find themselves within their ideal range of temperature if grown at 17°C?

   A   5.
   B   6.
   C   7.
   D   8.

17 How many of the plants in the diagram prefer some direct sunlight and thrive at 23°C?

   A   1.
   B   2.
   C   3.
   D   4.

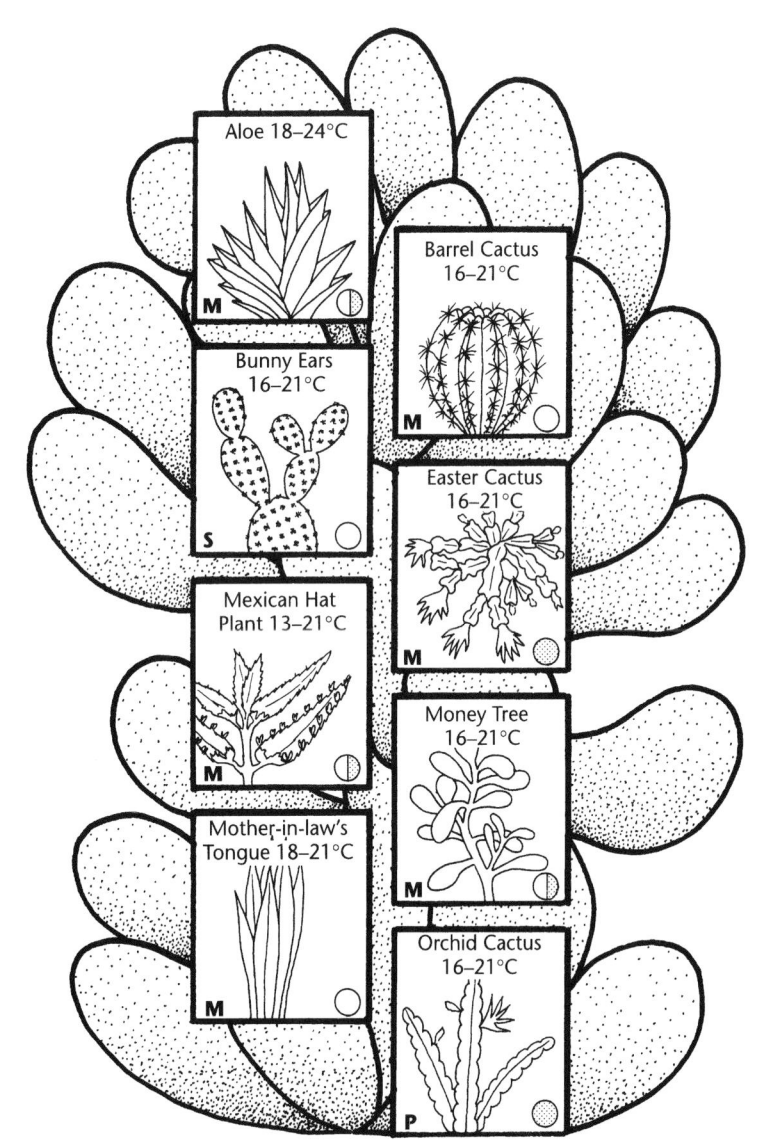

Aloe 18–24°C — M
Barrel Cactus 16–21°C
Bunny Ears 16–21°C — S
Easter Cactus 16–21°C
Mexican Hat Plant 13–21°C — M
Money Tree 16–21°C — M
Mother-in-law's Tongue 18–21°C — M
Orchid Cactus 16–21°C — P

Key to watering
 P = plentiful
 M = moderate
 S = sparing

Key to light
 ○ = full direct sunlight
 ◐ = bright, some direct sunlight
 ◌ = bright, no direct sunlight

Unit 3 Growing Plants

Multiple Choice Test 2 continued

Questions 18, 19 and 20 refer to the following information. The accompanying diagram shows the relative humidity values found at various locations in a school.

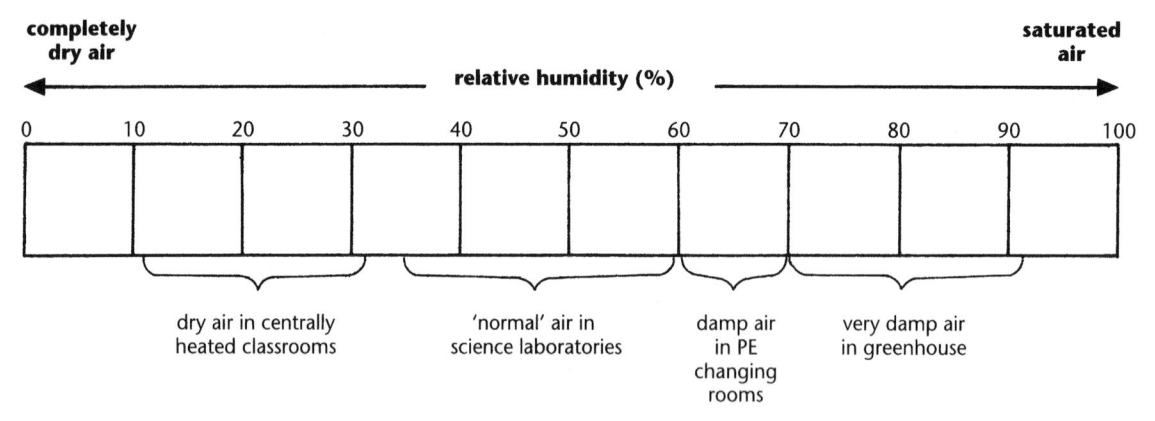

completely dry air ← relative humidity (%) → saturated air

0 10 20 30 40 50 60 70 80 90 100

- dry air in centrally heated classrooms
- 'normal' air in science laboratories
- damp air in PE changing rooms
- very damp air in greenhouse

Moisture-sensitive paper is blue when dry and pink when damp. In an experiment ten strips of this paper were placed in each of the four locations in the school for four hours. The average time taken for the paper to turn pink in each place was recorded as shown in the following table.

18 Which location was the greenhouse?
   A   1.
   B   2.
   C   3.
   D   4.

location	average time for paper to change colour (minutes)
1	30
2	1
3	60
4	more than 240

19 Which location was a centrally heated classroom?
   A   1.
   B   2.
   C   3.
   D   4.

20 How much longer (in minutes) did it take for the paper to change colour in a PE changing room compared with a science laboratory?
   A   29.
   B   30.
   C   59.
   D   180.

Multiple Choice Test 2 *continued*

21 Which of the following is wrong? A greenhouse needs to be ventilated when the air has become too

   A   hot.

   B   damp.

   C   cold.

   D   stale.

22 Carrying out 'dead-heading' on a plant often results in the

   A   production of more flowers.

   B   development of grey mould.

   C   setting of seeds.

   D   death of the plant.

23 The diagram shows four of the steps carried out during potting on. They are given in a mixed-up order. The correct sequence is

   A   3, 2, 4, 1.

   B   1, 2, 3, 4.

   C   3, 2, 1, 4.

   D   2, 4, 1, 3.

| 1. Firm the compost and add more until it is level with the original. Water carefully | 2. Invert pot and tap gently against table edge. Hold plant with one hand and remove pot with the other | 3. Choose a pot larger than the one containing the plant. Add crocks and a thin layer of potting compost | 4. Set the plant to be repotted in the larger pot. Fill the space with new compost |

Unit 3 Growing Plants

Multiple Choice Test 2 continued

24 The accompanying set of four diagrams shows common pests that attack plants. Which one shows greenfly?

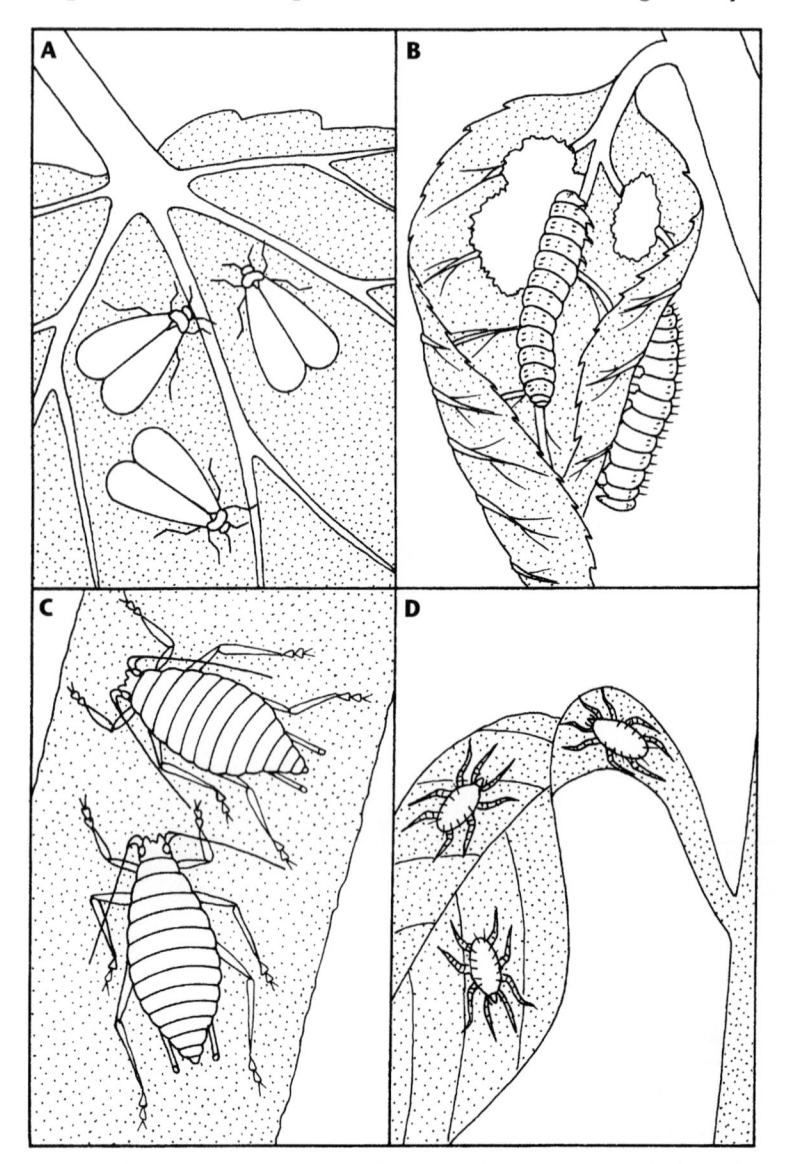

A

B

C

D

25 Methods of protected cultivation of germinating seeds are carried out in order to
  A stop the young plants from being harmed by frost.
  B enrich the soil with nutrients needed by the plant.
  C cross-breed the seeds with other plant strains.
  D delay the harvest until later in the year.

12 Specimen Exam Questions

Multiple Choice Exam 1

Choose the ONE correct answer to each of the following questions.

1. Which of the following sets contains the information in the accompanying diagram correctly paired up?

   A 1 = Z, 2 = X, 3 = Y.
   B 1 = X, 2 = Y, 3 = Z.
   C 1 = Y, 2 = Z, 3 = X.
   D 1 = Z, 2 = Y, 3 = X.

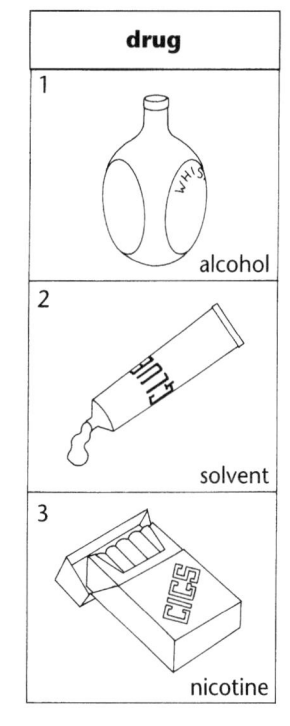

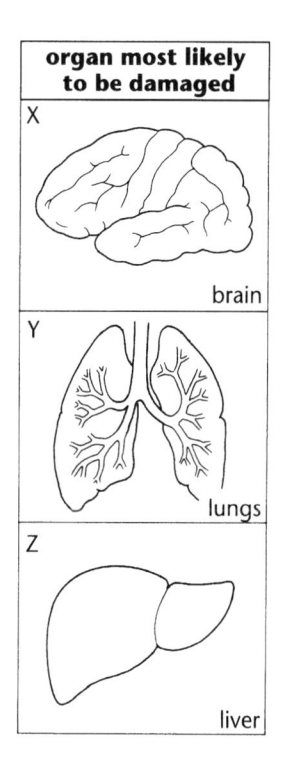

drug	organ most likely to be damaged
1 alcohol	X brain
2 solvent	Y lungs
3 nicotine	Z liver

2. Which of the following is *not* an aspect of the health triangle?

   A physical health.
   B mental health.
   C social health.
   D biotechnical health.

3. Which of the following diagrams of the heart shows blood flowing in the correct direction?

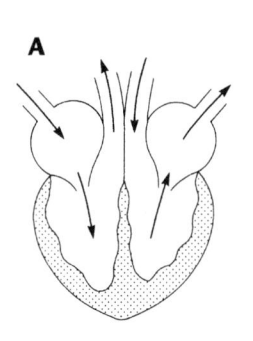

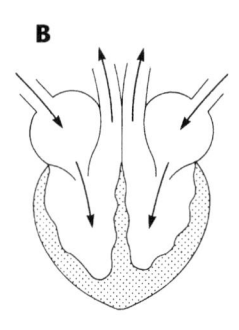

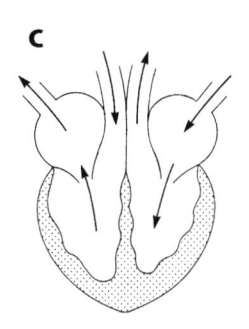

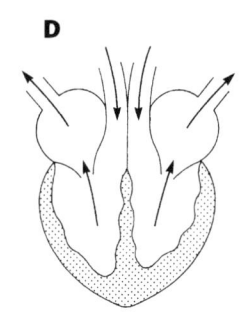

   A   B   C   D

Chapter 12 **Multiple Choice Exam 1**

4 The diagram shows a stopwatch.

To use it to measure a short period of time you would press buttons X and Y in the order

A   Y, X, Y.
B   X, X, Y.
C   X, Y, X.
D   Y, Y, X.

5 *Peak flow* is a measure of the
A   maximum rate at which air can be expelled from the lungs.
B   volume of air breathed in and out in one breath.
C   number of breaths taken per minute during exercise.
D   maximum volume of air that can be exhaled following a deep breath being taken in.

6 The data in the following table was obtained from an athlete during training.

activity	average volume of each breath (l)
resting	0.5
jogging	1.5
running a race	2.5

What is the percentage increase in volume of each breath from resting to running a race?

A   200.   B   300.   C   400.   D   500.

Questions 7 and 8 refer to the pie chart below. It shows the sources of fat eaten by a person on an unhealthy diet.

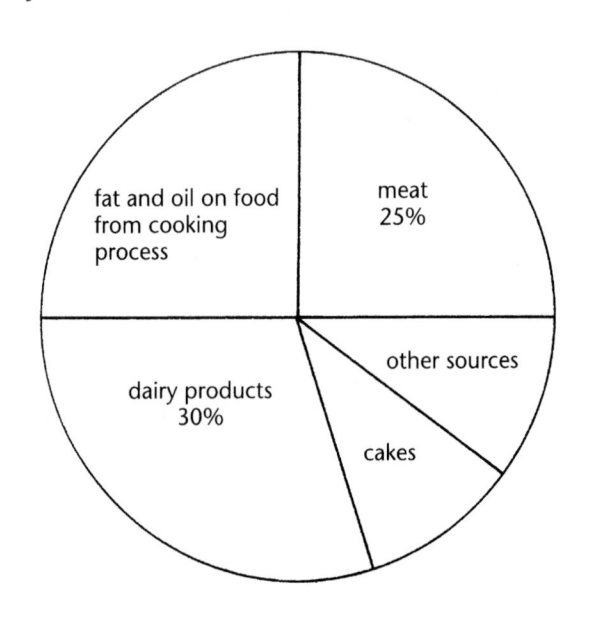

7 What percentage of fat in this person's diet came from cakes?

A   5.
B   10.
C   15.
D   20.

8 The total mass of fat eaten by this person in one day was 240 g. How many grams of fat were present in the meat that the person ate?

A   25.
B   60.
C   240.
D   960.

9 The following table shows the calcium content of four foods.

food	calcium content (mg/100 g)
cottage cheese	60
herring	100
milk	120
sardines	400

According to experts, 16-year olds need 600 mg of calcium each day to stay healthy. They could get this from
A 800 g of cottage cheese.
B 500 g of herring.
C 500 g of milk.
D 100 g of sardines.

Questions 10 and 11 refer to the diagram recording a hospital patient's body temperature taken over a period of five days.

10 What was the highest temperature (in °C) recorded?
A 40.1.
B 40.2.
C 40.4.
D 42.0.

11 On which day did the biggest drop in temperature take place between 6 am and 6 pm?
A 2.
B 3.
C 4.
D 5.

12 Reaction time can be decreased in length by
A drugs.
B practice.
C fatigue.
D alcohol.

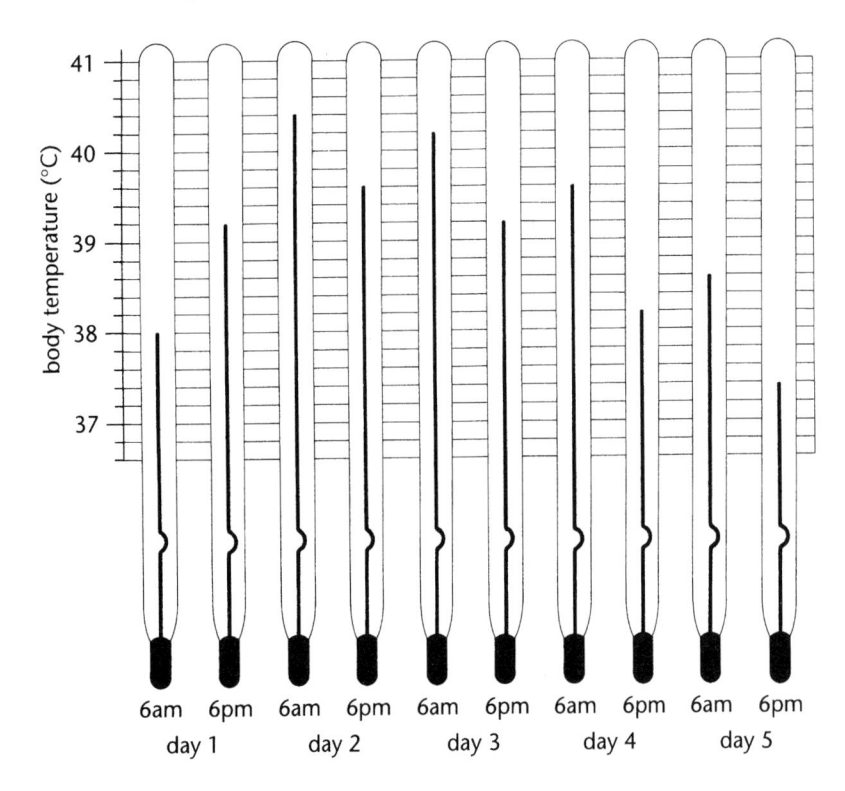

Chapter 12 **Multiple Choice Exam 1**

13 Which of the following treatments is carried out to produce UHT milk?
   A   Half of the fat is removed from the milk.
   B   Half of the water is removed from the milk.
   C   The milk is heated to 72°C for 15 seconds.
   D   The milk is heated to 140°C for 5 seconds.

14 Which line in the following table shows the most likely effects of adding a large volume of untreated whey to a river?

	number of bacteria in river	concentration of oxygen in river water	number of fish in the river
A	↓	↑	↑
B	↑	↓	↓
C	↑	↑	↑
D	↓	↓	↓

Key
↑ = increase   ↓ = decrease

15 Which of the following equations represents a method of treating whey before it is poured into a river?

   A   sugar in whey + alcohol $\xrightarrow{\text{yeast}}$ carbon dioxide (CO$_2$) + water.

   B   sugar in whey $\xrightarrow{\text{yeast}}$ alcohol + oxygen (O$_2$).

   C   sugar in whey + CO$_2$ $\xrightarrow{\text{yeast}}$ O$_2$ + water.

   D   sugar in whey $\xrightarrow{\text{yeast}}$ alcohol + CO$_2$.

16 In which of the following containers would cask-conditioned beer be stored?

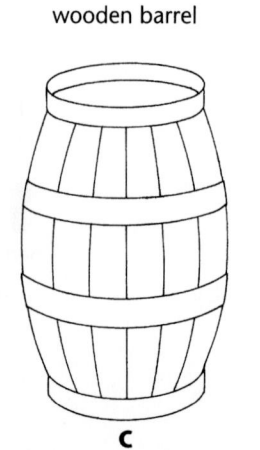

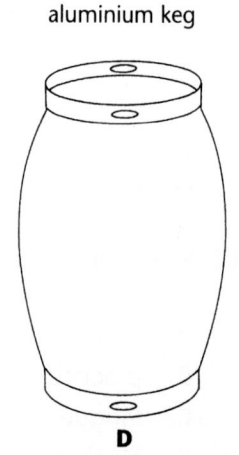

A aluminium can   B glass bottle   C wooden barrel   D aluminium keg

Questions 17 and 18 refer to the following information. Amylase is an enzyme present in some biological detergents. The graph shows the effect of pH on the production of amylase in an industrial fermenter.

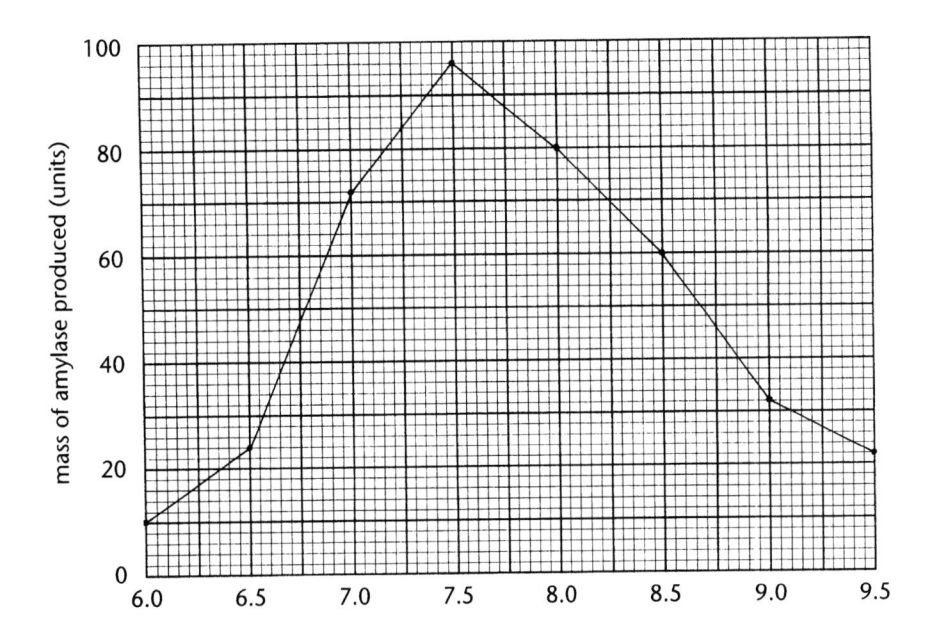

17 At what pH was a mass of 24 units of amylase produced?

A   6.0.

B   6.5.

C   9.0.

D   9.5.

18 What percentage decrease in mass of amylase occurred between pH 8.0 and pH 8.5?

A   20.

B   25.

C   60.

D   80.

Chapter 12 Multiple Choice Exam 1

19 The first of the diagrams on the right shows an experiment set up to test the effect of protease enzyme on photographic film.

Which test tube in the second diagram shows the best control for the experiment?

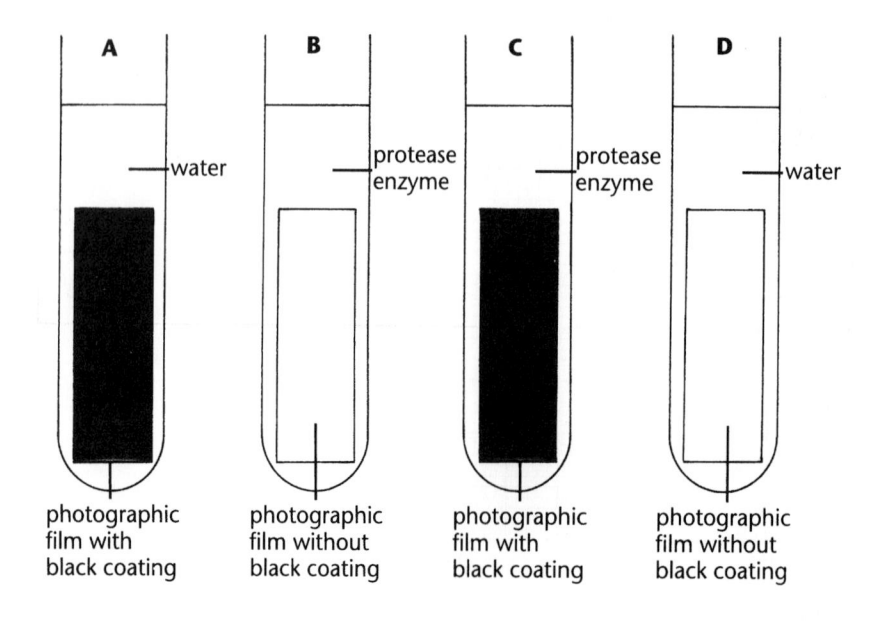

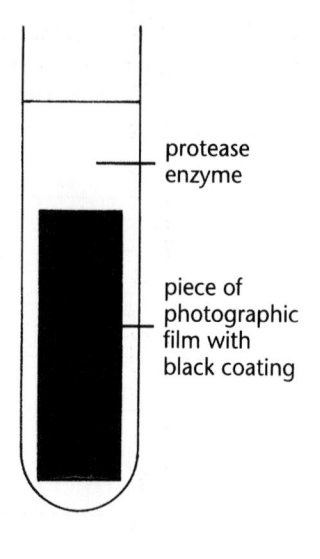

20 An antifungal chemical is a substance that
- A encourages the growth of bacteria.
- B encourages the growth of fungi.
- C limits the growth of bacteria.
- D limits the growth of fungi.

21 The diagram shows an experiment set up to investigate the conditions needed by cress seeds to germinate.

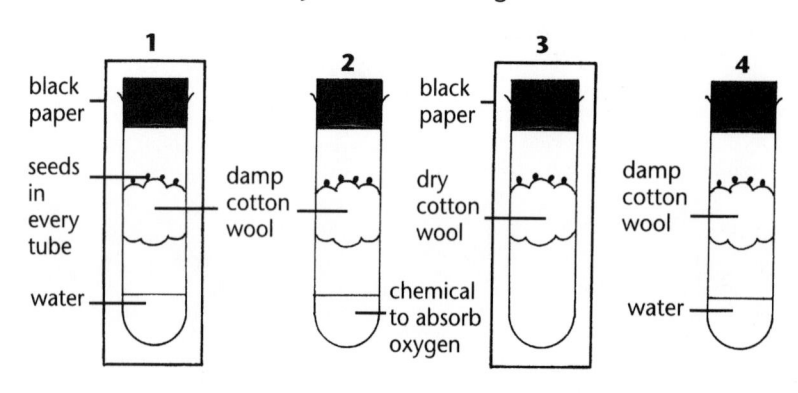

In which pair of test tubes will germination *not* occur?
A 2 and 3.   B 2 and 4.   C 1 and 3.   D 1 and 4.

22 The accompanying diagram shows the steps carried out when propagating a plantlet from a runner. The steps are in the correct order but stage 3 has been left out.

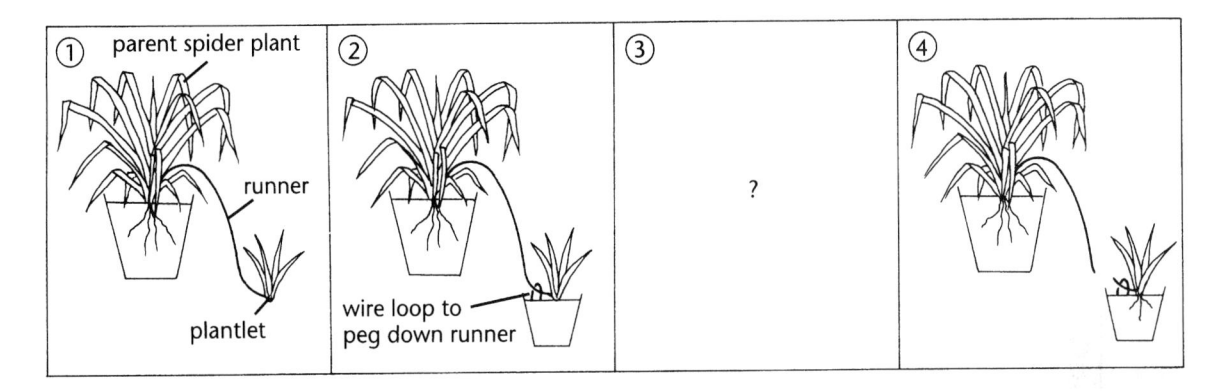

Which of the following takes place during stage 3?

A The parent plant's soil supply gets topped up.
B The wire loop is lifted out.
C The plantlet develops roots.
D The parent plant dies of old age.

23 The following table lists the properties of materials used to make different types of composts. Which line in the table is *correct*?

	material added	property of soil that is improved
A	perlite	aeration
B	peat	drainage
C	sand	water-holding capacity
D	fertiliser	crumb structure

24 Which of the following is *not* used in automatic watering systems?

A crystalline water-retentive gel.
B thick green capillary matting.
C plastic pipeline with nozzles.
D watering can with long spout.

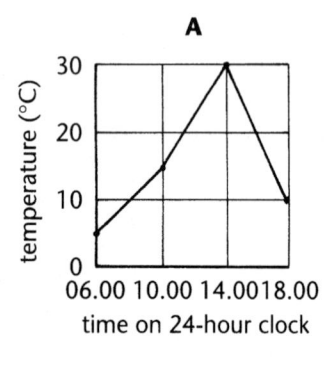

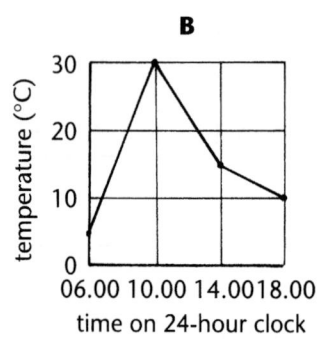

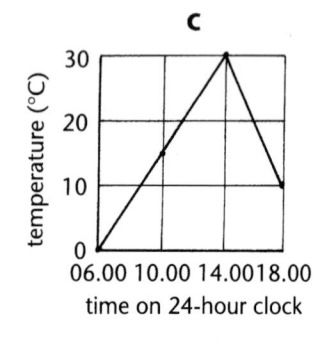

Chapter 12 Multiple Choice Exam 1

25 The following table records the temperature in a greenhouse over a period of 12 hours.

time on 24-hour clock	temperature (°C)
06.00	5
10.00	15
14.00	30
18.00	10

Which graph in the diagram correctly represents the data in the table?

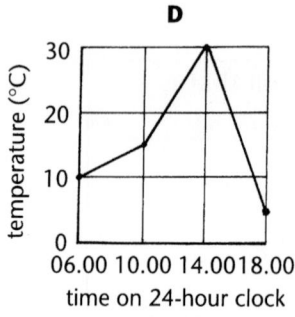

Multiple Choice Exam 2

Choose the ONE correct answer to each of the following questions.

1. Which of the following is a sign of good *social* health?
   A   having clear, sparkling eyes.
   B   being happy with your self-image.
   C   being able to relate to other people.
   D   having the ability to cope with stress.

Questions 2, 3 and 4 refer to the information in the following table about the health-related benefits of certain activities.

activity	possible benefit			
	increase in strength	increase in suppleness	increase in stamina	help to control overweight
archery	1	0	0	0
badminton	1	2	1	2
basketball	0	1	1	2
canoeing	2	1	2	1
cycling (hard)	2	1	3	2
dancing (disco)	0	3	2	2
digging garden	3	1	2	2
football	2	1	2	2
jogging	1	1	3	2
skating	0	0	1	1
weightlifting	3	0	0	0

Key to level of benefit
0 = of little or no benefit
1 = of some benefit
2 = of much benefit
3 = of very much benefit

2. Which activity is of very much benefit when trying to increase suppleness?
   A   badminton.
   B   digging the garden.
   C   disco dancing.
   D   jogging.

Chapter 12 **Multiple Choice Exam 2**

3 Which of the following activities are *both* of much benefit when trying to increase stamina?
   A   canoeing and football.
   B   archery and weightlifting.
   C   badminton and basketball.
   D   cycling and skating.

4 When trying to control overweight, cycling is found to be of
   A   no benefit.
   B   little benefit.
   C   much benefit.
   D   very much benefit.

5 Veins carry blood
   A   away from the heart to the body tissues.
   B   back to the heart from the body tissues.
   C   from the heart to the lungs.
   D   from the arteries to the capillaries.

6 Which of the following is a measurement of *breathing rate*?
   A   number of breaths taken per minute.
   B   volume of oxygen absorbed into the bloodstream.
   C   number of air molecules passing down the windpipe.
   D   volume of carbon dioxide breathed out.

7 At which site in the accompanying diagram of the breathing system does gas exchange occur?

8 Which line in the following table is *wrong*?

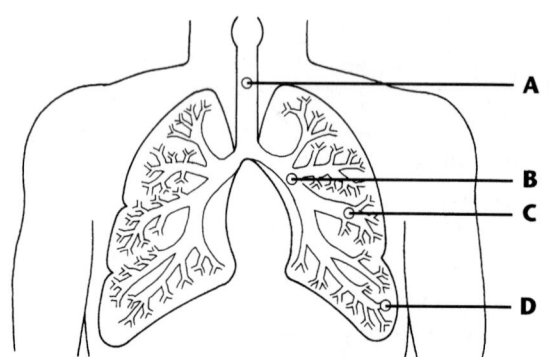

	type of food	to give the body energy	to build the body	to protect the body
		main function of food		
A	vitamin			✓
B	fat		✓	
C	carbohydrate	✓		
D	protein		✓	

Chapter 12 **Multiple Choice Exam 2**

9 Which of the thermometers shown in the diagram is *least* suitable for measuring body temperature?

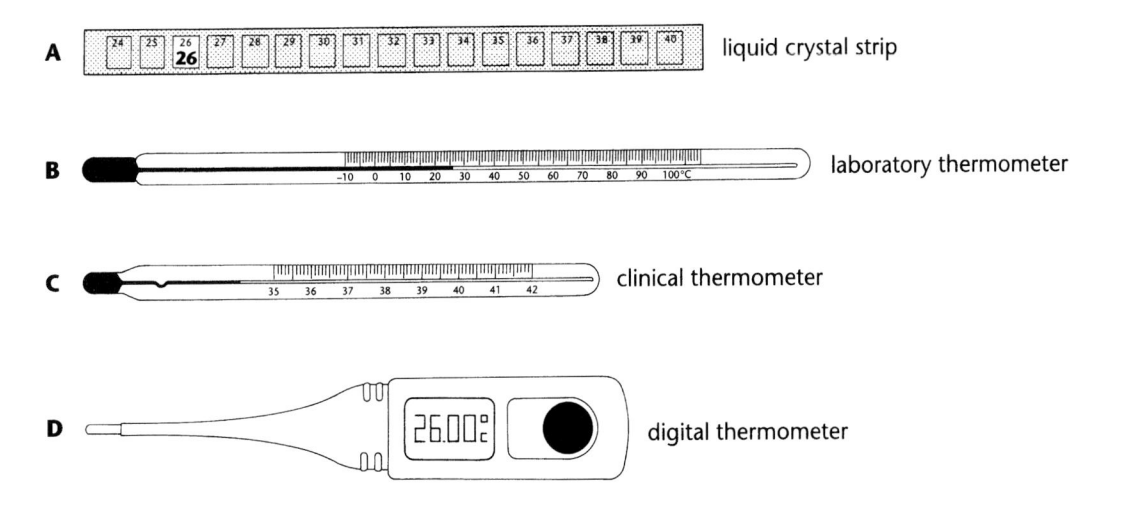

A — liquid crystal strip

B — laboratory thermometer

C — clinical thermometer

D — digital thermometer

10 Muscle strength and endurance are good indicators of a person's

  A physical fitness.
  B general health.
  C overall height.
  D excess weight.

11 The five measuring cylinders in the diagram show an experiment set up to separate milk into curds and whey.

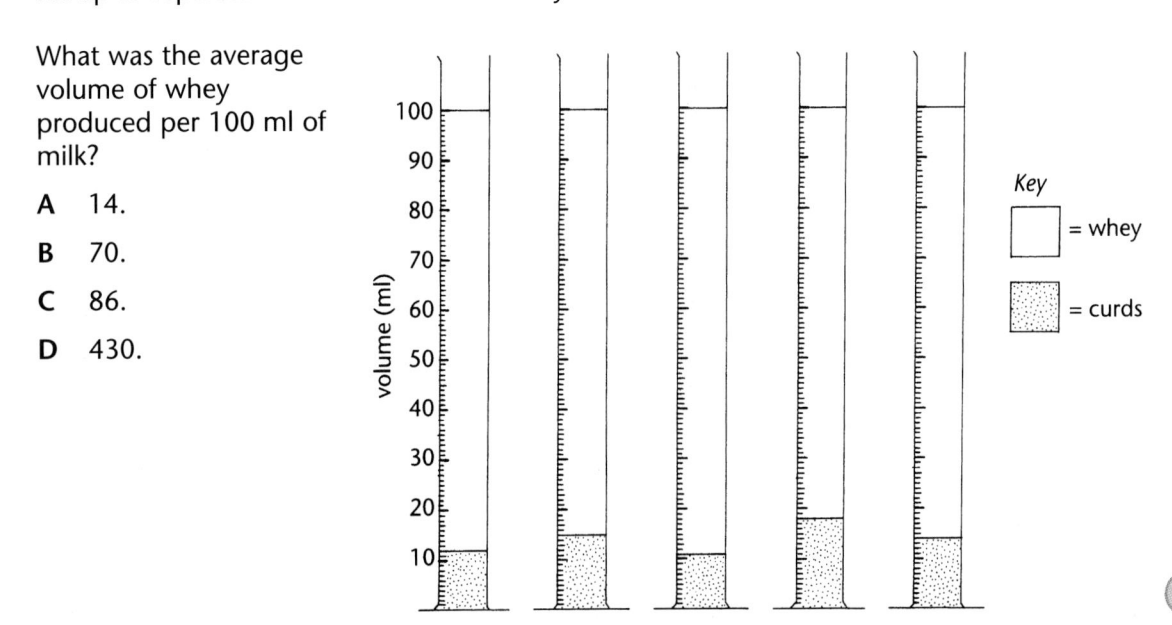

What was the average volume of whey produced per 100 ml of milk?

  A 14.
  B 70.
  C 86.
  D 430.

Key
□ = whey
▨ = curds

221

Chapter 12 **Multiple Choice Exam 2**

12 The diagram below shows the effect of polluting a river with untreated whey. What does graph X represent?

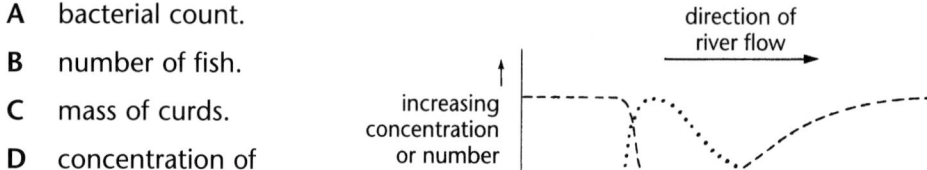

A bacterial count.
B number of fish.
C mass of curds.
D concentration of rennet.

Questions 13 and 14 refer to the following table.

drink	alcohol content (%)
export ale	4.5
lager	4.0
sherry	18.0
stout	4.2
strong cider	5.4

13 Which bar in the bar chart represents export ale?

14 By how many times is the alcohol content of sherry greater than that of export ale?

A 4.0.
B 4.5.
C 13.5.
D 18.0.

15 What is the reason for using sodium alginate solution when making a fermented drink by immobilisation techniques?

A It changes the sugar in milk to simple sugars.
B It acts on simple sugar and changes it into alcohol.
C It makes drops of liquid gel harden into beads of gel.
D It can be made into re-usable beads containing trapped cells and enzymes.

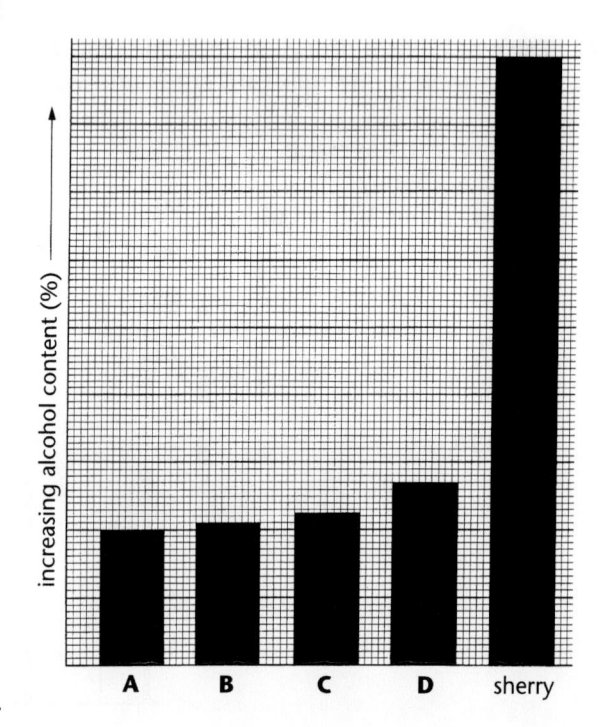

16 In an experiment bacteria of species F were spread evenly over the surface of a Petri dish of nutrient agar. A disc containing penicillin (P) and a disc containing streptomycin (S) were then added to the dish. The diagram shows the results after two days.

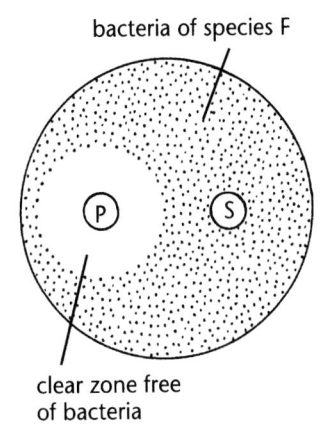

From this experiment it can be concluded that bacteria of species F are

A   sensitive to P.
B   resistant to P.
C   sensitive to S.
D   resistant to both P and S.

17 Which of the following is *not* a method of chitting seeds?

A   shaking them up with sharp gravel.
B   rubbing them with abrasive paper.
C   nicking their seed coats with a knife.
D   surrounding them with a pellet of clay.

18 What is the general name for a method of increasing the supply of a type of plant without using seeds?

A   sexual reproduction.
B   vegetative propagation.
C   asexual fertilisation.
D   zygote formation.

Chapter 12 **Multiple Choice Exam 2**

Questions 19 and 20 refer to the diagram. It shows four steps carried out when growing a plantlet from a Mexican Hat plant. They are given in a mixed-up order.

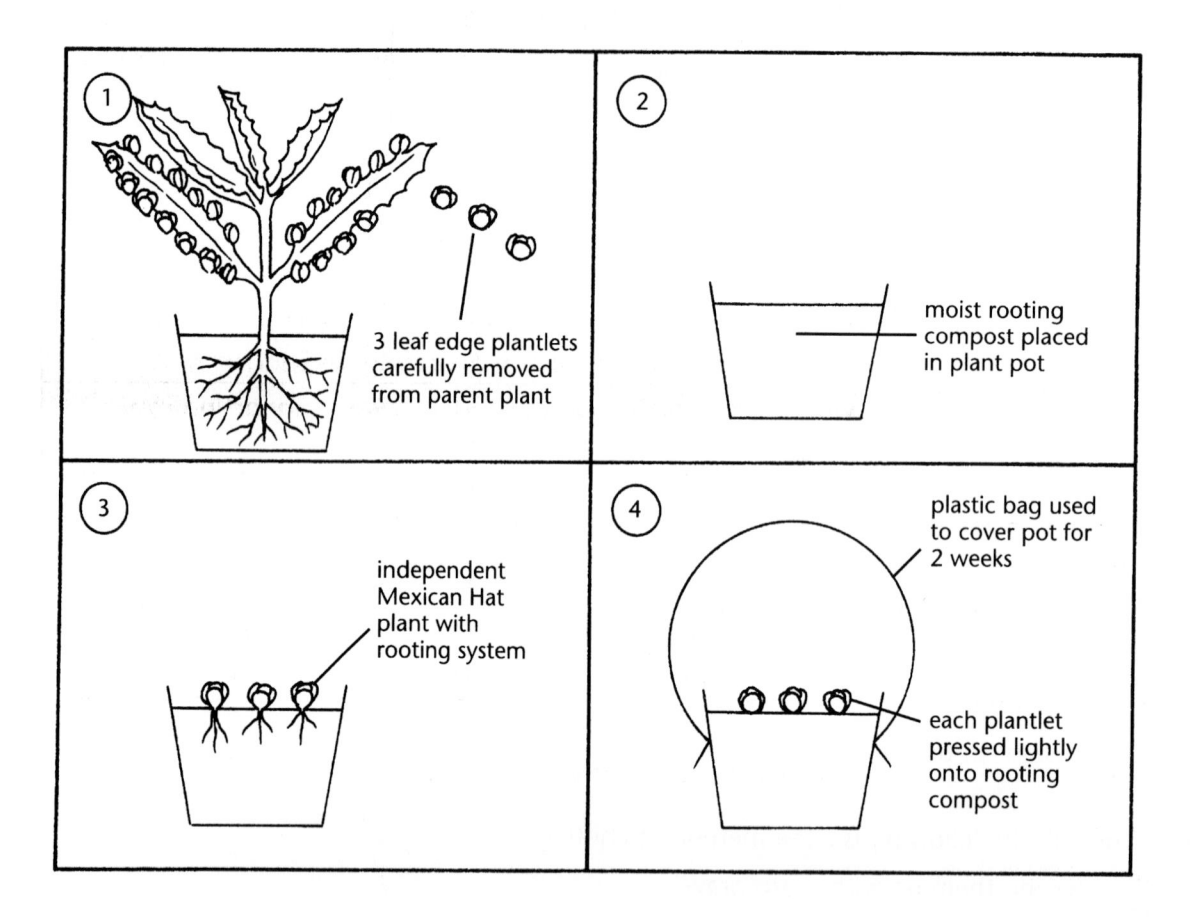

① 3 leaf edge plantlets carefully removed from parent plant

② moist rooting compost placed in plant pot

③ independent Mexican Hat plant with rooting system

④ plastic bag used to cover pot for 2 weeks; each plantlet pressed lightly onto rooting compost

19 What is the correct order of the four steps?
  A 1, 2, 3, 4.
  B 1, 3, 4, 2.
  C 2, 1, 4, 3.
  D 2, 4, 1, 3.

20 Why is the plastic bag placed over the pot?
  A to reduce water loss.
  B to increase light intensity.
  C to vary temperature.
  D to improve ventilation.

Chapter 12 Multiple Choice Exam 2

21 In an experiment the effect of the use of supporting canes during layering was investigated as shown in the accompanying diagram. The results are given in the table.

What percentage success rate should have been entered in box **X**?

A 25.
B 50.
C 75.
D 100.

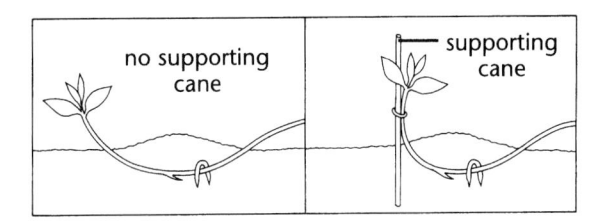

set of plants	number of plants (per set of 10) successfully propagated by layering	
	without supporting canes	with supporting canes
1	6	7
2	7	9
3	3	7
4	5	8
5	4	6
success rate (%)	[X]	74

22 Which of the following is *never* present in loamless compost?

A peat.
B nutrients.
C sharp sand.
D garden soil.

23 The following table shows the proportions of three chemical elements found in four brands of fertiliser.

brand of fertiliser	proportions of chemical elements present
A	7N : 7P : 14K
B	15N : 30P : 15K
C	3N : 8P : 4K
D	4N : 4P : 7K

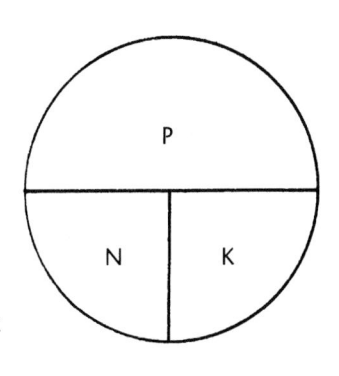

Which brand of fertiliser is correctly represented by the pie chart in the diagram on the right?

Chapter 12 **Multiple Choice Exam 2**

Questions 24 and 25 refer to the accompanying diagram which gives a temperature guide for the care of house plants.

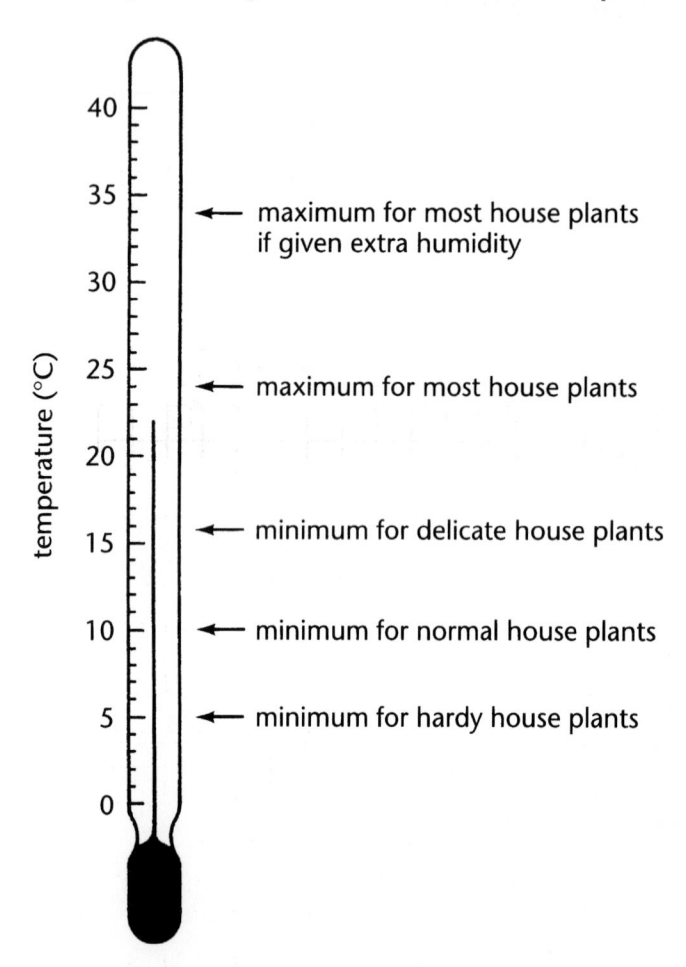

temperature (°C)

- 40
- 35 ← maximum for most house plants if given extra humidity
- 30
- 25 ← maximum for most house plants
- 20
- 15 ← minimum for delicate house plants
- 10 ← minimum for normal house plants
- 5 ← minimum for hardy house plants
- 0

24 Which of the following temperatures (in °C) would suit a delicate plant?

    A   3.

    B   8.

    C   13.

    D   18.

25 Which type of plant would be most successful at a temperature of 7°C?

    A   delicate.

    B   non-hardy.

    C   normal.

    D   hardy.

Chapter 12 **Multiple Choice Exam 1**

Intermediate 1 Biology Multiple Choice and Matching
ANSWER SHEET

QUESTION NUMBER

CHAPTER		1	2	3	4	5	6	7	8	9	10	11	12	13	14	15	16	17	18	19	20	21	22	23	24	25
1	1																									
	2																									
2	1																									
	2																									
3	1																									
	2																									
4	1																									
	2																									
5	1																									
	2																									
6	1																									
	2																									
7	1																									
	2																									
8	1																									
	2																									
9	1																									
	2																									
10	1																									
	2																									
11	1																									
	2																									
12	1																									
	2																									